TERTIARY LEVEL BIOLOGY

Developmental Microbiology

John F. Peberdy, B.Sc., Ph.D.

Senior Lecturer in Botany
University of Nottingham

Blackie

Glasgow and London

Blackie & Son Limited
Bishopbriggs
Glasgow G64 2NZ

Furnival House
14–18 High Holborn
London WC1V 6BX

International Standard Book Number
Hardback 0 216 91018 8
Paperback 0 216 91019 6

Filmset by Advanced Filmsetters (Glasgow) Limited
Printed in Great Britain by
Thomson Litho Ltd., East Kilbride, Scotland

Preface

SINCE THE EARLY DAYS OF MICROBIOLOGY IT HAS BEEN KNOWN THAT, during their life cycles, microorganisms exhibit developmental changes in common with other organisms. In the last decade interest in this aspect of microbiology has developed greatly, and research findings have provided an understanding of the genetic, molecular and biochemical bases of development. An important stimulus in this research has been the realisation that microbial development, in its various forms, provides interesting model systems that have relevance to a much wider understanding of the developmental processes in higher eukaryotes.

Many undergraduate and other courses in microbiology reflect these developments. Up to now, the only source material for these courses has been symposia publications, or books of a more specialised nature and at an advanced level. The aim in writing this book, which is based on a series of undergraduate lectures given at the University of Nottingham, was to bring together the relevant aspects of the biology of microorganisms, in particular the bacteria and fungi. The algae and protozoa have been excluded, partly because of the limits of space and partly because they are very different from the bacteria and fungi in most aspects of their biology. The early chapters deal with vegetative growth and development, leading into reproductive development. Each chapter begins by reference to the structural aspects of the subject and leads into the physiological and biochemical aspects. The chapter on Virus Replication was inserted to demonstrate the molecular basis of development. I have made the assumption that the reader already has a knowledge of first year microbiology and biochemistry.

I am very grateful to a number of people for their help: to Dr Susan Isaac, Miss Tina Such and several undergraduate students who have given helpful criticism of the manuscript, to the many research workers who have generously provided photographs for inclusion in the book, and to Mrs Linda Wightman for patiently typing the manuscript.

J.F.P.

ABBREVIATIONS

cAMP	cyclic adenosine monophosphate
ATP	adenosine triphosphate
BHB	β-hydroxybutyrate
DNA	deoxyribonucleic acid
dsDNA	double-stranded deoxyribonucleic acid
ssDNA	single-stranded deoxyribonucleic acid
DPA	dipicolinic acid
cGMP	cyclic guanosine monophosphate
GDP	guanosine diphosphate
$NADH_2$	nicotinamide-adenine dinucleotide, reduced form
PHB	poly-β-hydroxybutyrate
RNA	ribonucleic acid
mRNA	messenger ribonucleic acid
rRNA	ribosomal ribonucleic acid
dsRNA	double-stranded ribonucleic acid
ssRNA	single-stranded ribonucleic acid
TCA	tricarboxylic acid cycle
UDP	uridine diphosphate

Contents

INTRODUCTION

MICROORGANISMS DISPLAY PATTERNS OF DIFFERENTIATION OR CHANGE within the context of their life cycles that range from the simple to the complex. In bacteria such as *Escherichia coli*, we have an example of the simplest form where the life cycle and the cell cycle are synonymous, involving a continuum of growth and division—at least whilst assimilable nutrients are available. However, within the growth process of organisms such as this, differentiation of a biochemical nature can be identified within the cell as it ages. The changes that take place can be seen in the context of a "build up" to the division that is to follow. Looking more broadly at bacteria, we find that this apparently simple situation is not universal. For example, in the stalked bacterium *Caulobacter*, differentiation leading to functional differences in the cells at different stages in their life cycle is found. In other species, e.g. *Bacillus*, the pattern of development of the cells is influenced by the environment. Thus under certain conditions the cells cease vegetative growth and division and switch to a pattern of differentiation that terminates in the formation of a resting spore.

Not surprisingly, the fungi have more pronounced pathways of differentiation and development. In vegetative growth, the yeasts are similar to the bacteria, and current thinking interprets the growth of the hyphal apices in filamentous fungi in a similar cyclical pattern. Reproductive development, both asexual and sexual, is a dramatic switch from vegetative growth. Interestingly, asexual reproduction in most fungi is subject to minimal environmental control, but this may not be surprising in view of the fact that its use is primarily to provide the continuance and dissemination of a species on a large scale. Sexual reproduction is in contrast to this situation because it is subject to greater environmental control. Again this may be significant in the context of its purpose and also because the products of sexual reproduction are frequently more resistant than the asexual spores and so provide a mechanism for withstanding severe environmental stress. The patterns of differentiation that we see represented in these microorganisms, especially between the unicellular forms and the more complex filamentous forms, are diverse. The former are representative of a temporal differentiation where the change simply involves time, whereas the differentiation of reproductive structures in the filamentous structures is spatial in nature.

The underlying mechanism of control of differentiation must relate to the genome of the organism. The development of specific enzymes at a particular time in the cell cycle, the formation of specific surface appendages on a cell, or the production of a spore bearing structure are all expressions of a gene or genes that are presumably transcribed and translated a short time before the particular manifestation. The genome of an organism must contain all the necessary information that could possibly be translated into the various patterns of development that might be expressed by that organism. The efficient expression of these various patterns demands that the activities of the genome are subject to control. In the main this control is the environment in which the organism finds itself, and which influences internal triggers that regulate the activities of different parts of the genome. As will be clear from the subsequent chapters, our level of understanding of this complex interaction is variable from one system of microbial development to another. The challenge to the microbiologist is to delve further into these fundamental aspects of the biology of these organisms.

CHAPTER ONE

GROWTH OF BACTERIA

SEVERAL BACTERIAL SPECIES PROVIDE EXAMPLES OF THE FASTEST GROWING cells known to man. In the space of twenty to twenty-five minutes, a bacterium such as *Escherichia coli* can increase to a critical size and mass and then divide. The opportunity for such rapid growth is an indication of the neatly integrated metabolic system that exists in the bacterial cell. This system provides energy and metabolites, which are built up into macro-molecules, in turn providing the fabric of cell structure. The expression of the many biochemical events which begin at the "birth" of the cell and continue to its ultimate division are described as the cell cycle. Before the growth processes can be considered it is necessary to examine the nature of cellular organisation in bacteria. This discussion is limited to those aspects of relevance to the later parts of this chapter.

Morphology of the bacterial cell

Cell shape
The bacterial cell takes on one of three shapes: spherical, rod shaped or curved. The spherical cells, or cocci, occur in a variety of arrangements, each of which reflects the pattern of cell division exhibited by the particular organism. The cell arrangements may be as pairs, tetrads, chains or irregular clusters. The rod cells, or bacilli, divide only in one plane and normally the daughter cells separate, with short chains of cells forming only occasionally. Exceptions to this rule are the sheathed bacteria, e.g. *Sphaerotilus natans*, where long chains of bacilli are enclosed in a muci-laginous sheath. In other rod-shaped bacteria, a branching filamentous form may develop, e.g. *Nocardia*, and in *Streptomyces* and other genera this habit is extended, giving rise to a mycelial organisation as found in

the filamentous fungi. The curved cells have two basic forms: those with a slight curve and a comma-like appearance (i.e. the vibiros), and those which are spiral in shape.

Cell size

The range of size found in bacteria is enormous. The smallest cocci range from 0.5 μm to 1.5 μm in diameter, the rods from 0.5 μm diameter/1.5 μm long to 1–1.2 μm diameter/4–8 μm long, and some of the spiral forms are the largest with a length of 600 μm.

Ultrastructure and composition of the bacterial cell

Cell wall

The extremity of a bacterial cell is bounded by a wall layer which defines the shape of the cell. The only component present in walls of both Gram positive and Gram negative bacteria is peptidoglycan. However, the amount of the polymer present is very different. The walls of Gram positive organisms contain up to 95 per cent peptidoglycan and up to 10 per cent teichoic acids, which together form a matrix. The latter compounds are polymers of the alcohols glycerol and ribitol, and usually contain an amino acid, D-alanine, and a sugar as part of the complex. The organisation of the polymers in terms of wall architecture is unknown. Electron micrographs reveal a single layer of material which, in some species, has an outer covering of regularly organised protein subunits.

In contrast, the wall, or envelope as it is also known, of Gram negative bacteria is considerably more complex in both composition and ultrastructure (Costerton *et al.*, 1974). Electron micrographs of thin sections of *Escherichia coli* and other organisms show the wall to be comprised of several layers, which have been interpreted in terms of the structure shown in figure 1.1. The inner layer adjacent to the plasma membrane is peptidoglycan, which is variable in amount and can account for as little as 1–1.5 per cent of the cell weight. This is probably the most important wall component in determining the shape of the cell, but the other polymers

---

Figure 1.1   Diagrammatic representation of the Gram negative cell envelope.
bp, binding protein; ec, enzymes with functions directed to cytoplasm; em, enzymes involved in synthesis of wall macromolecules; ep, enzymes of the periplasmic space; es, cell surface enzymes; lp, lipid component of Braun lipoprotein; pt, protein component of Braun lipoprotein; p, proteins of inter membrane; ps, permease; s, structural protein of cytoplasmic membrane.
Adapted from Costerton, J. W., *et al.* (1974) *Bact. Rev.*, **38**, 87–110.

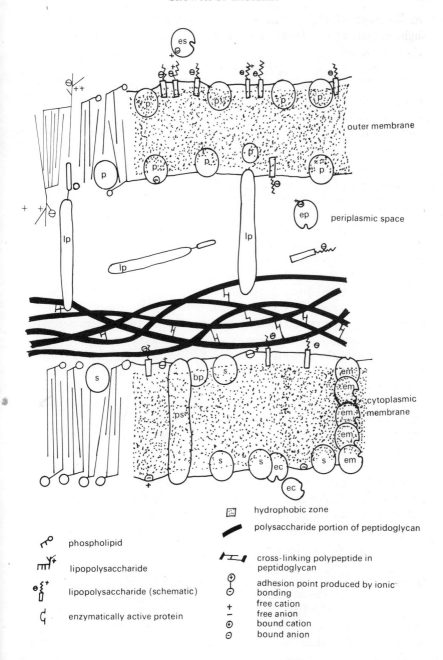

outer membrane

periplasmic space

cytoplasmic membrane

	hydrophobic zone
	polysaccharide portion of peptidoglycan
phospholipid	
lipopolysaccharide	cross-linking polypeptide in peptidoglycan
lipopolysaccharide (schematic)	adhesion point produced by ionic bonding
enzymatically active protein	+ free cation
	− free anion
	⊕ bound cation
	⊖ bound anion

may also provide some contribution to both shape and cell rigidity. The spaces within this skeletal layer and the large space located between it and the outer membranous layer form a periplasmic region. Several enzymes have been found in this region of the wall, some of which are assumed to be in transit to the outer layer, but the existence of products of certain of the enzymes has also led to the suggestion that these may be bound to static components in the region. Bridges of lipoprotein extend across the periplasmic space connecting the inner peptidoglycan layer to an outer layer of the cell envelope. This is a complex structure comprising lipo-protein phospholipid and glycoprotein. In thin section this layer is identical with other biological membranes, taking the form of a bilayer which is denatured during fixation to give the characteristic appearance of a double track. One function of this outer layer is the control of move-ment of molecules into and out of the periplasmic region.

In some bacteria the cell wall is covered by a capsule or a slime layer. Surface appendages, i.e. flagella and fimbriae, may also be present.

Plasma membrane
The composition of the bacterial plasma membrane is similar to that of eukaryotes with up to 30 per cent lipid and 75 per cent protein depending on the organism. The lipid fraction is represented by one or two phos-pholipids with phosphatidylglycerol and phosphatidylethanolamine being the principal types. Membrane structure in thin section is also similar to that in eukaryotes with two electron dense layers sandwiching an electron transparent layer. In freeze-etched preparations the membrane proteins are seen as "studs" that traverse the hydrophobic zone in the central region of the membrane. It is believed that some of these proteins may be permeases and others may have enzymic functions. The prokaryote cell lacks membrane-bound organelles and other cytoplasmic membranes such as endoplasmic reticulum and golgi bodies. However, specialised membranous structures are found, as exemplified by the mesosomes of some organisms (figure 1.2). Mesosomes are pocket-like invaginations of the plasma membrane which contain other membranous structures. They exhibit wide variation in shape, size, location and complexity in their structure. Three types of mesosome have been described according to their appearance in thin sections; these are lamellar, tubular and vesicular. Some bacteria have more than one type of mesosome depending on the physiology of the cell or the conditions to which the cell is exposed. Thus mesosomes in cells of *Bacillus cereus* change in structure from the lamellar to the vesicular form in the period between exponential and stationary

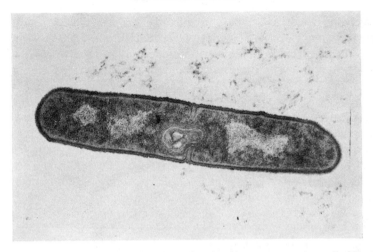

Figure 1.2 Electron micrograph of a thin section showing a mesosome in a cell of *Bacillus licheniformis* from an exponential culture. From Highton, P. J. (1970) *J. Ultrastruct. Research*, **31**, 247. By kind permission of Dr P. J. Highton and Academic Press.

growth phases prior to the commencement of spore development. However, the reality of the differences that have been described in many organisms has been questioned with the suggestion that the method of fixation is perhaps an important factor in determining the appearance of the structure. Removal of the cell wall or plasmolysis of the cell causes the mesosome to be extruded and it then takes the form of a string of small vesicles. The function of the mesosome is also a matter of controversy. One role that has been proposed is an involvement in the synthesis of the cell wall and of septa at cell division.

Bacteria with more specialised lifestyles, e.g. photosynthetic bacteria, also have internal membranous structures.

Nuclear material
A striking feature of the bacterial cell is the absence of a nuclear membrane, a typically prokaryotic feature. The nuclear material itself can be visualised as one or more discrete irregularly-shaped bodies in cells stained using DNA-specific staining procedures and viewed at the highest magnification with a light microscope. Thin sections of bacterial cells viewed with the electron microscope show areas of low electron density which have been interpreted as regions of densely packaged DNA and are called nuclear bodies or nucleoids. The appearance of these bodies is variable according to the conditions of fixation, and under certain

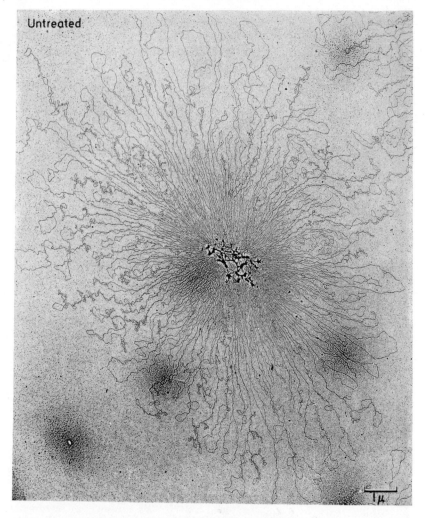

Figure 1.3 Nucleoid of *Escherichia coli* free of cell envelope material. From Kavenoff, R. and Bowen, B. C. (1976) *Chromosoma*, **59**, 89–101. Reproduced by kind permission of Dr R. Kavenoff.

treatments bundles of fibres are distinguishable. In serial sections of *Escherichia coli* the nucleoids were shown to be continuous with a body attached to the plasma membrane. In Gram positive organisms the nucleoid is frequently seen in association with a mesosome.

Studies carried out in the last decade by Pettijohn and his colleagues (Pettijohn, 1976) have provided the basis for current ideas on the function of nucleoids in relation to their appearance in bacterial cells. Using an extraction procedure involving detergents and highly concentrated salt solutions the nucleoids can be isolated from *Escherichia coli*. The isolated nuclear material is obtained in two forms; one in which the DNA is associated with materials from the cell envelope and the other in which the nucleoid is envelope-free. The presence of envelope material will obviously cause a difference in the chemical composition of the two preparations. RNA is found present in both and a major protein component is RNA polymerase. A question of particular interest relates to the association between the RNA and DNA in these preparations and its significance in the context of the form that the nucleoid takes in the cell. In both types of preparation the DNA, as seen in electron micrographs (figure 1.3), exists in a highly supercoiled state surrounding a central mass of RNA which can be removed if the preparation is treated with RNA-ase. It has been suggested that the form exhibited by the isolated nucleoid is an artefact, especially with regard to the relationship between the DNA and RNA, and several different lines of experimentation substantiate this view. Thus treatment of mRNA with highly concentrated salt solutions induces aggregation, and exposure of RNA polymerase-DNA mixtures to conditions equivalent to those used for nuclear material extraction initiates the formation of hybrid RNA–DNA molecules. At the *in vivo* level

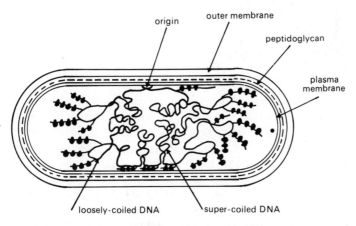

Figure 1.4 A diagrammatic model of the organisation of the nucleoid in *Escherichia coli*. Adapted from Kleppe, K., *et al.* (1979) *J. Gen. Microbiol.*, **112**, 1–13.

autoradiographic experiments have demonstrated that RNA synthesis occurs primarily in the cytoplasm and on the plasma membrane and not within the structure of the nucleoid. A reasonable summation of these observations is the possibility that the position of the RNA becomes inverted during isolation. The most recent proposal for the organisation of the nuclear body, at least in *Escherichia coli*, proposes that the DNA consists of regions in a highly supercoiled state possibly stabilised by histone-like proteins and regions that are more loosely packed (figure 1.4). The former are thought to form the central area of each nucleoid corresponding to the region of low electron density in micrographs of thin sections of cells. The other regions would be at the periphery of the nucleoid and correspond to sites of transcription with RNA molecules projecting into the cytoplasm or bound to ribosomes on the plasma membrane. Genetic studies on many bacteria have demonstrated the presence of a single linkage group which takes a circular form and for a long time it has been the convention to use the term chromosome to describe this unit.

Cytoplasm
The absence of a membrane around the nuclear bodies allows a close association between the genetic material and the cytoplasm and for a rapid movement of mRNA to the ribosomes which take up most of the space of the protoplast.

   A variety of other inclusions can also be found in the bacterial cell, their presence being determined by the growth conditions. These take the form of polyphosphate granules, which have no enclosing membranes, or polyhydroxybutyrate globules which are membrane bounded. In some spore-forming bacteria specialised inclusions occur in the form of protein crystals.

Organisation of Actinomycete cells
Actinomycetes resemble Gram positive bacteria with respect to cell structure. Mesosomes are found taking several forms including a tubular-vesicular form and a lamellar form. Whether these are different representations of one and the same structure, as discussed previously, is unknown. Septa are present in the hyphae and may arise in several ways. In the simplest mechanism the septum arises as a single ingrowth of the hyphal wall and plasma membrane. In some instances the septum may be thickened after it is formed and it may split to bring about separation of hyphal fragments. Another type of septal development involves a double

ingrowth of the hyphal wall which separates the new segments completion.

The bacterial cell cycle

The rapid growth exhibited by some bacterial species under favourable environmental conditions is the representation of an efficient coordination of a diverse range of synthetic processes. The level of activity of these activities in the individual cell is such that it is undetectable even by the most sensitive instruments that are currently available. It is necessary therefore to amplify these processes and so make them detectable. This requires large numbers of cells all at the same stage in their cell cycles. A batch culture of bacteria is therefore unsuitable for such investigations because the cell population is heterogeneous in terms of the cell cycle due to variations in the generation times of the individual cells. Whilst the majority of cells have a generation time close to the mean value the rest deviate, having either longer or shorter times. To understand the chronology of morphological and biochemical events in the growing cell and the relationship between these and its ultimate division, it is necessary to synchronise the cell population.

Synchronous cultures
Procedures for synchronisation of growing cells must be capable of coping with relatively large numbers of cells to be of value for biochemical investigations. Another important feature is that the procedure should not cause distortions to the metabolic processes of those cells, thus avoiding the introduction of artefacts into the system. The earliest methods used for induction of synchrony in bacterial cultures were based on the use of metabolic inhibitors, usually of DNA synthesis, or nutrient starvation, normally by limiting the availability of a precursor for DNA synthesis. Exposure of a batch culture to the inhibitor or nutrient starvation conditions blocks metabolism thus retarding the cells at some point in their development. As the restriction is released the cells begin to grow and subsequently divide in a synchronised manner. Fears have been expressed about the possibility of metabolic artefacts in these cultures because of the long exposure that is necessary to encompass the wide growth phase variation found in batch cultures.

To overcome these problems methods were devised to select cells of similar size and which were presumed, therefore, to be at the same phase in their cell cycles. The normal procedure is to select the smallest cells.

These are the result of the most recent divisions. A commonly used selection method involves a density gradient separation of cells in sucrose. The smallest cells remain at the top of the linear gradient and are readily removed. The second method is called the membrane elution technique. Here the cells are collected on a membrane filter to which they bind. The filter is inverted and fed with a constant supply of warmed medium which first washes away non-adsorbed cells and then the daughter cells from those that remain, as they divide. These cells are collected as separated fractions and used to set up a synchronous culture.

Cell growth, protein and RNA synthesis
Following its formation at division until its own subsequent division a bacterial cell increases in size and mass throughout the whole of its cycle to values double those at the start of the cell cycle (Donachie *et al.*, 1973). The rate of increase may be linear or exponential. Estimations of the total protein and RNA contents of the cell also follow similar patterns (figure 1.5). Examination of individual proteins, e.g. enzymes, shows a different situation. Enzyme synthesis proceeds throughout the cycle but at a specific time the rate of synthesis of a particular enzyme doubles. This change in rate has been shown to correlate with the time of replication of those structural genes which code for that enzyme. The pattern of enzyme

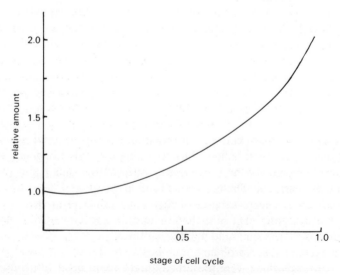

Figure 1.5   Pattern of protein synthesis in a synchronous bacterial culture.

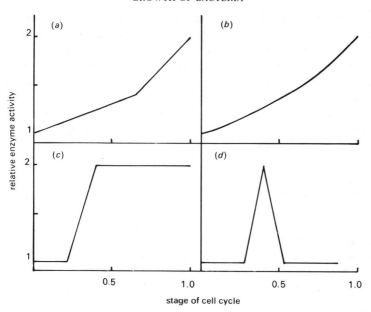

Figure 1.6 Patterns of enzyme synthesis in a synchronous bacterial culture; (a) linear, (b) exponential, (c) step and (d) peak.

synthesis in these instances may be either linear or exponential (figure 1.6). Not all enzymes follow a pattern of continual synthesis. This indicates that the rate of enzyme synthesis is controlled by other factors in addition to direct control by a specific number of genes associated with its formation. These enzymes show periodic synthesis and this may take one of two forms. Other enzymes show a similar specific timing for the increase in activity in the cell but this is short lived and the enzyme rapidly disappears. How might this periodic synthesis of enzymes be explained? Two possible explanations have been put forward. Those enzymes showing periodic synthesis that have been investigated so far have regulatory feedback mechanisms. The oscillation that is expected to arise in such a control system has been suggested as a mechanism which controls the rate of enzyme synthesis. The implication of this mechanism is a definite correlation between the oscillation of the controlling end-product and the cell cycle (figure 1.7). The alternative view states that the periodic synthesis of enzymes is a reflection of the periodic duplication of the relevant structural genes. If this is the case the sequence of synthesis of the

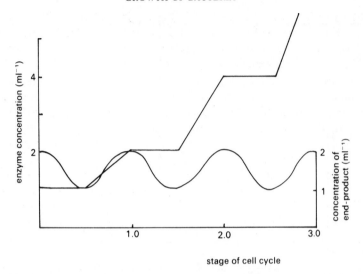

Figure 1.7   Control of synthesis of a periodic step enzyme mediated by oscillation of the concentration of the end-product in the cell. The troughs in end-product concentration are the stimulus for synthesis, and the peaks' concentration causes inhibition.

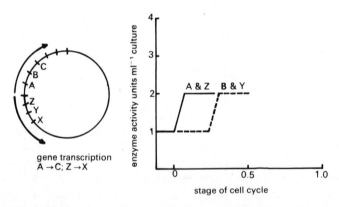

Figure 1.8   The correlation between the sequence of gene transcription and appearance of enzymes during the cell cycle.

periodic enzymes would be expected to mirror the sequence of gene transcription (figure 1.8).

DNA synthesis and chromosome replication

A model for the cell cycle of *Escherichia coli* proposed by Cooper and Helmstetter (1968) identifies three periods that follow in sequence; the I period which is the time in which key events essential for DNA synthesis occurred, the C period which represents the period of DNA synthesis and the D period which is the time interval between the termination of DNA synthesis and the subsequent cell division. Analysis of the duration of these periods in *Escherichia coli* cells grown under a range of environmental conditions showed that C and D were constant, at 40 minutes and 20 minutes respectively, over a range of doubling times from 20 to 70 minutes. The time taken for replication of the DNA is controlled by the rate of addition of nucleotides at the replication sites. The process of replication begins at a fixed point, the origin, and proceeds in both directions from this point to an opposite position, the terminus (figure 1.9). The rate of replication becomes longer than 40 minutes when the rate of growth is low. In fast growing cells the rate of DNA synthesis, as measured by the incorporation of ^{3}H-thymidine following pulse labelling, doubles at a particular time in the cell cycle. In view of the constancy of

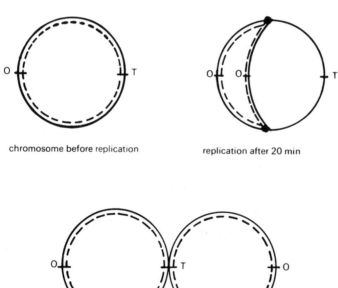

chromosome before replication

replication after 20 min

replication complete at 40 min

Figure 1.9 Diagrammatic representation of the replication of the bacterial chromosome. The process begins at the origin and proceeds around both sides of the circle until the terminus is reached.

generation time—60 min

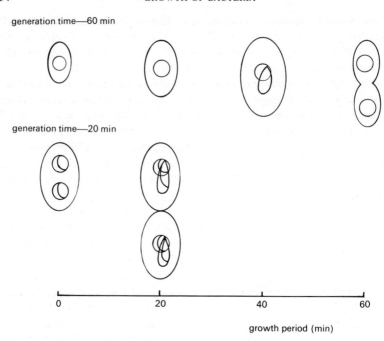

generation time—20 min

growth period (min)

Figure 1.10 Diagrammatic representation of the pattern of multiple rounds of chromosome replication occurring in fast growing cells.

the time for replication this increase in rate can only be explained on the basis of a doubling in the number of replication sites. In these cells the distribution of complete genomes is therefore ensured by some in-built mechanism and this is thought to be associated with changes in mass of the cells. In cells with a doubling time of 20 minutes the doubling of cell mass that occurs at this frequency would induce a new period of DNA synthesis and chromosome replication. Consequently a new round of replication will be initiated whilst one is in progress and the cells will be carrying nucleoids undergoing multiple rounds of replication, i.e. DNA synthesis is continuous (figure 1.10).

How is the initiation of DNA synthesis regulated? The model currently proposed stems from experiments on *Salmonella typhimurium* in which the relationship between cell mass and DNA content in exponentially growing cells with different specific growth rates was investigated. The results showed that both mass per cell and DNA per cell followed an exponential relationship over a range of doubling times and led to the proposition that a doubling of cell mass could control the initiation of a new round of DNA replication. Calculations made on *Escherichia coli* (Donachie, 1968) revealed that the cell mass designated M_i, at the time of initiation of DNA replication, was constant for doubling times of 30 to 60 minutes with a value twice this for doubling times of 20 to 30 minutes. This relationship between M_i and doubling time is similar to that for the proposed ratio of number of chromosome replication sites and doubling time, i.e. four for doublings of 20 to 30 minutes and two for doublings of 30 to 60 minutes. A constant ratio between these parameters, i.e. initiation mass and chromosome replication sites, over a wide range of growth rates could therefore provide the basis for an overall control system that regulates the "clock" that co-ordinates DNA replication and cell division.

Two theories have been put forward to explain the relationship between cell mass and chromosome replication. The first proposes the need for a protein, possibly involved in a replication complex, which is produced in the cell throughout the cell cycle, at a rate proportional to the growth rate, and reaching the critical concentration when M_i has doubled. Experiments with *Escherichia coli*, using the inhibitor chloramphenicol, showed that the protein(s) required for current rounds of replication were not affected but the initiation of new rounds was blocked. It was concluded that proteins required for the continued replication of DNA were stable molecules that once produced in the cell were functional for some considerable time, certainly long enough for the completion of the rounds of replication in progress. Conversely the protein(s) necessary to initiate new rounds of replication were concluded to be unstable and the presence of the inhibitor blocked their synthesis which in turn blocked further rounds of DNA replication. Temperature sensitive *dnaA* mutants, of *Escherichia coli* have been isolated, which grow normally at the permissive temperature (30°C) but at the non-permissive temperature (42°C) new rounds of chromosome replication are blocked. This may be caused by an alteration in a protein involved in initiation which makes it thermolabile.

The second theory, which has no experimental support, implicates an inhibitor which blocks the initiation of replication. As the cell volume increases during growth the molecule is thus diluted below a critical level with the concomitant relaxation of its control.

There is good evidence to suggest that the cytoplasmic membrane is involved in the replication of the bacterial chromosome. Cells of a leucine requiring strain of *Escherichia coli* were starved of the amino acid which prevented protein synthesis and as a consequence blocked further initiation of new rounds of chromosome replication. The effect of this block is to allow rounds of replication in progress to be completed (see above) and establish a condition whereby DNA replication will be synchronous when it recommences. This is achieved in this instance by supplying the limiting amino acid. If the cells are simultaneously given a short pulse label with ^{3}H-thymidine, regions of the chromosome adjacent to the origin will be labelled. Following a cold chase and a period of growth, cell envelope-nucleoid complexes were isolated (using a less drastic method excluding detergents) and analysed. This revealed that large amounts of the isotope were attached to the membrane. Although several sites of binding between DNA and the cytoplasmic membrane have been discovered the site that binds to the region of the molecule adjacent to the origin of replication appears to be unique. It is believed that a specific protein is involved which must recognise and bind to specific base sequences or some tertiary structure, close to the origin. The protein must also have a hydrophobic component by which it is attached to the membrane. Treatment with trypsin removes one protein component from the complex and also releases the DNA.

Co-ordination of chromosome replication and cell division

Cell division and chromosome replication are necessarily related pro-cesses since each daughter cell must receive a complete copy of the genome. Cell division does not occur immediately after a round of replication is completed, a lag of 20 minutes intervenes. Thus in cells with generation times of 40 minutes or shorter any division will relate to the completion of chromosome replication in an earlier cell generation. Therefore a division event is the result of a round of DNA replication started 60 minutes earlier. Thus if DNA replication is blocked in cells with a generation time of 20 minutes the division subsequent to any ongoing replication will be prevented. On the other hand if a replication had ended less than 20 minutes before the block is applied then one division will occur but any subsequent division is blocked. It was concluded from such observations that certain events must occur following completion of replication and before the cell can divide. It also seems that these events are associated with replication at least until the latter process is com-pleted. It has been suggested that the completion of a round of chromo-some replication triggers the synthesis of specific division substances, possibly proteins. The nature of these proteins remains unknown but it is possible that they may be associated with the cell membrane and might be involved in dissociating the chromosome from its replication complex. The cell cycle in an organism such as *Escherichia coli* may thus be looked

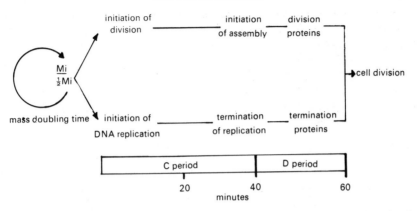

Figure 1.11 Co-ordination of cell division and DNA replication in the cell cycle of *Escherichia coli*. After Donachie, W. D., *et al.* (1973) *Symp. Soc. Gen. Microbiol.*, **23**, 9–44.

upon as at least two processes that occur in sequential manner. One of these is chromosome replication and the second involves the synthesis of all the necessary proteins that are required for cell growth and ultimately for division (figure 1.11).

Growth of the cell wall and septum formation
The increase in mass and volume of a bacterium during its cell cycle demands a simultaneous increase in the surface area of the cell surface. The growth of the cell envelope layers, the plasma membrane and the cell wall, results from the co-ordinated synthesis of the many polymers that make up these structures. Several fundamental questions arise, but of major interest is the question of sites or locations in the wall for insertion of the new polymers and the relationship between wall growth and septum development.

The mechanism of cell wall growth is not fully understood although several interesting models have been put forward. The most clear cut evidence is found in studies on *Streptococcus faecalis*, a Gram positive coccus. Detailed electron microscopic observations have been made on thin sections of cells of this bacterium and these have indicated the addition of new wall material to the existing wall in a band which runs around the cell. This band of wall growth also represents the site for the next septum when the enlarged cell divides (figure 1.12). The position of the wall band is determined during the previous cell division cycle. It is thought that as wall growth commences autolytic enzymes, acting in a

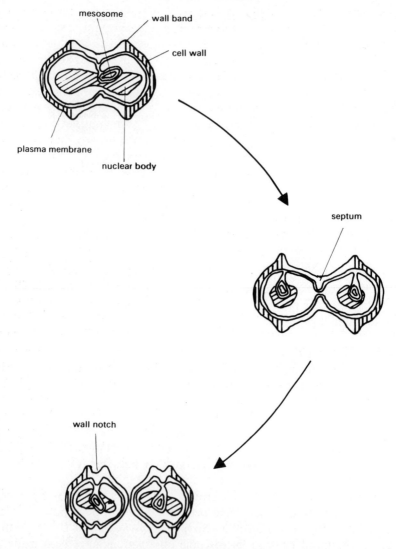

Figure 1.12   Model for cell wall growth in *Streptococcus*. Adapted from Higgins, M. L. and Shockman, G. D. (1971) *CRC Crit. Rev. Microbiol.*, **29**, 29–73.

very localised manner, bring about a cleavage in the outer side of the wall around the wall band. This results in the formation of a small notch around the cell which represents the position of insertion of the new wall polymers. As the new wall is synthesised it is laid down at the base of the notch and gradually pushes outwards over the cell surface, so increasing the area of the wall. As the cell volume doubles the direction of cell wall growth changes to become centripetal, resulting in septum formation and separation of two daughter cells. The mesosome is thought to have an important role in these events; a mesosome is present at each wall band, attached to the plasma membrane and to the nuclear body. Prior to cell division the original mesosome becomes disorganised and is replaced by new ones at the sites where cell wall growth will occur in the daughter cells.

Our knowledge about wall growth in other bacteria is less well defined. Investigations carried out on the rod-shaped bacteria *Escherichia coli* and *Bacillus subtilis* using various techniques have given rather different results. Studies in which specific envelope components (e.g. diamino-pimelic acid) have been labelled by radioisotopes, and other investigations in which the distribution of cell surface markers (e.g. flagella) amongst the daughter cells following division has been followed have led to the view that one or possibly several envelope growth sites occur. In contrast, experiments in which the distribution of peptidoglycan between daughter cells has been followed, using immunofluorescent techniques, have led to the view that many sites exist. However, an unknown factor in all these studies is the possibility that turnover of the component polymers making up the fabric of the envelope may occur. For this reason it is more generally accepted that only a small number of envelope growth sites are functional. Where a single site of wall growth occurs it is believed to be located at the end of the cell at the junction of the curved polar wall and the linear cylinder wall (figure 1.13). Simultaneously with chromosome replication the linear wall increases in length unidirectionally. When chromosome replication is complete a new attachment site is formed on the membrane and cell division proceeds with septum growth.

When the cell divides a septum is formed at one of these sites. Where only one site exists its location will determine the pattern of envelope growth prior to septum formation. Where the site is central then the extension of the envelope on either side might occur as in the case of *Streptococcus faecalis*. If the site is towards one end of the cell as has been suggested for *Escherichia coli*, then the intercalation of new material will be polarised.

The mechanism of partition of daughter cells may be different between Gram positive and Gram negative organisms. Thus in bacteria such as *Bacillus subtilis* electron microscopic evidence indicates that a septum is formed (as in *Streptococcus faecalis*) by the centripetal growth of the

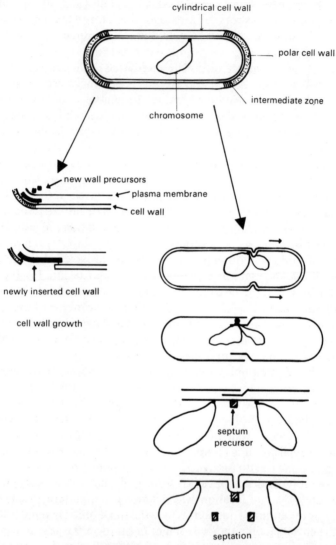

Figure 1.13 Model for wall growth in rod-shaped bacteria. Adapted from Higgins, M. L. and Shockman, G. D. (1971) *CRC Crit. Rev. Microbiol.*, **29**, 29–73.

envelope, and the separation of cells is brought about by the action of hydrolases. The time period for septum formation in this bacterium is constant for a wide range of growth rates. Under conditions of most rapid cell growth, therefore, extension of the cell is faster than septum development. In such cultures multiseptate cells may be seen which slowly separate. Septation in *Escherichia coli* is brought about by the invagination of the cytoplasmic membrane and the peptidoglycan layer of the wall. The outer part of the wall is not involved. It is assumed that the release of the covalent linkage between the peptidoglycan and the lipoprotein bridges is a necessary associated event, and this could be of significance in the septation process. Attempts to establish this have involved the isolation and study of mutants deficient in the lipoprotein bridge component. These mutants were isolated by a method of suicide selection devised by Torti and Park (1976) which is based on the fact that lipoproteins are deficient in a number of amino acids. Auxotrophic strains with requirements for these substrates were starved so blocking growth but allowing lipoprotein synthesis to continue. Simultaneously the cells were supplied with high levels of a radioactively labelled amino acid that is a component of the lipoprotein. Incorporation of large amounts of the isotope kills the cells, but a small number in the population survive. These are cells that did not synthesise lipoprotein because of some mutational block. These lipoprotein deficient mutants were isolated and were subsequently shown to be unable to make septa. Unfortunately this observation did not confirm a role for the lipoproteins in septation because subsequent analysis showed that other envelope proteins were also absent and these may also have some function in the process.

Two fundamental questions arise concerning the relationship between the synthesis of peptidoglycan and both cell elongation and septation— are the polymers similar or different and are the enzymes involved the same or different? Answers to these questions have come forward in recent years as a result of some elegant experiments based on the effects of the β-lactam antibiotic, penicillin (Spratt, 1975). The natural product, penicillin G, has two effects. At low concentrations septation is blocked by the antibiotic and the cells grow as elongate filaments containing multiple copies of the chromosome, but at higher concentrations the cells are lysed. The implication of these results is that two individual patterns of peptidoglycan synthesis exist for the septum and for cell elongation with two separate enzyme systems each exhibiting different sensitivities to penicillin G. Cephalexin, a cephalosporin and another β-lactam, also blocks septum development but has no other effect on the cells indicating specificity for the enzymes involved only in septation. A totally different morphological effect, namely the development of spherical cells, is caused by a semi-synthetic penicillin, amidinopenicillinamic acid. In this case septation is not blocked nor is lysis induced, indicating inhibition of the enzyme(s) involved in elongation.

Subsequent experiments were carried out to ascertain the sites of penicillin binding in the cell envelope in order to elucidate further those mechanisms involved in wall growth and septation. Electrophoresis of extracts from the cytoplasmic membrane treated with ^{14}C-penicillin G gave six separate protein bands which were assumed to be enzymes sensitive to the antibiotic. Pretreatment of the membrane with the two antibiotics mentioned previously gave interesting results. In each case the protein profile was deficient in one band. The missing band was different for each antibiotic. Mutants resistant to the two antibiotics were subsequently found to be lacking in the two specific proteins identified in the previous experiments. The conclusion from these studies is therefore an interesting one. It is implied that the specific enzymes involved in peptidoglycan biosynthesis have significant functions at different stages in cell development. Identification of the two enzymes has not yet proved possible. Comparison of activities of three enzymes involved in the formation of the peptide chains of the muramic acid residues during the cell cycle, has revealed that one, carboxypeptidase II, does peak at the time of septation, however, this enzyme is not sensitive to cephalexin. This should not be surprising because it is unlikely that only one enzyme is the key to the switch in pattern of peptidoglycan synthesis.

Environmental control of cell shape

Most bacteria, through repeated growth and division, yield populations of cells that are regular in shape and form irrespective of the medium on which they are cultured. A few species diverge from this giving different cell shapes in response to environmental differences. This pleomorphism is well expressed in representatives of the genus *Arthrobacter*. In media which support a low growth rate, e.g. a glucose salts medium, the cells assume a spherical shape (figure 1.14). The addition of more complex nutrients, such as peptone, stimulates faster growth and a change in shape to the rod or bacillus form (Ensign and Wolfe, 1964).

Analyses have been made on the peptidoglycan component of the walls of the two growth forms and three differences have been found. In the rod-shaped form there is more extensive cross-linking between the peptides of the N-acetyl muramic acid residues; glycine is present in the cross links between the peptide chains in the spherical cells but not in the rods, and thirdly the polysaccharide chain is shorter with forty hexosamine residues

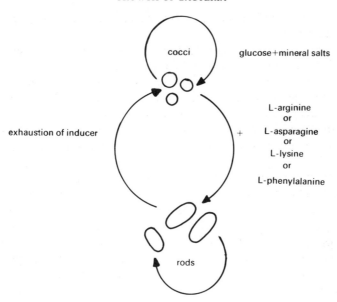

Figure 1.14   Environmentally controlled changes in cell shape in *Arthrobacter*.

in the spherical cell as opposed to one hundred and twenty residues in the rod shaped cells. A further difference is a higher N-acetylmuramidase activity in the coccal form. The nature of the trigger that induces this morphological switch remains unknown.

Cell dimorphism in *Caulobacter*

Caulobacter is an interesting deviation from the normal pattern of bacterial cell development exhibiting differentiation in regard to both cell morphology and function. The cells of this organism have a unique structural feature, a stalk or prostheca, which provides attachment for the cell to some suitable substratum. The stalk is an extension of the cell, its surface being an elongation of the wall of the main body of the cell. The stalk is essentially a non-growing structure except for a region at its junction with the body of the cell. The stalk is variable in length and environmental factors have some influence in this respect.

Development of the stalk cell is also unique (figure 1.15). After the main body of the cell has enlarged to form the pre-divisional cell an asymmetric division follows to give one daughter cell that retains the stalk and the

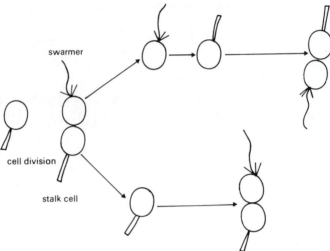

Figure 1.15   The cell cycle of *Caulobacter*.

other which develops a flagellum and fimbriae becoming a swarmer cell. These two cell types are out of phase in their cell cycles, the stalked cell commences a new cycle immediately with the initiation of a new round of chromosome replication. The swarmer cells, however, are immature and of necessity are required to undergo some as yet unknown differentiating steps before becoming stalked mother cells and embarking on division. Most obvious is the repression of DNA replication in these cells, with the event proceeding only when stalk development has taken place some 30 minutes after cell division.

The underlying mechanism of control of differentiation clearly involves segmental gene transcription and the regulation of gene activity but the ways in which these are expressed remains to be discovered. Cyclic GMP has been implicated to be involved at certain levels especially in the regulation of surface change (Shapiro, 1976). Thus cells grown in the presence of derivatives of cyclic GMP fail to develop flagella and fimbriae but retain the capacity for stalk formation and elongation.

SUMMARY

1. Despite the apparent simplicity of the bacterial cell in terms of structure and organis-
    ation the processes and events associated with its growth and replication are clearly
    complex.

2. An understanding of the events associated with growth and cell replication requires the
    use of synchronous cultures. These can be obtained by using inhibitors which block cell
    metabolism at a specific stage or by selection of cells based on size. The latter procedure
    is preferred to avoid the possibility of metabolic artefacts which may arise from the use
    of inhibitors.

3. Cell mass, total protein and total RNA increase throughout the whole of the cell cycle
    following either an exponential or linear pattern. At the level of individual enzymes the
    situation is different. There are two basic patterns; those enzymes which are synthesised
    continuously and those which are synthesised in a periodic fashion.

4. DNA synthesis and chromosome replication demonstrate an aspect of the uniqueness of
    bacteria. Over a range of growth rates, the rate of DNA synthesis is constant so that cell
    division may occur over time periods shorter than those required for chromosome
    replication. Clearly the two daughter cells of a division event need to receive copies of
    the complete genome. To achieve this a model has been proposed which requires that
    the initiation of new rounds of chromosome replication be related to doublings of cell
    mass. In fast growing cells multiple rounds of replication are assumed to be in progress.

5. Cell wall growth is an essential part of cell growth. New wall polymers are believed to be
    incorporated into the existing wall at only a few sites. In cocci the site of wall growth and
    septum formation, are believed to be one and the same at the time of division. A similar
    situation may exist in the Gram positive bacilli but in the Gram negative forms there is
    evidence to suggest that septation is independent of wall growth.

6. Regularity in cell shape whilst a feature of the majority of bacteria is not so for all.
    Environmental influences dictate cell shape in *Arthrobacter* and associated alterations in
    the cell wall may explain the morphological change.

7. The life cycle of *Caulobacter* provides an interesting diversion from the typical cell
    growth and division cycle of bacteria. The developmental sequence provides an example
    of differential gene activity whereby the products of cell division show morphological
    and biochemical differences. In one of these, the swarmer cell, the cell cycle is elongated
    commencing with an initial period in which DNA replication is arrested. A switch in
    behaviour of the swarmer cell coincides with the initiation of DNA synthesis.

CHAPTER TWO

GROWTH OF YEASTS

THE YEASTS ARE A GROUP OF ORGANISMS THAT EXHIBIT HETEROGENEITY
in virtually all aspects of their biology. Although the name yeast is widely
used it has no taxonomic significance. Thus yeasts are typically unicellular
fungi which, on the conventional criteria of mechanism of sexual reproduction, belong to one of the three major groups—the Ascomycetes, the
Basidiomycetes and the Fungi Imperfecti. As we saw with bacteria in the
previous chapter, the processes of cell growth and division are closely
integrated and, although cell division is in fact a reproductive process, it is
clear that the event is very much influenced by the growth of the cell that
proceeds it. For this reason these aspects are treated together in this
chapter.

Cell morphology

Yeast cells are diverse in shape (figure 2.1) but most common are types
which are ellipsoidal and a smaller group where the cells are elongated.
Dimensions of the cells are variable and subject to environmental factors
but average sizes for ellipsoidal cells are 5 μm long axis by 4 μm short axis,
and for the elongated cells are 3.5 μm diameter by 5 μm to 20 μm long.
These two groups have different patterns of cell division. In the ellipsoidal
forms division involves the formation of buds whereas in the elongated
forms the process is a conventional fission of the cell into two equal parts.
In the budding yeasts some variation is found in the relationship of the
mother and daughter cells. In some the daughter cell becomes detached
when another bud starts to form and the position of the first bud is
marked by a bud scar on the wall of the mother cell. In other species the
daughters remain attached to the mother cell and they in turn produce

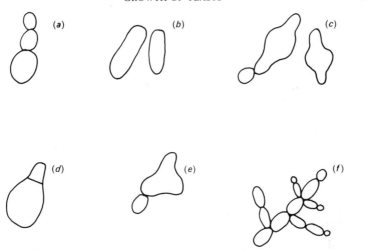

Figure 2.1 Diversity in cell shape in yeasts; (a) spheroidal—*Saccharomyces*, (b) elongate—*Schizosaccharomyces*, (c) apiculate—*Hanseniaspora*, (d) flask-shaped—*Pityrosporum*, (e) triangular—*Trigonopsis*, (f) pseudomycelial—*Candida*.

daughters as does the mother cell. This type of association of cells can take on the appearance of a pseudomycelium and in some yeasts this type of morphology is characterised by differentiation of the cells. Cells of the main chains become elongated and cylindrical producing clusters of buds at their shoulders (figure 2.1). A few yeasts, mainly those which are pathogenic on animals, have a dual morphology and are said to be dimorphic. These organisms grow in either the unicellular or filamentous form and the switch in morphology is environmentally controlled. In the Basidiomycete yeasts this dimorphism also occurs with the mycelial forms representing the dikaryon stage in the life cycle.

Ultrastructure

The cell wall
The wall surface of yeast cells is characterised by the presence of scars which are the sites of bud formation and fission. In the budding yeasts there are two types of scar; the birth scar which marks the site of attachment of the cell to its mother cell, and the bud scars which are the sites where buds were formed (figure 2.2). The birth scar is normally sited at one end of the cell on the long axis, and the bud scars occur either randomly or at fixed sites depending on the species.

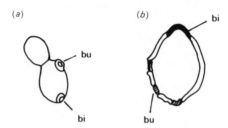

Figure 2.2 Budding in *Saccharomyces cerevisiae*. (*a*) Mother and daughter cell showing birth scar (bi) and bud scars (bu) (line drawing from micrograph by Dr E. Streiblova). (*b*) Diagrammatic representation of scars.

Is there a limit to the number of buds a cell can form? It seems there is and some intricate experiments on *Saccharomyces cerevisiae* were done to prove it. To prevent nutrient exhaustion being a limiting factor in bud formation cells were subjected to microsurgery such that after a bud had formed it was removed by micromanipulator so maintaining the cell population constant. The cells produced variable numbers of buds from 9 to 43 with a median value of 24. Yeast cells are therefore subject to ageing, the period between budding, i.e. the generation time, lengthens as the number of buds increases. Eventually budding stops and the cells die. The pattern of budding in haploid cells of this organism is organised for a given cell, but can vary between cells taking the form of rings or spirals. Interestingly the pattern of bud formation by diploid cells is totally random.

The scars on the surface of fission yeast cells are the sites of separation of two daughter cells and arise from the particular mechanisms of septum development and cell wall growth.

The ultrastructure and chemistry of the yeast cell wall has been investigated most extensively in *Saccharomyces* using a combination of chemical analysis and enzyme dissection on purified wall preparations. The enzyme dissection techniques involve a systematic treatment of the wall material with purified enzymes, either singly or in specific combinations, followed by an electron microscopic examination to observe changes in texture that result. The observations made so far indicate the wall to be comprised of three layers. These are an inner microfibrillar layer of β-glucan which is alkali-insoluble, a middle layer of alkali-soluble β-glucan and the outer layer of mannan-protein and phosphate.

The inner layer of glucan accounts for about 35 per cent of the wall, and is made up primarily of a β-1,3-linked polymer with a small number of β-

1,6-linkages that form branch points. Electron micrographs of this material reveal a dense microfibrillar network. A second (more highly branched) polymer is also present in small quantity and this has a greater number of β-1,6-linkages. The two glucans are separable using hot acetic acid in which the highly branched polymer solubilises. Alkali extraction of *Saccharomyces cerevisiae* wall removes the soluble glucan and the mannan-protein complex and the addition of Fehlings Solution separates the two components by precipitation of the mannan-protein. The glucan can be precipitated by neutralising the alkaline extract with acetic acid. The alkali soluble glucan is amorphous in texture and comprises 20–22 per cent of the wall, it also differs from the inner layer of glucan in having β-1,6-linkages inserted in the β-1,3-chains. Small quantities of mannose have been discovered in the alkali-soluble glucan fraction suggesting possible linkage of this middle layer to the outer mannan-protein-layer.

The outer mannan-protein complex makes up about 30 per cent of the wall. The polysaccharide component of this complex has a backbone of D-mannose units with α-1,6-linkages about 50 residues in length and side chains of variable length with α-1,3- and α-1,2-linkages.

Other types of yeasts show differences in the wall polysaccharides. The Basidiomycete budding yeasts have chitin as the skeletal component, replacing glucan. Chitin is also present in *Saccharomyces cerevisiae* walls, but in very small quantity, and is highly localised in the septum which is formed during the budding process. The fission yeast *Schizosaccharomyces pombe* lacks both chitin and mannan in its walls. A polysaccharide found only in this latter species is a nigeran-like α-1,3-glucan.

The protein component of the wall has several roles. In bakers yeast (*Saccharomyces cerevisiae*) it may account for up to 10 per cent of the dry wall, the amount varying in response to environmental conditions, age of culture and species. Some of the protein is enzymatic occurring in the form of invertase and acid phosphates, and is found in the mannan-protein layer. An important feature of the structural protein in this layer is the high content of sulphur-containing amino acids which most probably form disulphide bridges. It has been proposed that these bridges have an important role in maintaining the structural integrity of the wall and are thus involved in the initiation of budding.

The other component of yeast walls is lipid and this may make up about 12–13 per cent of the wall.

The protoplast
The organisation of the protoplast is typically eukaryotic, its limit is the

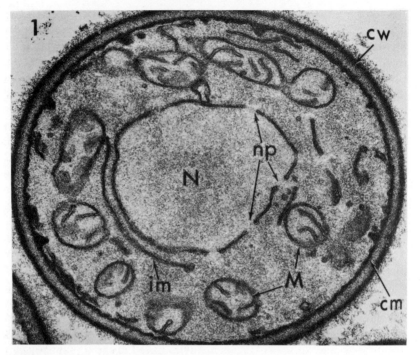

Figure 2.3　Transmission electron micrograph of *Hansenula wingei*.
CW, cell wall; N, nucleus; M, mitochondria; np, nuclear pores; im, endoplasmic reticulum; cm, cytoplasmic membrane (×46 000). From Conti, S. F. and Brock, T. D. (1965) *J. Bact.*, **90**, 524–533. By kind permission of Dr T. D. Brock.

plasma membrane. In *Saccharomyces cerevisiae* this is characterised by the presence of particles, 15 nm diameter, organised in parallel rows. The particles are of mannan and protein and are thought to be the units of construction of the outer wall layer. The particles have been found embedded at varying depths in the plasma membrane and this has been interpreted as an expression of their passage through the membrane. Another feature of the plasma membrane is the presence of many deep invaginations. In thin sections these are seen to be up to 50 nm deep and about 30 nm wide.

An internal membrane system comprised of endoplasmic reticulum and nuclear membrane is readily distinguishable in electron micrographs of *Saccharomyces cerevisiae* (figure 2.3). The nuclear membrane has typical pores and, as in other Ascomycete fungi, remains intact at division. In

Basidiomycete yeasts the membrane breaks down at division. The presence of a golgi apparatus is a point of controversy. This organelle has been described in micrographs of freeze-etched preparations. However, the function of this organelle in wall synthesis may well be taken over by the endoplasmic reticulum. Alternatively the golgi may be an ephemeral structure arising prior to wall synthesis during bud growth and being consumed in the process. Vacuoles and mitochondria of typical eukaryotic form are present.

Associated with the retention of the nuclear membrane during division are certain other unique features, at least in *Saccharomyces cerevisiae* (Byers and Goetsch, 1975). In the life of a cell a distinctive region becomes apparent on the nuclear membrane called the spindle or centriolar plaque and associated with it are microtubules, some projecting into the body of the nucleus and the rest into the cytoplasm. Prior to nuclear division the plaque duplicates and the copies lie adjacent to each other. Later they rapidly migrate to opposite sides of the nucleus and become connected by the intra-nuclear microtubules which form a spindle. These events occur simultaneously with bud development and immediately after the migration of the nucleus to the neck which connects mother and bud. Both the nucleus and the microtubular spindle subsequently increase in length very rapidly. The nuclear membrane then pinches inwards at the neck region forming two nuclei. Genetic studies have indicated that *Saccharomyces cerevisiae* has at least seventeen chromosomes but these cannot normally be seen during nuclear division.

In the Basidiomycete types the nucleus becomes elongated, part in the mother cell and part in the bud. The chromosomal component moves into the region of the nucleus in the bud and the nucleolus stays in the mother cell. The nuclear membrane in the bud breaks down and the chromatin material divides. What happens to the nucleolus is not clear, it seems to break up but reappears again within the newly formed nuclei which arises through the formation of new membrane around the two chromatin components. When the nuclei are formed one moves back to the mother cell, the second remaining in the bud.

Cell growth and division in budding yeasts

The cell cycle
Synchronisation of yeast cells for cell cycle investigations (see Chapter 1) is normally achieved using centrifugation selection methods. In most budding yeasts the cell cycle follows the conventional eukaryotic pattern

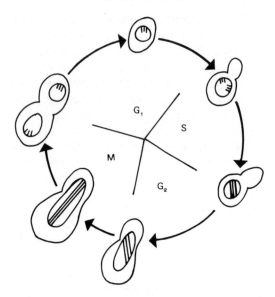

Figure 2.4   The cell cycle of *Saccharomyces cerevisiae.*

with four distinct phases, G1, S, G2 and M. S and M represent periods of DNA synthesis and mitosis, respectively and G1 and G2 are periods in the cycle separating the two events. Cell division follows mitosis, although *Saccharomyces cerevisiae* deviates in this respect because they are temporally separated with cell division occurring during the G1 phase (Hartwell, 1974). Various other events associated with the budding process can also be used as markers in the cycle as shown in figure 2.4. After mitosis the mother and daughter cells start the G1 phase of the next cycle, the daughter cells may increase in size during this time but this depends on environmental influences. The end of G1 and the start of S are marked by the events of plaque duplication and bud initiation.

Budding

The development of a new bud begins with a localised weakening of the mother cell wall. The reduction of the sulphydryl bridges in the wall protein has been implicated in this event. Within the protoplast small vesicles accumulate adjacent to the budding site. Electron micrographs of freeze-fractured yeast cells show the plasmalemma to have small circular invaginations which could arise from fusion of these vesicles with the plasmalemma. The bud continues to grow in size during the cell cycle and this involves the *de novo* synthesis of wall polymers. Investigations using autoradiographic and fluorescent staining procedures have shown that deposition of wall material occurs at a site distal to the parent cell.

The pattern of budding is a variable feature in different yeasts. In *Saccharomyces cerevisiae* and some other Ascomycete yeasts it is multipolar and can occur at any point on the cell surface except at a previous budding site. Other Ascomycete yeasts have bipolar budding which occurs repeatedly at the two ends of the cell. The Basidiomycete yeasts also produce buds at random sites but several buds can be formed at one site. The mechanism of orientation of the new bud in *Saccharomyces cerevisiae* is unknown. The spindle plaque has been implicated because at the stage of duplication it becomes orientated in the direction of the new bud with the extranuclear microtubules extending into the bud.

The migration of the spindle plaque and bud growth are continuous through both the S and G2 phases of the cell cycle. At the end of G2 the nucleus has migrated to the neck connecting the bud and the mother cell. Mitosis then follows during which the spindle plaque exhibits the spectacular behaviour already described.

The budding process and the cell cycle, are completed with the formation of the septum. This apparently simple event in fact represents a highly significant morphogenetic process and has been the subject of intensive investigation (Cabib, 1975). The interest in septum development

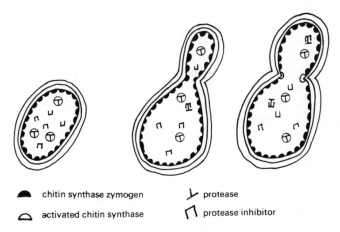

- ◖ chitin synthase zymogen
- ◖ activated chitin synthase
- ⅄ protease
- ⊓ protease inhibitor

Figure 2.5 Model for the initiation and control of chitin synthesis in the primary bud scar of *Saccharomyces cerevisiae*. Adapted from Cabib, E. and Farkas, V. (1971) *Proc. Nat. Acad. Sci. USA*, **68**, 2052–2060.

resides in the fact that the first formed wall is composed of chitin and septa are the only site in which this polymer is found. The localised deposition of chitin, both spatial and temporal during the cell cycle raises fundamental questions relating to the mechanisms controlling such morphogenetic events. The model proposed (figure 2.5) is the result of many years of investigation and is based on the activities of three components. The enzyme concerned in synthesis of the polymer, chitin synthase, appears to exist in an inactive zymogen form bound to the plasma membrane. Activation is achieved through the action of a proteolytic enzyme which is contained in vesicles and is presumed to be released at the neck region. The third component is an inhibitor molecule, also a protein, which has the proposed function of inactivating any stray proteolytic enzyme which is released into the cytoplasm. The only weak point in this elegant model is the role of the protease activator which might be expected to be very specific in its action. It has been shown that the endogenous protease that activates chitin synthase also activates tryptophan synthetase.

Cell growth and division in fission yeasts

The fission yeast *Schizosaccharomyces pombe* has been used extensively as a model system for the first three-quarters of the cell cycle (about 105 minutes) in an almost exponential manner. For the majority of cells of a culture, wall synthesis occurs only at one end of the cell. During the remainder of the cycle the size remains constant. The centrally located nucleus divides at the end of the growth phase and this is followed by the centripetal growth of the inner wall layer to produce a septum or scar plug. The septum then splits transversely allowing the two daughter cells to separate. At the site of septum formation a scar remains where the outer wall layers are severed (figure 2.6). Where daughter cells have a scar plug at each end then new wall growth will occur at both ends of the cell.

DNA synthesis during the yeast cell cycle

Location of DNA
Haploid strains of *Saccharomyces cerevisiae* contain approximately 1.2×10^{10} daltons of DNA. Most of this is located in the nucleus and genetic studies suggest that it is organised into seventeen chromosomes. Mitochondrial DNA accounts for 5–20 per cent of the total and this occurs as circular molecules 25 μm long. The ratio of mitochondrial to

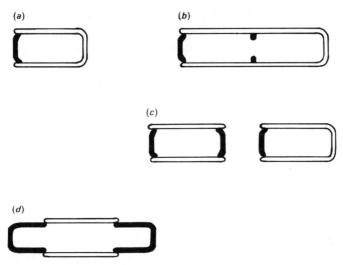

Figure 2.6 Diagrammatic representation of cell division in *Schizosaccharomyces pombe*; (*a*) cell with single birth scar, (*b*) cell elongation and the initiation of septum development, (*c*) separation of daughter cells, one cell has a single birth scar and the other has two, (*d*) growth at both poles in the cell with two birth scars. Adapted from Streiblova, E., *et al.* (1966) *J. Bact.*, **91**, 428–435.

nuclear DNA remains fairly constant under a variety of growth conditions. A few years ago an additional DNA molecule was discovered in the form of closed circles 2 μm in circumference. These small molecules have since been shown to have properties similar to bacterial plasmids, and the term plasmid is now used to describe them. Yeast plasmid DNA accounts for 1–5 per cent of the total. It can be separated as a distinct component independent of nuclear and mitochondrial DNA but its location is as yet unknown.

DNA synthesis
A constant time relationship between growth rate and DNA synthesis has also been suggested for yeasts and there is some experimental support for the idea. When *Saccharomyces cerevisiae* was grown in a chemostat at different growth rates induced by glucose limitation it was found that the time period between bud emergence and cell separation was similar over a wide range. At the slower growth rates the phase that did vary was the period prior to bud emergence. A corollary of this finding concerns bud emergence and DNA synthesis which are generally co-incident, in which the time from the initiation of DNA synthesis to cell division is also

constant. This observation led to the proposal by Carter (1978) of two phases to the growth cycle of the yeast cell, an expandable phase which will vary according to growth rate and a constant phase.

Further support for this hypothesis was derived from experiments in which a numerical analysis technique devised to determine the duration of cell cycle phases in asynchronous populations of cells (Hartwell *et al.*, 1973) was used with temperature sensitive cell cycle (*cdc*) mutants which have blocks at different stages of the cycle. The experiment involves the culture of the mutant at the permissive temperature at which the cycle is normal and then switching to the non-permissive temperature. The cells in the culture that have passed the stage at which the block occurs will

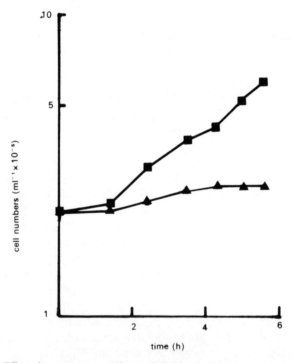

Figure 2.7 Effect of a temperature shift on cell division in *Saccharomyces cerevisiae cdc 7* (a temperature sensitive mutant). The cells were taken from steady state growth at 24°C, diluted in fresh growth medium, and samples were incubated at 24°C (■) and 38°C (▲) (the restrictive temperature). The increase in cell number was followed in the two cultures. The cells grown at the permissive temperature increased exponentially after a short lag but only a small increase (about 17 per cent) occurred at the restrictive temperature. This represents the proportion of the population that had commenced DNA synthesis at the temperature shift. Redrawn from Carter, B. L. A. (1978) *Adv. Microb. Physiol.*, **17**, 243–302.

continue their cycles but the remainder will be subject to arrest when they reached the blocked stage. The percentage of cells in the population that have passed the block is determined and this information is used to calculate the timing in the cycle that the block occurs using the equation

$$X_1 = \frac{1 - \ln(N/N_0)}{n2}$$

where X_1 = stage of cell cycle block

N_0 = number of cells at the time of the temperature shift

N = final number of cells

Carter (1978) applied this approach to a mutant of *Saccharomyces cerevisiae, cdc 7,* which is defective for the initiation of DNA synthesis. Cultures of the mutant were grown at different glucose-limiting rates in a chemostat and cells then transferred to the non-permissive temperature (38°C). The cells that continued to divide were measured (figure 2.7). As the growth rate declined the block on DNA synthesis was apparent later and later in the cell cycle, but with the exception of very low growth rates, the time from initiation of DNA synthesis to cell division remained constant over a wide range of growth rates (figure 2.8).

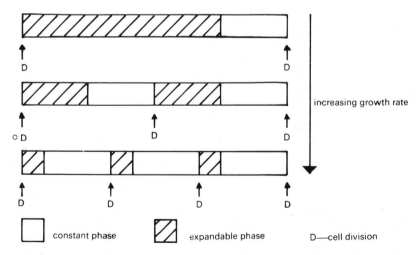

Figure 2.8 Schematic model for the cell-division cycle in *Saccharomyces cerevisiae.* Adapted from Carter, B. L. A. (1978) *Adv. Microb. Phys.,* 17, 243–302.

The initiation of DNA synthesis in the yeast nucleus is dependent upon active protein synthesis but completion of a round of synthesis will occur if protein synthesis is stopped. In experiments involving the use of the inhibitor cycloheximide it was shown that exposure up to 10 minutes prior to the start of S had no effect on DNA synthesis, clearly the synthesis of the requisite proteins can occur in a relatively short time. The significance of protein synthesis to the mechanism of initiation of DNA synthesis remains obscure, however, it is hoped that this might be resolved as more detailed studies are made on the *cdc* mutants.

The pattern of mitochondrial DNA synthesis is variable in different yeasts, in some it occurs continuously throughout the cell cycle in others the timing is specific. Details on the control of the process are restricted. Thus it is not known whether the nuclear genome or the mitochondrial genome carries the message for synthesis of the components of the replication system. It does appear, however, that mitochondrial DNA replication is independent of nuclear DNA replication, at least in part. Cells in which nuclear DNA synthesis is blocked continue to replicate their mitochondrial DNA for a period equivalent to two generations.

Macromolecule synthesis

The general patterns of synthesis in growing yeast cells are the same as

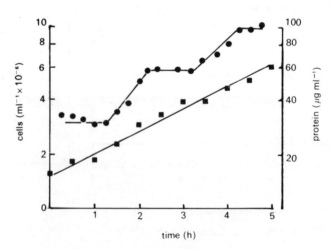

Figure 2.9 Growth (●) and protein synthesis (■) in a synchronous culture of *Schizosaccharomyces pombe*. Adapted from Stebbing, N. (1971) *J. Cell Sci.*, **9**, 701–717.

described for bacteria. Total cell mass, total protein and total RNA all increase continuously throughout the cell cycle (figure 2.9).

The various patterns of enzyme synthesis recounted for bacteria have also been shown to occur in yeasts. The most favoured model to explain these events is the sequential chromosome transcription model which assumes that the order of appearance of the different enzymes is determined by the order of genes on the chromosomes. Evidence cited in support of this model involves comparison of the sequence of enzyme production which is coded by chromosome II. The genes for lysine requirement and the utilisation of galactose are closely linked and this is reflected in the close timing of their translation. In a particular mutant strain this region of chromosome II has been altered due to a translocation event, and the two genes are a greater distance apart. This genetical difference correlates with the biochemical situation in which the timing of synthesis of the two enzymes is altered (figure 2.10).

Synthesis of cell wall polymers

Information on the biosynthesis of the major cell wall polymers is limited and relates primarily to the mannan component. Preparations of intra-

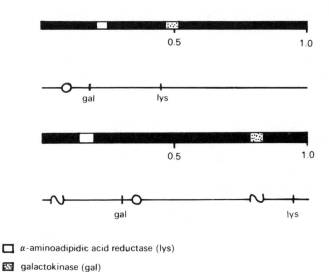

☐ α-aminoadipidic acid reductase (lys)

▨ galactokinase (gal)

Figure 2.10 Cell cycle and genetic maps showing the relationship between timing of enzyme synthesis and gene location.

cellular membranes have been isolated that utilise guanosine diphos-
phate-mannose as the mannosyl donor for the synthesis of the mannan
component of the mannan-protein complex. Mannosyl transferases,
highly specific for the synthesis of α-1,6-, α-1,3- and α-1,2-linkages, transfer
the mannosyl residues for the polymerisation of the chains. Attachment of
the mannan chains to the protein involves a lipid intermediate, dolichol
monophosphate.

A β-glucan synthase system has yet to be isolated from yeast cells, and a
lipid intermediate has not been identified to date. The evidence for β-
glucan synthesis is therefore rather limited and rests with studies in which
cells, treated with lipid solvents and made permeable, were found to
incorporate UDP glucose into the β-1,3-linked glucan.

The pattern of cell growth during the cell cycle suggests that wall
synthesis proceeds continuously.

Co-ordination of growth and cell division

An obvious but still fascinating feature of growth and division of yeast
cells is the order associated with the various events. This order has to be
maintained and perpetuated to ensure that viable daughter cells are
produced and a fundamental question relates to how it is maintained.
Studies using mutants with blocks at specific cycle events and using
inhibitors have shown that a block early in the cycle may also cause
inhibition in some other later events, but not all. These observations have
led to the hypothesis that the cell cycle of *Saccharomyces cerevisiae* is
organised into two independent pathways, but each pathway comprised
of dependent steps. Thus mutants which are blocked at bud emergence
continue to synthesise DNA and undergo nuclear division and conversely
strains which can be blocked at DNA synthesis do initiate bud formation
and nuclear migration. The concept of the cycle as a progression of events
has recently been questioned (Carter, 1978) following the suggestion of
two phases, the expandable and constant phases, in the life of the cell with
the constant phase being equivalent to the cell cycle.

There is, as yet, little sound information on the mechanism of integration of growth and division. One proposal suggests that increments
of growth might be controlled by the occurrence of particular cell cycle
events, alternatively the requirements for one of these particular cell cycle
events may be satisfied only when a specific size is reached.

The possible involvement of cell size as a controlling factor in the cell
cycle raises interesting implications in relation to the newly formed buds.

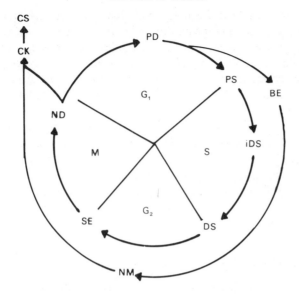

Figure 2.11 Dependent and independent events in the cell cycle of *Saccharomyces cerevisiae*.
PD, plaque duplication; PS, plaque separation; iDS, initiation of DNA synthesis; DS, DNA synthesis; SE, spindle elongation; ND, nuclear division; BE, bud emergence; NM, nuclear migration; CK, cytokinesis; CS, cell separation. Adapted from Hartwell, L. E. (1974) *Bact. Rev.*, **38**, 164–198.

After a cycle of budding the mother cell remains at a size about the same as its pre-division size. This cell might then be expected to commence another cycle immediately. In contrast the bud is considerably smaller and a period of growth will be required before bud emergence and the initiation of DNA synthesis commences. In cultures of fast growing cells this period will be short but in slow growing cultures the cells will attain the required status after a much longer period. Consequently the population will be comprised of two groups of cells with different generation times. This period of growth to attain the critical size prior to the commencement of the next round of division, could be interpreted as the expandable phase.

In the fission yeast *Schizosaccharomyces pombe* a slightly different view of the integration of cell cycle events has been put forward. There is evidence for at least two sequences, the DNA-division cycle which involves DNA synthesis, mitosis and cell division, and the growth cycle which includes the processes of macromolecule synthesis, including

GROWTH OF YEASTS

enzymes. The two sequences can be dissociated by a variety of experimental procedures. Inhibiting DNA synthesis or nuclear division was found to have no effect on the growth cycle markers but the cells grow to unusual lengths. Acceleration of the DNA-division cycle caused the formation of small cells even though the rate of events in the growth cycle were not affected.

The growth of the yeast cell provides a simple yet elegant system for the study of "biochemical differentiation". The ordered sequence of events occurring during growth and division are an expression of the genome of the organism under a particular set of environmental conditions. Our knowledge of these important organisms has expanded greatly but the challenge of some of the fundamental questions still remains.

SUMMARY

1. Yeast cells show diversity in shape, but characteristically show only two patterns of division, budding and fission.

2. Yeast cells are typically eukaryotic in their general cellular organisation.

3. The cell wall is comprised mainly of β-1,3-, β-1,6-linked glucan and α-1,6-linked mannan. The outer surface of the budding yeasts is characterised by scars that mark the site of bud formation. Part of the scar is comprised of chitin and its synthesis is thought to involve an intricate molecular control system.

4. The cell cycle of yeasts is divided into the four phases, G1, S, G2 and M, characteristic of eukaryotes. In the fission yeast *Schizosaccharomyces pombe* the G1 phase may be missing under certain cultural conditions.

5. In budding yeasts, the bud develops at a site of weakening in the cell wall, thought to be a region where disulphide bridges in wall protein are reduced. Development of the bud involves *de novo* wall synthesis which in the case of the mannan component is believed to be intracellular. Variety exists in the pattern of budding with differences being found between different species. In fission yeasts cell wall growth is polarised to one end of the cell.

6. DNA in the yeast cell is located in the nucleus, mitochondria and in plasmids. Nuclear DNA synthesis occurs during the S phase but the timing is not so specific for mitochondrial DNA. The timing and mechanism of replication of the plasmids is unknown.

7. Protein and mRNA synthesis are continuous processes, but specific molecules are produced at particular times in the life of the cell.

8. The overall picture of growth and division in yeast cells is one of an ordered sequence of events. Current thinking supports the idea that these events form into two independent pathways, one involving cell growth the other concerned with division, as in bacteria.

CHAPTER THREE

VEGETATIVE GROWTH OF FILAMENTOUS FUNGI

In the filamentous fungi the basic unit of structure is the hypha. When massed together the hyphae form a mycelium. The individual hyphae are tube-like structures which exhibit polarised growth and may produce branches at sub-apical sites. In effect hyphal growth involves two components, an increase in volume which results from extension of the tip and an increase in protoplasmic contents. These involve a complex interaction of biosynthesis of macromolecules and their subsequent organisation into recognisable physical structures. The latter aspect of growth occurs over long distances within an individual hypha. In recent years fungal hyphae have been the subject of broad investigation in regard to their ultrastructure, biochemistry and physiology and it is now possible to devise models relating these features to the growth process.

Hyphal cytology

Light microscope studies, some of the earliest reports appearing in the latter part of the last century, provided a lot of fundamental information about the fungal hypha which has stood the test of time and still remains central in our thinking on hyphal growth. Of particular interest were the reports on apical growth of hyphae and the discovery of the Spitzenkörper, a zone at the extreme apex of septate fungi that can be stained with iron-haemotoxylin. More sophisticated methods, e.g. autoradiography, fluorescence microscopy and phase contrast microscopy (figure 3.1), have confirmed these early descriptions. The Spitzenkörper appears to be associated with active growth because it is not present in non-growing hyphae. Another feature of growing hyphae, just resolvable by phase contrast microscopy in good preparations particularly of the

44

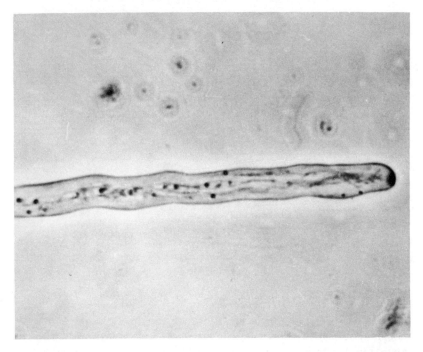

Figure 3.1   Phase contrast micrograph of the hyphal tip of *Neurospora crassa* showing the Spitzenkörper. From Grove, S. N. and Bracker, C. E. (1970) *J. Bact.*, **104**, 989–1009. By kind permission of Dr S. N. Grove.

large hyphae of Zygomycetes, is the presence of small particles which can be seen migrating towards the hyphal apex.

The tip region involved in increasing hyphal volume is known as the extension zone. The length of this zone has been determined in various ways including observations on the displacement of markers placed on hyphae and more recently by the use of optical brightener compounds, manufactured for incorporation into detergents, which bind to the extension zones of hypha of many fungi.

Hyphal ultrastructure

Many of the early observations made by light microscopy, e.g. the Spitzenkörper and movement of particles, have been further resolved by the use of electron microscopy. However, since the proliferation of the

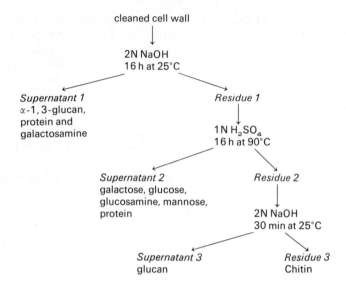

Figure 3.2   Fractionation procedure for fungal cell walls containing chitin and glucans.

fungal hypha involves the syntheses of new components of the rigid hyphal wall the following discussion will start with this component of the hypha.

Composition and architecture of the hyphal wall
The boundary of the fungal hypha is the rigid cell wall. The analysis of the chemical composition of the wall involves a detailed procedure and

Table 3.1   Wall composition of fungi representative of different taxonomic groups.

	% Composition		
	Phycomycete *Phytophthora heveae*	Ascomycete *Chaetomium globosum*	Basidiomycete *Agaricus bisporus*
cellulose	36	—	—
chitin	—	13.9	43
α-1,3-glucan	—	—	14
β-1,3-glucan	54	54.1	27
lipid	2.5	3	1.5
protein	4.6–6.7	29	16

preparation of the material prior to investigation. An unknown factor is the possibility of changes in composition during these preparative procedures. Once the wall material is prepared a protocol for fractionation such as shown in figure 3.2 is used and the results from an analysis are given in table 3.1.

From the many reports on hyphal wall composition of different fungal species several basic features arise. Typically the walls are comprised of polysaccharides (75–80 per cent on a dry weight basis), protein, lipid, and melanin. A variety of polysaccharides occur—the homopolymers β-1,3-glucan, β-1,4-glucan, α-1,3-glucan, chitin, chitosan, and a variety of heteropolymers which are made up from mannose, galactose, fucose and xylose (Rosenberger, 1976). Of these different polymers the β-1,3-glucan is found more broadly across the various taxonomic groups of fungi. The analyses of wall composition of the many fungi investigated has revealed the interesting situation shown in table 3.2 where there is a relationship between the nature of the two major polymers present and the different taxonomic groups.

Examination of the organisation of the various polymers in the fungal wall, using a combination of biochemical and chemical techniques in association with electron microscopic observations, has shown the wall to be a highly structured entity (Hunsley and Burnett, 1970). Of the two major polymers present in the wall, one occurs in microfibrillar form making up a skeletal network and the other is a matrix material that forms a filling for the spaces of the network. Additional polysaccharide polymers occur in either of these forms and in some Ascomycetes another network comprised of glycoprotein is also found. In thin sections viewed with the electron microscope, the wall is seen to be made up of two or more layers. In every case the microfibrillar skeletal material forms the

Table 3.2 Cell wall composition and fungal taxonomy.

Major polymers	Taxonomic group
cellulose-β-1,3-glucan	Oomycetes
cellulose-chitin	Hyphochytridiomycetes
chitin-chitosan	Zygomycetes
chitin-β-glucan	Chytridiomycetes
	Euascomycetes
	Homobasidromycetes
mannan-β-glucan	Hemiascomycetes
chitin-mannan	Heterobasidiomycetes

After Bartnicki-Garcia (1968)

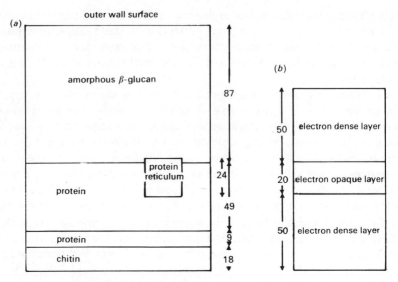

Figure 3.3 Organisation of polymers in the hyphal wall of *Neurospora crassa*, observations made on 5-day cultures. (*a*) Model of the wall based on experiments in which wall material was subjected to specific enzyme treatments. Five layers are distinguishable, (i) outer layer of amorphous glucan with β-1,3- and β-1,6-linkages, (ii) coarse strands of glycoprotein network, (iii) easily removed protein, (iv) more resistant protein and (v) inner layer of chitin microfibrils probably containing protein also. The thickness of the layers (in nm) is indicated by the numbers and arrows. (*b*) Structure of the wall as seen in thin section by transmission electron microscopy (diagrammatic representation). The wall has three layers distinguishable by differences in electron density. Redrawn from D. Hunsley and J. H. Burnett (1970) *J. Gen. Microbiol.*, **62**, 203–218.

inner layer adjacent to the plasma membrane, with the amorphous matrix, and other material when present, as the outer layers. Differences are found, however, between the wall structure in the apical extension zone and in the sub-apical region. The wall of the extension zone is called the primary wall and is comprised almost entirely of the microfibrillar wall component but may have some amorphous component (figure 3.3). In the sub-apical region the secondary wall is deposited on the outer surface of the primary wall and involves the thickening of existing microfibrils, the addition of new ones and the formation of the amorphous and other wall components.

The hyphal wall can be removed by digestion in a mixture of the enzymes specific for the major polysaccharide components. If this digestion is done in an osmotically stabilised medium the cytoplasmic contents of the hyphae are then released as discrete units termed protoplasts (figure 3.4). Protoplasts have proved useful for studies on wall biogenesis in fungi because when incubated in an osmotically stabilised growth medium they regenerate a new wall and revert to the normal hyphal form (Peberdy, 1978).

Septa
Septa or crosswalls occurring irregularly along the length of a hypha are a feature of all fungal groups (Gull, 1978). The septa are produced in the apical region in what appears to be a controlled manner (see later). With certain exceptions, the septa found in representative species of particular taxonomic groups are characteristic for the group. The simplest type is that which forms a total barrier across the hypha but more common are septa with pores (figure 3.5). These pores are central in location, unless the septum is multiperforate. In many fungi with porous septa, each pore has a characteristic structure. The Woronin body—a membrane bounded,

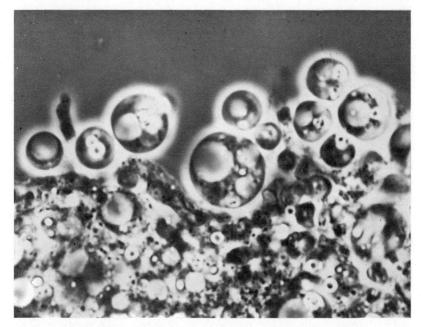

Figure 3.4   Phase contrast micrograph of protoplasts isolated from hyphae of *Aspergillus nidulans*. The hyphae are treated with a lytic complex containing chitinase and β-1, 3-glucanase in the presence of potassium chloride which acts as an osmotic stabiliser (× 400).

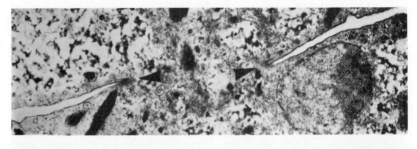

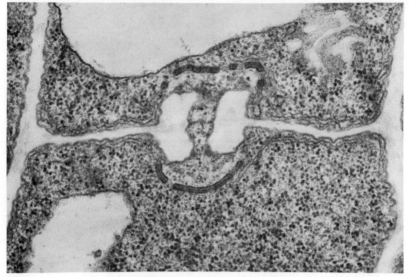

Figure 3.5   (*a*) Electron micrograph of a septum from a 24 h culture of *Neurospora crassa* (× 15 750). From Hunsley, D. and Gooday, G. W. (1974) *Protoplasma*, **82**, 125–146. By kind permission of Dr G. W. Gooday.
(*b*) Electron micrograph of a dolipore septum in the Basidiomycete *Agrocybe praecox*, as seen in hyphae from the hymenial layer of the fruit body (× 43 750). From Gull, K. (1978) in *The Filamentous Fungi*, Vol. III (ed. J. E. Smith and D. R. Berry) Arnold, London, 78–93. By kind permission of Dr K. Gull.

electron-dense proteinaceous structure—always remains adjacent to the pore despite cytoplasmic streaming. In species lacking the Woronin body, a proteinaceous crystal is found. Both structures are thought to have the same function, namely to block the pores of septa in older regions of the hyphae.

The septa of Basidiomycete fungi, except the rust and smut fungi, are more complex. They have a central pore but the margin of this is swollen and is known as the dolipore (figure 3.5). On each side of the pore is a hemispherical cap of perforated membrane which is thought to be formed from an extension of the endoplasmic reticulum.

The chemical composition of the septa is unknown except for two species, *Neurospora crassa* and *Schizophyllum commune*. In the former microfibrils of chitin are found in septa of young (one day old) mycelium but as time passes both sides of the septum are covered with an amorphous proteinaceous material. The β-1,3-glucan and glycoprotein com-

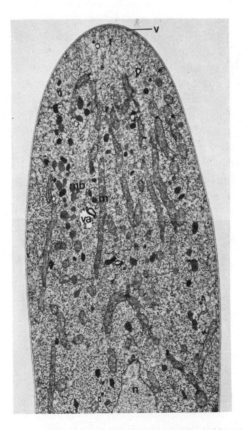

Figure 3.6 Electron micrograph of a near median longitudinal thin section of the hyphal tip of the Phycomycete *Allomyces arbuscula*. The apical zone contains only vesicles (v) and ribosomes (r). Other organelles seen in the sub-apical zone are mitochondria (m), microbodies (mb), a small vacuole (Va) and a nucleus (n) ($\times 15\,000$). From Roos, U-P and Turian, G. (1978) *Protoplasma*, **93**, 231–247. By kind permission of Dr U-P Roos.

ponents of the hyphal wall are not found in the septum. In *Schizophyllum commune* the septa contain chitin and a *β*-glucan, both of which are also found in the hyphal wall. The *α*-glucan found in the wall is absent from the septa. Dissolution of the septa in this and other Basidiomycetes is an important feature of reproductive development (see chapter 7).

The protoplast

Ultrastructural observations on the fungal hypha have revealed an interesting picture of organisation (Grove 1978). The apical region of a hypha may be conveniently sub-divided into two zones; the tip or apical zone, characterised by the presence of vesicles and ribosomes, and the sub-apical zone in which the organelles characteristic of a heterotrophic eukaryote are found (figure 3.6).

The presence of vesicles at the tip zone is of particular interest and has led to the formulation of models explaining their involvement in wall formation and hence hyphal growth. The small particles seen by light microscopy have been interpreted as vesicles and the organisation of the latter at the apex provide an understanding of the nature of the Spitzenkörper. The vesicles fall into two groups on the basis of size. The smaller ones, termed microvesicles, have been shown to contain chitin synthase in several fungi, and their involvement in wall synthesis must therefore be presumed.

The arrangement of vesicles in the tip zone is a variable feature with different patterns being characteristic for the different taxonomic groups (figure 3.7). In the Oomycetes both sizes of vesicles are found distributed

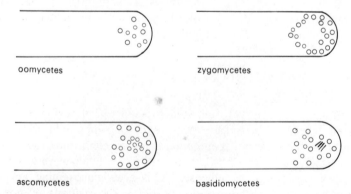

oomycetes

zygomycetes

ascomycetes

basidiomycetes

Figure 3.7 Diagrammatic representation of the organisation in hyphal apices of fungi from different taxonomic groups. Adapted from Grove, S. N. (1978) *The Filamentous Fungi*, Vol. III (ed. J. E. Smith and D. R. Berry) Arnold, London, 28–50.

in a random fashion. In electron micrographs, however, the larger one is seen to contain electron opaque, granular material whereas the micro-vesicles have more uniform contents. The sub-apical zone of these fungi is characterised by large numbers of dictyosomes frequently seen in associ-ation with cytoplasmic vesicles. Some micrographs have shown the ves-icles to occur in lines between the dictyosomes and the apex, strongly suggesting a relationship between the two organelles and events in the tip zone. In representatives of other taxonomic groups the organisation of the apical vesicles shows more order. In the Zygomycetes the larger vesicles form a distinct layer beneath the plasma membrane giving the appearance of a hemispherical cap. The microvesicles occur randomly in the region behind this cap. The microvesicles in the apical zone of Ascomycete fungi occur as a spherical cluster surrounded by the large vesicles and the complete cluster is located just behind the apical wall. The Basidiomycete arrangement is somewhat smaller with a spherical arrangement of large vesicles surrounding a vesicle free zone which includes a dense core of unidentifiable structure. The vesicular arrangements seen in the tip zones of these fungi are probably the Spitzenkörpers described from light micrographs.

Vesicles are also seen in the sub-apical zones of the hyphae of fungi. Regions of cytoplasm occur that are free of ribosomes and in these, membranous structures corresponding to the cisternae of golgi bodies are present, associated with vesicles. In the sub-apical region vesicles also occur intermingled with the other organelles, nuclei, mitochondria, endo-membrane components and ribosomes. Involvement of the vesicles in events at the apex, including the synthesis of the hyphal wall, necessitate their transport through the mass of other organelles, but a mechanism for this process remains to be discovered.

Biosynthesis of cell wall polymers

Location of synthesis
As mentioned previously the existence of an apical region of hyphal extension was described many years ago following light microscope observations. Substantial experimental evidence confirming these obser-vations has come from investigations in which hyphae were fed with radioactive sugars, e.g. ^{14}C glucose, ^{14}C N-acetylglucosamine, and then subjected to autoradiography (Gooday, 1971). The sugars were shown to be rapidly incorporated into polymers such as chitin and glucan at the extreme apex (figure 3.8). When a pulse feeding of isotopic sugar is

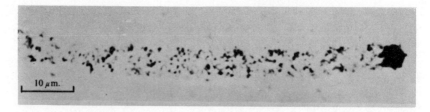

Figure 3.8 Light microscopic autoradiograph of the growing hyphal tip of *Schizophyllum commune*. The hyphae were given a 10 min pulse feed with ^{3}H-glucose. The autoradiograph shows silver grains marking the sites of incorporation of the isotope into the hyphal wall. The density of grains is greatest at the apex decreasing in the sub-apical zones. From Gooday, G. W. (1971) *J. Gen. Microbiol.*, **67**, 125–133. By kind permission of Dr G. W. Gooday.

followed by a so-called cold chase, i.e. replacement of the isotope by the normal sugar, autoradiographs reveal that the area of wall just behind the apex has become labelled, but the apical zone itself is free of label. Quantification of the autoradiographs can be achieved by counts of the silver grains. The grain density is highest at the extreme apex falling sharply at a distance of 10–15 μm behind the apex. The conclusion of these observations is that *de novo* wall formation occurs at the apex, but some sub-apical wall deposition cannot be ruled out. In the autoradiographs referred to above, a low but uniform number of silver grains can be seen in the wall of sub-apical regions. This incorporation is believed to reside in the microfibrils which increase in size. In *Neurospora crassa* the glycoprotein reticulum of the wall is laid down in the sub-apical zone and not at the tip. The dominance of the apex in relation to the deposition of wall polymers can be overcome experimentally, e.g. by growth in the presence of cycloheximide or by osmotic shock, and under these conditions radioactive substrates are incorporated uniformly throughout the wall. The effect of these treatments therefore is to overrule the mechanism that controls apical wall synthesis.

Biochemical aspects of wall synthesis
Of all the wall polymers described in the filamentous fungi, the biosynthesis of chitin is the most extensively documented. The enzyme involved in the final stage of polymer formation is chitin synthase which catalyses the reaction

$$UDP - N\text{-acetylglucosamine} + (N\text{-acetylglucosamine})_n \xrightarrow{Mg^{2+}} UDP + chitin$$

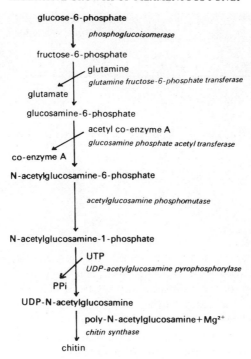

Figure 3.9   Biosynthetic pathway leading to the formation of UDP-*N*-acetylglucosamine.

The supply of UDP − *N*-acetylglucosamine, which is necessary for continued synthesis, is from a pathway starting with fructose-6-phosphate and glutamine as precursors (figure 3.9). The complete pathway has not been followed in a single organism but there are descriptions of the four enzymes involved from different fungi.

The cytoplasmic location of chitin synthase has not been fully established although there is strong evidence to support a membrane site. In cell homogenates the highest levels of chitin synthase are found in the microsomal fraction which is rich in membrane. In the intact hypha the functional site of the enzyme is assumed to be on the outer surface of the plasma membrane. Evidence for this view stems from several experimental sources, in autoradiographs viewed with an electron microscope silver grains were found on the membrane surface and in the wall, and never in the cytoplasm, and protoplasts isolated from hyphae by digestion of the walls are able to synthesise new wall material and revert to the normal morphology (figure 3.10). Recent studies (Ruiz Herrera *et al.*, 1977) on the

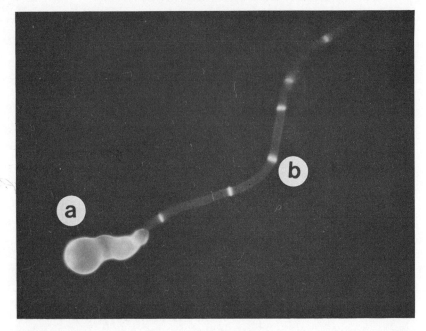

Figure 3.10   Reversion of hyphal protoplasts of *Aspergillus nidulans* to the normal hyphal form. The protoplasts are cultured in an osmotically stabilised growth medium. The process begins with the development of an abnormal hypha (*a*) which later undergoes transition to the normal hyphal form (*b*). The preparation was stained with the optical brightener Tinopal and viewed with a UV fluorescence microscope (× 400).

yeast form of *Mucor rouxii* (see later) showed that microfibrils of chitin could be produced *in vitro*. The preparation of chitin synthase used took the form of particles obtained by a detailed purification procedure (figure 3.11). The particles, called chitosomes, were subsequently shown to be microvesicular structures, 40–70 nm in diameter. During microfibril synthesis the chitosomes undergo a transformation such that when the microfibril is formed the shell of the membrane is shed. The *in vivo* function of the chitosome, which has since been described in several other fungi, is presumed to be that of conveyor of chitin synthase to the cell surface where the chitin polymer is normally synthesised.

Data on glucan synthesis in growing hyphae is more limited. In *Neurospora crassa* where a β-1, 3-glucan is present as an amorphous component in the wall, a β-1, 3-glucan synthase has been found in cell wall preparations. Also in *Phytopthora cinnamomi*, which has a β-1,3-, β-1,6-

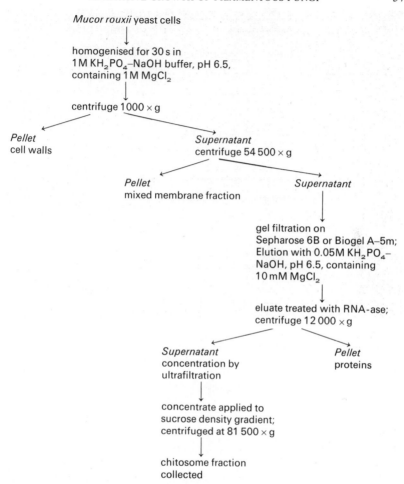

Figure 3.11 Procedure for the isolation of chitosomes. Adapted from Ruiz-Herrera, J., Lopez-Romero, E. and Bartnicki-Garcia, S. (1977) *J. Biol. Chem.*, **252**, 3338–3343.

glucan fibrillar wall component, a synthase was also found in the wall fraction, that catalysed the synthesis of the polymer from UDP-glucose. When the fungus was grown under conditions of high glucose concentration, thus reducing the level of protease in the hyphae, a membrane bound enzyme was also found that catalysed the formation of a polymer which contained only β-1, 3-linkages. A synthase system associated with the formation of the wall β-1,4-glucan has been found in *Saprolegnia*

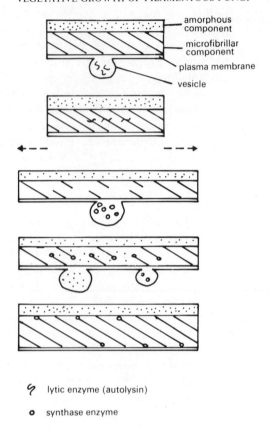

φ lytic enzyme (autolysin)

o   synthase enzyme

Figure 3.12   Model of cell wall growth in fungi. Autolysins are released from vesicles (1) which sever the microfibrils of the skeletal component (2) and allows the wall to stretch (3). The enzyme involved in the synthesis of the skeletal component becomes bound to the fibrils (4). The microfibrils are extended and new amorphous material is incorporated into the wall. Adapted from Bartnicki-Garcia, S. (1973) *Symp. Soc. Gen. Microbiol.*, **23**, 245–267.

monoica, an Oomycete fungus. The enzyme has been detected in fractions containing wall and microsomal material and more recently in vesicles believed to originate from the golgi system.

Model for wall growth

A proposed model for wall growth (figure 3.12) involves both wall lytic enzymes as well as synthases (Bartnicki–Garcia, 1973). The lytic enzymes are believed to function by cleaving the existing wall polymers to allow extension and insertion of new material. Evidence for the significance of these enzymes is claimed firstly from experiments on the bursting of hyphal tips and secondly from studies on the release of sugars from walls during incubation. Bursting of hyphal tips can be obtained by treatment with various chemicals which have been suggested increase the activity of those lytic enzymes located in the walls. This idea has been challenged by the suggestion that the treatments caused changes in the wall matrix materials, these changes in turn led to bursting. Evidence for wall lytic enzymes from a second group of experiments is more convincing. Up to 3 per cent of the polymers were found to be released from walls of *Aspergillus nidulans*, in the form of glucose, N-acetylglucosamine, mannose and galactose. In further experiments using isotopically labelled walls it was shown that the release of sugars was preferentially from the newly formed wall at the apex rather than from sub-apical regions. More recent studies (Polacheck and Rosenberger, 1978) on the same fungus revealed the presence of six autolytic enzymes (autolysins) that hydrolysed chitin, laminarin, α-glucoside, β-glucoside, protein and β-N-acetylglucosaminide respectively. These enzymes were found bound to the wall fraction and in the soluble protein of the cytoplasmic fraction of cell homogenates. The attachment of the wall bound enzymes was mediated by lipids. The cytoplasmic vesicles in the hyphae are assumed to function again as carriers of these enzymes but confirmation of this and the role of the autolysins in wall formation and hyphal growth must await further research. Despite this evidence for the existence of wall-bound lytic enzymes direct information relating to their involvement in hyphal growth is lacking.

Whatever the precise details of the system, the synthesis of the hyphal wall clearly demands the secretion of a variety of materials at the surface of the plasma membrane in the region of the growing tip. Transport of these compounds is an obvious role for the vesicles described earlier in this chapter. Cytochemical data suggests that some of the vesicles may be carriers of carbohydrate material and recently there have been interesting reports that the microvesicles are carriers of chitin synthase as described earlier. Discharge of the vesicle contents will occur following fusion of the vesicle with the plasma membrane the latter event also provides a mechanism for membrane growth which is also a necessary part of hyphal extension.

The mechanism for vesicle transportation is not known, but two hypotheses have been proposed, both of which are based on reports of a gradient in membrane potential of some 100 mV in the apical zone,

7 nm long, in *Neurospora crassa* hyphae. The first hypothesis proposes that this gradient could generate enough current for the electro-phonetic movement of vesicles through the apical zone. The second view is based on the assumption that the gradient is a function of a decrease in the number of potassium pumps (ATP-ase dependent) in the membrane towards the hyphal tip. A consequence of this would be an osmotic flow forwards to the tip which could carry the vesicles.

Control of localised synthesis

The previous discussion has stressed that wall synthesis is localised at the hyphal apex, so how is this localisation controlled? In several fungi there is now evidence for the existence of an active and a zymogen form of chitin synthase (a similar situation to that described for the yeast *Saccharomyces cerevisiae*) and that the latter form can be activated by protease enzymes found in the hyphae. The significance of these two components in relation to the mechanism of control remains unknown. An attempt to understand their distribution within the hyphal organisation was made using the technique of protoplast isolation as a fractionation system (figure 3.13). Protoplasts released from hyphae of *Aspergillus nidulans* during the first hour of wall digestion are predominantly from the apical tips. In the subsequent time period the cytoplasm from sub-apical and distal zones is also released as protoplasts. Comparison of active and zymogen chitin

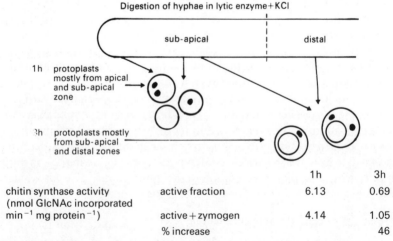

chitin synthase activity (nmol GlcNAc incorporated min^{-1} mg protein^{-1})		1h	3h
	active fraction	6.13	0.69
	active + zymogen	4.14	1.05
	% increase		46

Figure 3.13 Chitin synthase activities in hyphal protoplasts from *Aspergillus nidulans*. Data from Isaac, S., *et al.* (1977) *J. Gen. Microbiol.*

synthase in the different preparations showed that protoplasts released in the first hour had a high level of active chitin synthase but no zymogen, and the protoplasts released later had a much reduced level of the active enzyme and higher amounts of the zymogen.

From the limited data available a possible working hypothesis would suggest that chitin synthase is released at the apex following fusion of the chitosomes with the plasma membrane. The chitin synthase, which is probably synthesised in zymogen form, is activated either in the chitosome prior to fusion, or on the membrane surface following fusion. As the hyphal tip advances the newly inserted membrane and the newly formed wall become lateral to it. In this position the majority of the enzyme molecules would become inactivated either reversibly or irreversibly.

The presence of inactivated enzyme in the lateral regions of the hyphae is one conclusion drawn from experiments on *Aspergillus nidulans* in which hyphae were either treated with cycloheximide or subjected to osmotic shock. In both instances the treated hyphae were pulse labelled with radioactive carbohydrate and examined by autoradiography. In this case the hyphae had a uniform distribution of silver grains over their whole length and not the restricted location as referred to previously. The changed pattern of incorporation and therefore presumed wall synthesis could be an expression of the reactivation of zymogen, however, an alternative explanation cannot be ruled out at this stage. This suggests that the cycloheximide treatment or osmotic shock disrupts the normal mechanism of vesicle transportation and discharge at the apex resulting in a random discharge over the whole hyphal surface, cannot be ruled out at this stage.

Branch initiation is also an important part of the model; in the case of a reversible inactivation situation the enzyme molecules would be reactivated. If the enzyme is inactivated irreversibly then the insertion of new active enzyme molecules would be required to initiate growth of a branch.

Additional control of chitin synthase can be effected through *N*-acetylglucosamine, known to be an activator of the enzyme *in vitro*. In the hyphae this molecule would be released at localised sites following lysis of chitin by wall bound enzymes. If this lysis occurs only at the apex this would enhance the rate of synthase activity at this region.

Hyphal growth and the duplication cycle

In the unicellular bacteria and yeasts the events of growth and division are integrated, forming the cell cycle. It is now believed that similar in-

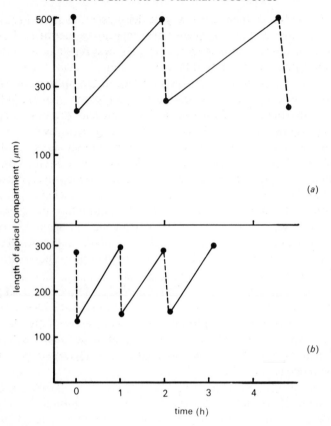

Figure 3.14   The duplication cycle showing growth and septation of the apical compartment of fungal hypha in (*a*) *Aspergillus nidulans* and (*b*) the dikaryotic mycelium of *Schizophyllum commune*. Adapted from Trinci, A. P. J. (1978) *The Filamentous Fungi*, Vol. III (ed. J. E. Smith and D. R. Berry) Arnold, London, 132–163.

tegration of growth and nuclear division occurs in the apical compartment of hyphal fungi but owing to the absence of cell separation the term duplication cycle is used to describe these events (Trinci, 1978). Some diversity exists in relation to the organisation of the apical compartment in different fungi. In some species the compartment is uninucleate, e.g. the Phycomycete *Basidiobolus ranarum*, and in the monokaryotic mycelium of many Basidiomycetes. In the dikaryotic mycelium of these latter fungi each hyphal compartment has two nuclei. In coenocytic species, e.g.

Aspergillus nidulans, there are many nuclei present, in some instances up to 90. In all cases a regular sequence of events can be identified. Following septation the apical compartment elongates as a result of growth at the tip. In the species with uni- and binucleate compartments the nucleus(i) is seen to remain in a constant position relative to the tip and consequently must migrate at a rate equivalent to the rate of tip growth. When the apical compartment reaches a critical size nuclear division occurs followed by septation (figure 3.14). The timing of these events is regular indicating a cyclic nature. The situation in coenocytic fungi is identical, with certain minor modifications. Nuclear division is not completely synchronous and where a large number of nuclei are involved the division event may last for up to 20 minutes, until each nucleus has divided. Septation is also different in coenocytes. The formation of several septa divides the compartment into an apical segment and a number of other segments each of variable size and nuclear number. In all cases the apical compartment is reduced to half its length at septation thus maintaining constancy in size.

An essential feature of the duplication cycle is the as yet unexplained relationship between the volume of cytoplasm and the DNA content of the apical compartment. As the cytoplasm attains a doubling in volume, division of the nucleus or nuclei and septation occur, thus restoring the nuclear-cytoplasmic ratio. The observed events suggest that a positive control system is operating.

It has been proposed that a cytoplasmic factor is involved, similar to that suggested for bacteria. If such a factor is produced during the interphase period, at a rate proportional to the rate of increase of the cytoplasm, then mitosis would be induced when a critical level is attained. The apical cells of hyphae in a mycelium show no synchrony in respect of their duplication cycles, which suggests that if such a cytoplasmic factor is involved its effect is very restricted to individual apices. This would suggest that cytoplasmic mixing is very restricted even in those fungi in which the septa have pores.

Our understanding of the duplication cycle will hopefully improve in future years through the study of mutants. Several temperature sensitive mutants have been isolated in *Aspergillus nidulans* that have blocks in nuclear division and in septation. The nuclear division mutants fall into several groups including those blocked at the stage of DNA synthesis and others blocked during mitosis. Investigations on these strains may tell us more about the control of nuclear division in the fungal hypha and the relationship between this event and septation.

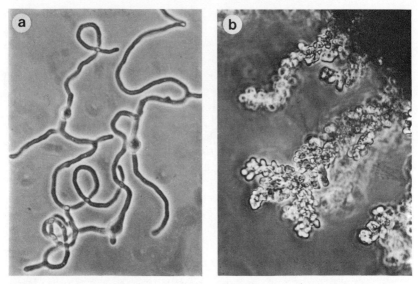

Figure 3.15 Light micrographs of hyphae of (*a*) wild-type and (*b*) a morphological mutant of *Aspergillus nidulans* which exhibits an abnormal branching pattern (× 400).

Hyphal branching

Branch formation is a feature of all fungal hyphae which allows the organism to rapidly colonise a particular substratum. A variety of patterns of branching are seen and the frequency of branch formation is variable—both aspects are subject to environmental and genetic control (figure 3.15). Branches arise either adjacent to septa or on the lateral walls of apical or sub-apical hyphal compartments. In the former instance the septa are believed to be involved in branch formation, acting as a barrier to the flow of vesicles towards the hyphal apex. Fusion of the vesicles with the plasma membrane, as is also believed to occur at the apex, results in the discharge of their contents. This initiates changes in the hyphal wall and branch formation.

Where branches arise independently of septa then the location is presumed to be random and is determined only by the sites at which vesicles accumulate. The stimulus for such accumulation is unknown. On occasions the hyphal apex is seen to branch dichotomously, this could also be an expression of vesicle accumulation. In this case a greater supply is required than is normally needed to maintain the normal polarised growth.

Dimorphism

As mentioned in the previous chapter some fungal species grow in two or more morphological forms, i.e. they exhibit dimorphism. In the majority of cases the forms are distinct, yeast-like and mycelial. It is of interest that many of the species involved are pathogenic. The transformation from one form to the other is influenced by specific environmental conditions. These are diverse and may be nutritional, e.g. in *Candida albicans*, or physical factors, e.g. temperature in *Paracoccidiodes brasilieusis*, or the gaseous environment, e.g. in *Mucor rouxii* (figure 3.16).

The morphological switch from a dividing or budding cell to a cell growing by elongation is presumed to be related to changes in the cell wall. However, examination of the cell wall composition of the three fungi mentioned above reveals major differences between each example and underlies the fact that a single mechanism cannot explain dimorphism in all fungi.

Research on *Paracoccidiodes brasiliensis* and *Candida albicans* has centred on the cell wall and in the former there is good evidence to suggest that a switch in wall biogenesis is the basis for the morphological change. Analysis of walls from the yeast and mycelial forms has shown significant

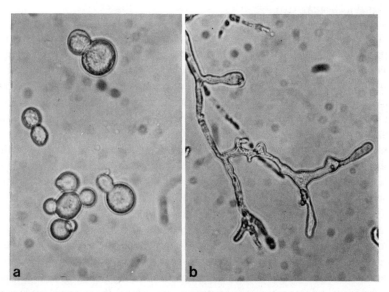

Figure 3.16 Light micrograph of (*a*) the yeast and (*b*) the mycelial forms of *Mucor rouxii* (× 400).

differences in composition and structure. In the yeast form the major polymer is an α-glucan with chitin and in the mycelial form a β-glucan and a galactomannan are the major components. What remains to be discovered is the nature of the underlying control mechanism which influences the pathway of wall synthesis and how this is affected by a temperature change. A much simpler change in the cell wall has been proposed for *Candida albicans* which involves the disulphide component of the wall protein. It is suggested that growth in the yeast form is maintained by high levels of sulphydryl residues in the protein, mediated by a $NADH_2$ dependent protein disulphide reductase. The availability of the hydrogen donor stems from an excess generated during carbon metabolism. The experimental evidence for this proposal resides in the demonstration of the presence of the reductase enzyme, however, other causes for the dimorphic change cannot be ruled out and further study of this organism is necessary.

The biochemical basis of dimorphism in *Mucor rouxii* and related species appears to be different from the fungi described previously. The problem has been actively researched in recent years and whilst several mechanisms have been proposed (Sypherd *et al.*, 1978) one hypothesis implicated cAMP as the endogenous initiator of the dimorphic switch from the yeast to hyphal form. Yeast cells growing in CO_2 and shifted to an aerobic environment switch to the mycelial form and a simultaneous decrease in the intracellular level of cAMP (about 3–4 fold) was found. Supportive evidence also came from the observation that the lipid derivative dibutyryl cAMP transformed hyphal cells growing in air, to the yeast form and also from the fact that yeast cells growing in a gaseous environment of 100 per cent CO_2 have high levels of cAMP. Other evidence does not support an involvement for cAMP. In cultures in which the growth form is controlled by the flow rate of gaseous nitrogen into the culture both yeast and hyphal cells have similar levels of cAMP and the addition of dibutyryl cAMP to hyphal cultures failed to bring about the transformation as reported previously. It can only be concluded, at this time at least, that the dimorphic switch is not linked, in an obligatory way, to the intracellular concentration of cAMP.

Another explanation for the phenomenon was sought in the relationship between the yeast form and a high rate fermentative metabolism based on growth on hexose. In this respect the yeast form of *Mucor rouxii* contrasts with *Saccharomyces cerevisiae* because fermentative metabolism in the former does not repress mitochondrial development. *Mucor* species cultured aerobically in the presence of high concentrations of glucose are fermentative and take the yeast form. It could be argued that the importance of hexose for the yeast pattern of development is an indication that the enzymes of carbon catabolism are some significance in the morphogenetic switch, however, differences in metabolic patterns between the yeast and mycelial form under certain environmental conditions do not necessarily occur under another set of conditions. One case in point relates to the utilisation of the glycolytic and the pentose phosphate pathways. In aerobically grown yeast cells 14 per cent of the glucose is metabolised through the pentose phosphate cycle compared to 28 per cent in the mycelial form. Comparison of yeast and mycelium under anaerobic conditions revealed that the balance of carbon metabolism through the two pathways was the same for both growth forms. Several other reports have been made of differences between enzymes produced in the two growth forms, e.g. isoenzymic forms of pyruvate kinase, but in no case so far described has a clear cut correlation between specific enzymes and a particular morphological type been shown.

The two patterns of development in dimorphic fungi are clearly the phenotypic expression of different parts of the genome. Attempts to unravel molecular differences that are associated with morphogenetic switches have been few, and mostly with the dimorphic species of *Mucor*. The RNA polymerases of the two growth forms have been found to be similar so differences might therefore be expected at the translational level. The switch from yeast to hyphal form is accompanied by a noticeable increase in the rate of protein synthesis but the nature of the newly formed proteins still requires elucidation.

SUMMARY

1. Growth of the fungal hypha is apical and a model to explain the process can now be formulated from the ultrastructural and biochemical data available.

2. The ultrastructure of the hypha is typically eukaryotic but certain features are fairly unique being found only in specialised structures of plants, e.g. rhizoids of mosses, root hairs of plants.

3. The cell wall has a variable composition in different fungi. Polysaccharides account for up to 80 per cent of the wall and of these two major components, skeletal or

microfibrillar and amorphous are found. The wall has a distinctive architecture being made up from two or more layers. The septa which are present in many fungi vary in their morphology and are normally composed of some, but not all, wall polysaccharides.

4. A distinctive feature of the hyphal protoplast is the apical zone which is free of all organelles except vesicles and ribosomes. The size of this zone and the organisation of vesicles within it varies in different fungi. Nuclei, mitochondria, golgi bodies, endoplasmic reticulum and vacuoles are present in the sub-apical zone.

5. Extension of the hypha depends on the continual synthesis of new cell wall. This process occurs primarily in the apical zone although some synthesis does take place in the sub-apical region. Synthesis of the skeletal wall component is believed to occur on the surface of the plasma membrane, with the specialised micro-vesicles playing a central role in the transportation of wall synthesising enzymes to this functional site. Some control system must operate to restrict wall polymer synthesis to the apical zone but its mechanism remains to be discovered. Lytic enzymes present in the wall are believed to be involved in wall formation. Their suggested role is to cleave the existing components to allow the insertion of new material.

6. Observations on elongation and nuclear division in the apical compartment of fungal hyphae have shown that a cyclic pattern exists that is equivalent to the cell cycle in unicellular organisms. The exception being that cell separation does not occur following septation. This cycle has been designated the duplication cycle.

7. Branch formation is a characteristic feature of hyphae. A variety of branching patterns is found. In some instances the origin of a branch can be related to septum development. The underlying cytoplasmic mechanism appears to be the aggregation of vesicles and a septum acting as a barrier can clearly bring this about. The mechanism for aggregation where septa are not involved remains to be elucidated.

8. Some fungi exhibit dimorphic growth, i.e. they develop as a yeast or mycelial form, or in some cases other intermediate forms as well, subject to various environmental controls. The underlying mechanism for dimorphic development is thought to involve changes in the cell wall. In some fungi changes in cell wall composition associated with the particular cell morphology have been identified. The basis of the interaction between environment and cell metabolism involved is not known. cAMP has been proposed as the key to this interaction.

CHAPTER FOUR

REPLICATION OF VIRUSES

VIRUSES ARE CHARACTERISED BY MANY UNIQUE FEATURES THAT SET THEM apart from other groups of organisms which find a place within Microbiology. A discussion on the nature of viruses and their relationships to other organisms was fashionable 10–20 years ago but no satisfactory definition ever emerged. No doubt as our knowledge of viruses expands still further some insights into their relationship may emerge.

Viruses are very different from micro-organisms in their organisation and mechanism of multiplication. The only feature that they share in common with a few bacteria and fungi is that they are obligate pathogens and are totally dependent upon some host for their replication. The unit of structure of a virus is the particle or virion. These range in size from the smallest having a diameter of 10 nm to those having one dimension, e.g. length, around 250 nm. Viruses are therefore essentially submicroscopic and an electron microscope is required to study their architecture. The larger particles may just be visible with a light microscope equipped with ultra-violet light to maximise its resolution.

The interest of the developmental microbiologist in viruses and their multiplication must inevitably reflect their unique position. Virus replication involves macromolecular replication and assembly and in the latter respect contrasts sharply with replication patterns seen in unicellular organisms. Central to the process of replication is the involvement of the host and the control of host metabolism by the invading virus.

Virus organisation and architecture

Viruses lack any form of cellular organisation—the majority are comprised of only two macromolecular components, nucleic acid and protein.

69

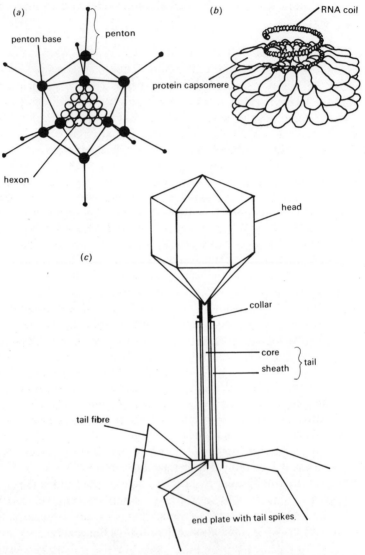

Figure 4.1 Diversity of virus architecture. (*a*) Polyhedral virus—Adenovirus. Adapted from Russell, W. (1971) in *Strategy of the Viral Genome* (ed. G. E. W. Wolstenholme and M. O'Connor) Ciba Foundation Symposium. (*b*) Helical virus—Tobacco mosaic virus. Adapted from Klug, A. and Caspar, D. C. D. (1960) *Adv. Virus Res.*, **1**, 225. (*c*) Complex virus—Bacteriophage T_4.

In some of the larger viruses the virion is contained within a membranous capsule or envelope which is comprised of lipoproteins and glycoproteins (figure 4.1, 4.2).

Nucleic acid components
Viruses show a remarkable constancy in their basic organisation despite the diversity of the hosts on which they depend. The nucleic acid component of the virion is either DNA or RNA and in both cases may occur in double-stranded (ds) or single-stranded (ss) forms. In the ds DNA viruses the molecule occurs as a covalently closed circle or as in some bacteriophages (viruses infecting bacteria) as a linear molecule but with single-stranded ends which are complimentary in base sequences so forming "sticky ends". It is likely that these DNA molecules can assume a circular form and may in fact do so when in the host cell. The amount of nucleic acid in virus particles, expressed in terms of number of proteins that can be coded, is very variable. In the smallest RNA bacteriophages, e.g. phage M52, the nucleic acid codes for only three proteins whereas in the larger particles some 200–300 proteins may be coded.

The protein components
The nucleic acid forms the central core to the virion and is enclosed by the protein, or one of the protein components, which takes the form of a coat or capsid. The capsid is comprised of many sub-units or capsomeres which may be formed from one or more polypeptides. The capsid fulfils several roles; it gives the particle its shape, it provides protection for the nucleic acid whilst the virus is outside its host, and it is involved in the initial attachment of the virion to the host cell. With respect to shape, virions fall into two groups, the helical forms and the polyhedral forms. The major exception to this generalised pattern are the "tailed" or T bacteriophages where the virion is a complex of a head region with a polyhedral form, and an attached tail that is helical.

Only in the tobacco mosaic virus, which has a helical structure, is the relationship between the two virion components known. The ss-RNA takes a helical form lying in a groove located in each capsomere. The virion has 2000 identical capsomeres orientated in a helical manner giving it its overall rod-shaped appearance. Many of the polyhedral viruses, where the relationship of nucleic acid to capsid is unknown, are iscosahedral in form composed of 12 corners, 20 triangular faces and 30 edges with a total of 162 capsomeres. The latter are of two types depending on their location within the capsid; the pentons are located at the 12 corners of the virion and have 5 other capsomeres surrounding them, and the hexons make up the triangular faces of the capsid and have 6 other capsomeres as neighbours. A further distinction is the presence of an attached fibre and knob on each penton. The smallest number of capsomeres in a capsid is 12 in the bacteriophage ϕX, and each one is a penton, but a large number of viruses have 162 capsomeres, e.g. adenovirus and herpes virus.

The protective function of the capsid is a fundamental one enabling the virion to survive outside the host. Packaging the nucleic acid in this way enables its genetic capabilities to be maintained for indefinite periods of time even in fairly harsh environmental situations. Thus in many viruses the capsid is resistant to proteolytic enzymes and is also stable in solutions of varied ionic strengths over a wide range of pH.

The role of capsid proteins in attachment to the host cell is also an important one. It is most likely that this function involves an interaction based on the molecular structure of the polypeptide involved. The best known examples of this function are found in the bacteriophages, e.g. the spike proteins of ϕX174, the "A" protein in the capsid of M52 and the tail fibres of the T bacteriophages.

In some viruses the virion contains protein additional to that present in the capsid. These proteins are enzymes which are usually absent from the host cell and are contained within the capsid. These enzymes are normally those essential for the first step, or steps, in virus replication. They are inactive in the intact virus but removal of the capsid brings about activation by mechanisms as yet unknown. Other non-enzymatic proteins have been reported in some viruses. These are rich in arginine and are believed to have a neutralising function with respect to the charge on the nucleic acid. Other virus coded proteins are found in the membranes which form the envelope around certain types of virus particles.

Virus replication

Our knowledge of virus replication stems from the detailed study on the T-even bacteriophages which infect *Escherichia coli*, however, subsequent investigations on many other viruses have shown that the sequence of events involved in replication are very similar. The events of virus replication are summarised in figure 4.3.

Attachment to the host
The infection process commences with the attachment of the virus to its

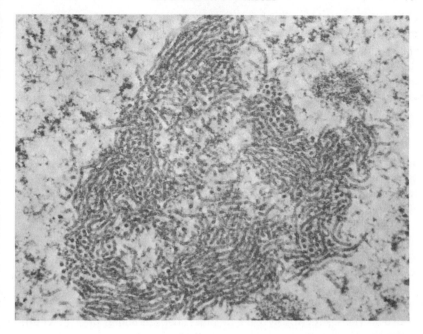

Figure 4.2 Electron micrograph of monkey cells infected with measles virus showing nucleocapsids in the nucleus (× 70 000). From Fields, B. N., *et al.* (1977) *Microbiology*, 1977 (ed. D. Schlessinger) American Society for Microbiology, Washington DC, 462–469. Reproduced by kind permission of Dr B. N. Fields.

susceptible host cell. This is essentially a random event; the virus reaches its host by diffusion. The efficiency of infection will be increased if adsorption of the virion can be restricted only to potentially susceptible host cells. As mentioned previously specific components of the protein capsid are known to be involved in the attachment process and these attachment proteins interact with specific receptor sites on the host cell surface (Simon and Anderson, 1967). Such sites have been identified in *Escherichia coli* for many of the T-phages, with some located in the outer lipoprotein layer, e.g. T_2 and T_6, and others in the peptidoglycan layer, e.g. T_3, T_4 and T_7. Eukaryotic cells also have surface recognition sites to which virus particles become attached. Some of the best evidence for these is derived from experiments involving the haemoagglutination property exhibited by many animal viruses. When viruses are added to a suspension of red blood cells, an individual particle may adsorb to the surface of several cells so bringing about agglutination. The myxovirus and the influenza virus have some 200 attachment sites over the capsid surface. Specificity may also be expressed in relation to the cell types that are infected, thus the polio virus only infects cells of the digestive tract and the nervous systems of primates. This specificity is believed to be related to a specific receptor on the host cell membrane and is found only in the membranes of these two cell types.

The adsorption of virus particles to their host cell is influenced by various environmental factors. At temperatures lower than normal for virus growth, the adsorption process is a reversible one but it can be blocked by the addition of antibodies specific either to the virus or to the host receptor site. At normal growth temperatures, however, these effects are not found, virus adsorption is irreversible and antibody inhibition does not occur. It is assumed that this change results from some alteration(s) in either the virus or the host receptor site. The capsids of adsorbed virus particles have been shown to be less resistant to the actions of proteolytic enzymes than are free particles and this change has been interpreted as significant in relation to the adsorption process.

Entry into the host
Entry of the virus into its host cell involves the penetration of various barriers: the plasma membrane and the cell wall in the case of micro-organisms and plants, the plasma membrane in animal cells. Again research into this aspect of virus replication has centred on the T-phages, in particular T_2 and T_4 (Simon and Anderson, 1967). However, as we shall see there are important differences between bacteriophages and other viruses in relation to the nature of the virus material that enters the host.

In the bacteriophage the tail component of the virion is vital to the mechanism of entry into the host. Following attachment of the phage to its receptor site, the tail fibres fold upon themselves and in doing so bring the base of the tail, with its spikes, into close contact with the cell wall to which these spikes become attached. This event is the stimulus for the contraction of the tail sheath but the nature of the interaction involved in this event is not understood. Many molecules of ATP are localised in the tail of the phage and this is utilised during contraction. The ultimate outcome is the penetration of the cell wall, and presumably the plasma membrane, by the tail core and the simultaneous transfer of DNA from the head of the virion into the host cytoplasm (figures 4.4, 4.5). An intriguing feature of this event is how the DNA molecule, some 50 000 nm long and 2.4 nm diameter, is transferred through the core, which

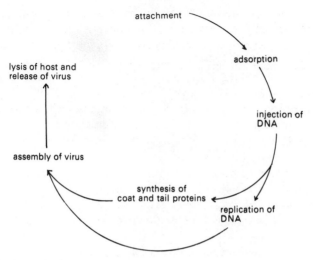

Figure 4.3 Synopsis of the steps in the replication of Bacteriophage T$_4$.

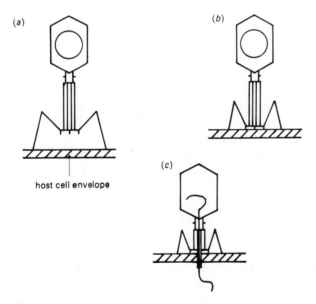

Figure 4.4 Attachment and infection of a bacterial host cell by a T-phage. (*a*) Adsorption of the virus to its receptor site on the cell envelope, by the tail fibres. (*b*) Attachment of the tail spikes to the cell wall. (*c*) Contraction of the tail sheath causing penetration of the envelope by the core and injection of phage DNA.

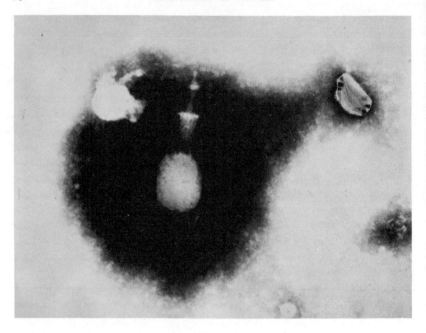

Figure 4.5   Electron micrograph of a shadowed preparation of bacteriophage T_4 attached to *Escherichia coli* cells. Note the contracted tail sheath ($\times$ 180 000).

is 2.5–3 nm diameter, in only one minute. It is possible that the host cell plays some part and in the case of phage T_5, protein synthesis appears to be a requirement for the transfer step.

Many bacteriophages of course do not have the specialised tail component and the mechanism of transfer of their nucleic acid is yet to be discovered. After the initial adsorption (involving the capsid spike) of phage ϕX174, close contact between the particle and its host cell quickly follows. Only the viral DNA enters the host, leaving the capsid on the cell surface. The sexpili found on the outer surface of "male" or "donor" strains of *Escherichia coli* are the receptor sites for several "tail-less" phages and these structures may provide a mechanism of entry for the viral nucleic acid into the host. These phages include certain small RNA types f2 and Q, and the filamentous DNA phages f1 and fd. Some workers have demonstrated the presence of phage RNA and the so-called "A" protein, a specific capsid protein involved in the attachment and adsorption process, in sexpili. It might then be envisaged that the pili provide channels of entry into the host. An alternative suggestion is that the pili could contract, similarly to the sheath of the tailed-phages, and consequently bring the virus into contact with the surface of the host cell.

The mechanisms of entry of plant and animal viruses into their host cells is even more speculative. Plant viruses are dependent upon some damage to the cell wall to gain entry into their host. This damage may occur by mechanical means or by an insect vector which, during feeding, pushes its stylet through the cell wall and plasma membrane into the cytoplasm. After passage through a wall, damaged by mechanical means, the virions are confronted with a second barrier, the plasma membrane. This may be breached by an endocytotic process. Investigations using isolated protoplasts from plant cells have demonstrated that viruses can be taken up in this way.

Entry of viruses into animal cells requires the penetration of only one barrier, the plasma membrane. Three theories have been proposed to account for this process. The first is also based on endocytosis, with the virus particles entering the host cell in small vesicles (figure 4.6a). The latter may be expected to make contact and fuse with liposomes, the enzymes of which could then be involved in the removal of the virus coat. Subsequently the nucleic acid and other proteins contained in the capsid would be liberated into the cytoplasm as the vesicles break down. What is not clear is the mechanism whereby these other virus components are not degraded in a similar manner as the capsid. The second theory was devised to explain the entry of smaller, simpler viruses into the animal cell. It proposes that the virions are transported directly across the membrane with, in some instances, the capsid proteins being deposited within the membrane or on its outer surface. The third proposal was put forward to explain what might happen in the case of viruses with membranous envelopes. It is assumed that the first step involves the fusion of the virus membrane with the plasma membrane of the host cell (figure 4.6b). As a result a channel is created through which the virus can pass into the cytoplasm of the host cell.

Comparing this aspect of virus replication in bacteriophages and other viruses the clear difference relates to the uncoating process and the location of its occurrence. The external uncoating as seen in the bacteriophages clearly allows a more rapid beginning to the next stage of the replication process. In the case of plant and animal viruses the entry mechanism involves events which are part of normal membrane activity and requires these processes for uncoating and liberating the viral nucleic acid. This latter type of mechanism would also appear to be most

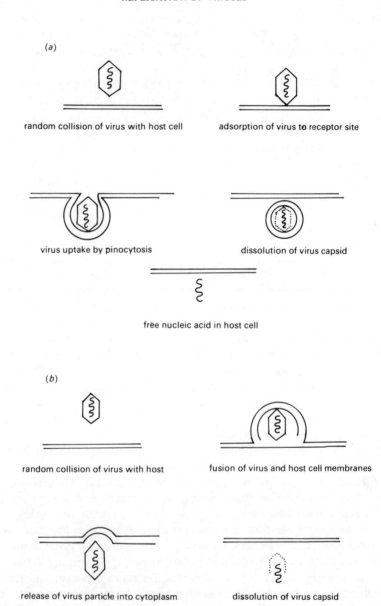

Figure 4.6 (a) Entry of virus particle into host cell by endocytosis.
(b) Entry of membrane-bounded virus into host cell by fusion of virus and cell membranes.

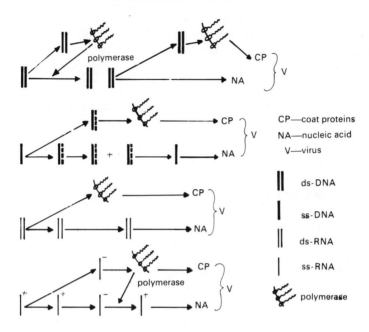

CP—coat proteins
NA—nucleic acid
V—virus

ds-DNA

ss-DNA

ds-RNA

ss-RNA

polymerase

Figure 4.7 Schematic replication of virus nucleic acids. Adapted from Newton, A. A. (1974) in *Companion to Biochemistry* (ed. A. T. Bull *et al.*), Longman, London, 277–306.

reasonable in the case of viruses that release proteins, as well as nucleic acid, into the host cytoplasm.

Replication of viral nucleic acids
The nucleic acid component of viruses takes on a variety of forms, as discussed previously. A successful infection will result in the production of many replicas of those molecules vital for subsequent incorporation into mature particles. The enzymes involved in nucleic acid replication, in different virus-host systems, are derived from a variety of sources (figure 4.7). They may be host enzymes, enzymes taken into the host by the virus, or enzymes synthesised *de novo* based on a coding determined by the viral nucleic acid (Bachrach, 1978).

Many of the DNA viruses utilise the polymerase enzymes of the host cell for the replication of their nucleic acid, others induce the synthesis of new DNA polymerase or cause modification to the host enzyme. These virus-mediated enzymes, however, are not template specific and their purpose is consequently obscure. With the exception of the pox-viruses, nucleic acid replication in the ds-DNA viruses occurs in the nuclei of the host cells and so does transcription. The synthesis of virus mRNA is again dependent on host enzymes in the majority of DNA viruses. Following viral infection the host DNA-directed RNA polymerases become more efficient in utilising the viral DNA template for transcription than that of the host cell.

In the ss-DNA viruses, e.g. ϕX174, the first step of nucleic acid replication is the synthesis of a strand of DNA complementary to the infecting strand, involving the host polymerase enzyme for this purpose. The first-formed duplex, called the replicative form, of the viral nucleic acid functions as a template for the synthesis of additional copies. These are used as templates for the synthesis of the single-stranded molecules required for the new virions. This step requires enzymes coded by the virus genome. The ds-DNA replicative form also serves as the template for mRNA transcription.

The replication of RNA molecules does not occur in either prokaryotic or eukaryotic organisms, consequently host cells infected with RNA viruses become involved in a unique process. In the case of ss-RNA viruses, e.g. polio virus, the infecting strand acts as a template for the sequential production of a number of complimentary strands. The latter strands are subsequently used as templates to make copies identical to the infecting strand. The mechanism of RNA replication in the ds-RNA viruses is not fully understood. Initially single-stranded molecules are produced from the double-stranded template. These newly formed molecules function as mRNA and as templates for the synthesis of complimentary strands in the formation of new ds-RNA. The uniqueness of RNA replication to the virus situation is reflected by the absence of RNA polymerases in the host cells. To overcome this deficiency ss-RNA viruses code for the early synthesis of the enzyme and the ds-RNA viruses carry their own enzyme.

The RNA tumour viruses have a more intricate mechanism of nucleic acid replication. These viruses have ss-RNA molecules which, following infection of the host cell, become copied through several steps finally appearing as ds-DNA. A copy of this molecule is then inserted into one of the host chromosomes and is replicated at subsequent cell divisions. The integration, in this case, of a "re-cast", of the viral nucleic acid is somewhat analogous to the lysogenic situation that is found in some bacteriophages (see later).

Replication of viral nucleic acids, not surprisingly, causes several changes in the metabolism of the host cell. The original ideas on virus

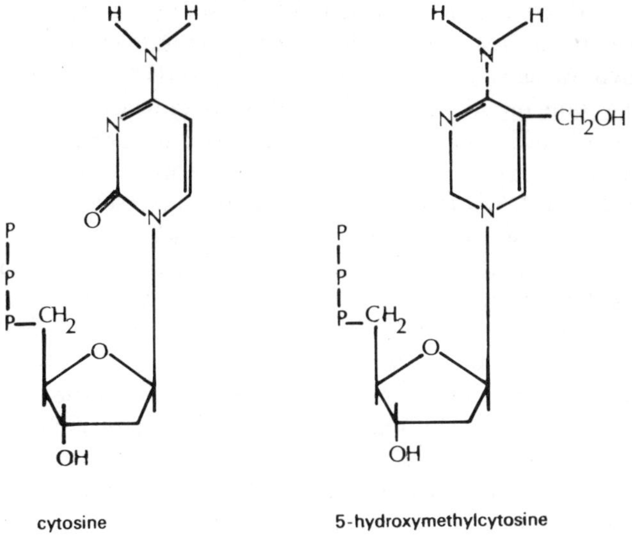

Figure 4.8 Structure of cytosine and 5-hydroxymethylcytosine.

replication suggested that the events taking place were maintained at the expense of the existing metabolic processes occurring in the host. Modification of these views followed the discovery that certain component molecules, i.e. monomers of the nucleic acid and proteins, were specific to viruses, e.g. hydroxymethylcytosine, a constituent of the DNA of T phages (figure 4.8). The synthesis of such molecules demands that the host cell be programmed to produce the necessary enzymes required for that synthesis. Another alteration in the metabolism of the host cell might be the depression of a host enzyme which is required for viral replication, e.g. when virus infects a non-dividing cell. New forms of a polymerase enzyme will also be required if the host enzyme has a cytoplasmic location different from the site at which nucleic acid replication occurs, e.g. as in the pox viruses.

Where nucleic acid replication is dependent on a *de novo* synthesis of an enzyme, this latter process must occur very soon after infection has taken place. Early transcription implicates the involvement of host DNA-directed RNA polymerase for mRNA synthesis. Although, as we have seen in some RNA viruses, the infecting nucleic acid itself serves as a messenger, attaching to the host ribosomes.

Protein synthesis

From the previous discussion it is clear that several new proteins will be synthesised by the host cell following virus infection. The appearance of a particular protein will reflect its function, either as an enzyme or as a component of the virus particle. Synthesis of virus proteins utilises the host ribosomal system, responding to virus mRNA. Where novel amino acids are required, i.e. those not normally produced by the host cell, new forms of tRNA will by synthesised. In virus infected cells host protein synthesis is normally stopped usually as a result of the degradation of polyribosomes which occurs as an early response to infection.

Assembly of new virions

The process of assembly of the individual components into functional units differentiates viruses from organisms that reproduce by division or cell fusion events (Casjens and King, 1975). Our knowledge of the assembly process is enhanced from *in vitro* experiments utilising the tobacco mosaic virus. When virus RNA and protein are incubated together they become assembled into normal infectious particles. If the protein component is incubated alone, under suitable conditions, the sub-units become aggregated into the rod structures that are typical of the virus. Assembly ceases when all the sub-units are linked together. The presence of RNA, however, determines the length of the rod structure. Subsequent experiments with other plant viruses have given the same results and it has also been demonstrated that particles can be assembled which are comprised of the nucleic acid of one virus and the protein of a second.

These observations clearly demonstrate that the formation of the virus capsid is a self-assembly process, independent of enzyme activity. The structure of the protein sub-units determines their orientation with respect to each other as the capsid is built up. As a consequence, the final shape of the capsid is determined by the orientation of the capsomeres as they become joined together. In other words the construction of the virus capsid complex is controlled by structural information built into the individual sub-units (Murialdo and Becker, 1978; Showe and Kellenberger, 1975).

Involvement of membranes in virus replication

Membranes of the host cell are involved in virus replication in a number of ways. By definition, those viruses that have membranous envelopes will necessarily involve membrane activity at some stage in their formation. The membranous envelope is derived from both host and virus coded

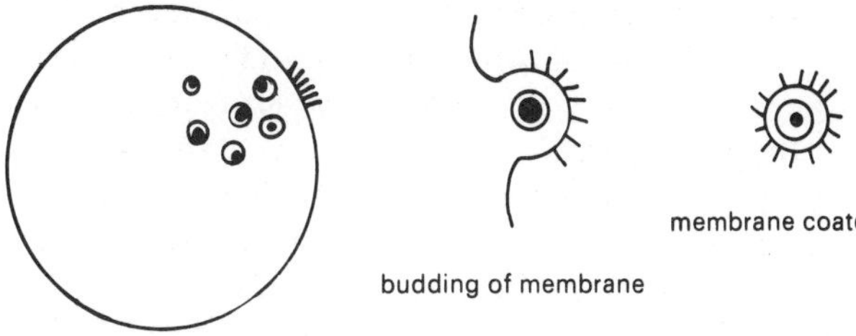

Figure 4.9 Release of membrane bounded virus from an infected cell.

components. The host component is lipid and the virus component is protein (figure 4.9). In some viruses the protein has a carbohydrate component, i.e. a glycoprotein, and this is also synthesised by host coding. The virus coded protein becomes inserted into the plasma membrane of the infected cell, at localised sites, replacing the membrane protein. This begs the question as to the relationship between these membrane sites and virus replication. Two possibilities exist; the change in the membrane may result from the replication and assembly of the virus at an adjacent site or alternatively the changed membrane may initiate the viral activity in the adjacent cytoplasm.

Release of mature viruses

The intracellular phase of virus development terminates with the release of mature virus from the host cell. The release of virus particles may or may not cause damage to the host. In those viruses having envelopes, the units are budded through the plasma membrane. Certain bacteriophages, e.g. the filamentous phages, are extruded in some way through the cell membrane causing no damage to the host. Where the host cell survives and can multiply, a clone of virus producing cells results.

The other method by which viruses are released, causes the death of the host cell. When the virions are assembled the host cell is induced to lyse. In infections involving the T-phages cell lysis is brought about by the action of a virus-coded lysozyme which is synthesised as one of the later products in the infection cycle.

Pattern of virus replication

The overall pattern of virus replication and infection can be readily demonstrated experimentally, using a bacteriophage-bacterium system.

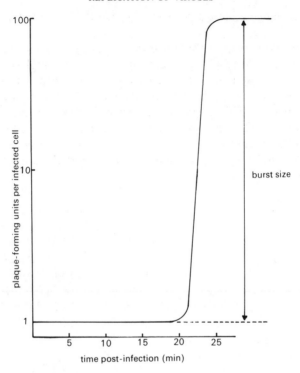

Figure 4.10   One-step growth curve of a bacteriophage culture.

The phage is added to a broth culture of the host bacterium, which should be in the exponential phase of growth, at a ratio of 1 phage particle per 10 host cells. This low ratio ensures that multiple infections will be extremely rare. After a few minutes phage antiserum is added to the culture to inactivate any phage particles that remain free. The antiserum is then inactivated after a further short incubation period and the culture is sampled at intervals to determine the number of phage particles using the plaque assay procedure (figure 4.10). The number of phage particles remains at the input level (1 per infected cell) for a certain time, known as the *latent period*. This may be some 20 minutes at optimal conditions and then there is a rapid increase in the number of particles free in the culture which attains a maximum in a matter of a few minutes. The particles are released as the host cells are lysed and the input ratio is known, thus the number of particles produced per infected cell, known as the burst size, can be determined. This experiment is called the one-step growth experiment.

The events taking place within the host cell during the latent period can be monitored in a similar experiment in which the samples taken for phage assay are first treated, e.g. by shaking with chloroform, to break open the cells. In this way it is found that the infecting phage particle quickly disappears. This might be expected in view of the infection process, however, infectious particles can be detected in the cell extracts a few minutes before the latent period ends and at the point when normal lysis would occur. The period when no infectious particles are extractable is called the *eclipse phase*.

Lysogeny

Infection of host cells with the subsequent release of mature virions is not the pattern of development for all viruses. Certain bacteriophages, called temperate or lysogenic phages, infect their bacterial host by the mechanism described previously. Their DNA does not commence replication, instead it becomes integrated in the chromosome of the host cell forming a

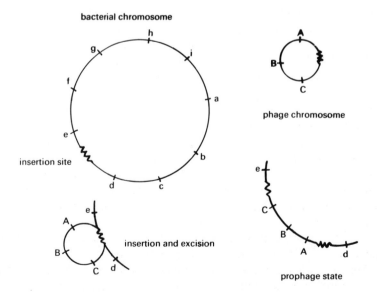

Figure 4.11 Integration and excision of bacteriophage DNA into the host bacterial chromosome.

unified structure. Integration of the phage DNA may occur at one or several sites on the chromosome, depending on the particular virus. Integration occurs at regions of homology in the base sequences (figure 4.11). The DNA in the virion, and on entering the host cell, becomes a linear duplex with short single-stranded or "sticky ends". A circular duplex is formed before the molecule is integrated into the bacterial chromosome.

The phage in this integrated state is known as a prophage and the association between the virus and its host is known as lysogeny. This condition can be maintained for many generations of the host with each daughter cell receiving a copy of the prophage. The lysogenic state is maintained by a repressor protein, a product of one of the few phage genes that is transcribed, whilst it exists as the prophage. The repressor protein inactivates the other phage genes and continues to do so whilst it is maintained at a certain critical level in the cell. The repressor protein also has an immunity function and is responsible for the condition known as super-infection. Cells in the lysogenic state are immune to further infection by the same phage.

The prophage state can be broken by various treatments known as induction, with a brief exposure to UV light being the simplest. These treatments apparently cause a decrease in the concentration of the repressor protein. As a result of the induction process the phage DNA is extruded from the bacterial chromosomes, undergoes replication and initiates synthesis of phage proteins. Eventually mature virions are assembled and released from the host cell following lysis.

SUMMARY

1. Most viruses are complexes of two macromolecules, a nucleic acid and protein, organised into distinct structural entities called particles or virions.

2. The nucleic acid component is either DNA or RNA which are present as either single-stranded or double-stranded form.

3. The protein component forms a coat, or capsid, that encloses the nucleic acid. It is comprised of a number of sub-units, the orientation of which gives the particle its

shape. The coat provides protection for the nucleic acid whilst outside the host cell and is also involved in the initial attachment of the virus to its host cell at infection. In some viruses additional proteins are present, mostly enzymatic; these are enclosed within the particles.

4. Virus particles are totally dependent on a host cell for their replication. A number of stages are recognised, (i) attachment to the host, (ii) entrance into the host, (iii) replication of the viral nucleic acid, (iv) synthesis of virus proteins, (v) assembly of new particles and (vi) release of virus from the mature cell.

5. Virus attachment is a random process, but its efficiency and that of subsequent infection is increased by the specificity existing in relation to the adsorption of particles to the host cell. Specific proteins in the virus coat and specific receptor sites on the host cell surface are involved in the adsorption process.

6. Viruses infecting various host types differ in relation to their entrance into host. In bacteriophages, at least those investigated so far, only nucleic acid enters host cell. This is achieved through a specialised infection process which is related to the structure of the virus particles. In the case of plant and animal viruses the whole particle is taken into the cell and then uncoated to release the nucleic acid. Plant viruses enter their hosts, in natural infections, via insect vectors which during feeding insert their stylets into the cell and eject virus particles with their secretions. Viruses can also infect cells through walls that have suffered mechanical damage. The virus is then thought to enter the protoplast by pinocytosis in a similar manner to the animal viruses.

7. The diversity of form among virus nucleic acid is also reflected in the mechanisms of replication. The DNA viruses normally utilise the host DNA polymerases. In contrast RNA replication is not a mechanism found in prokaryotic and eukaryotic cells and consequently RNA polymerase is not produced. To overcome this the viruses carry their own enzyme or induce its synthesis in the host cell.

8. Virus proteins are assembled on the host ribosomal system in response to viral mRNA. The unique amino acids found in some virus proteins require the production of novel forms of tRNA.

9. Virus particle assembly is a non-metabolic process and is independent of the host cell. The protein sub-units fit together in a specific form determined by their own structure.

10. In those viruses enclosed in membranous envelopes both the virus and the host cell contribute to its production. The host cell provides the lipid and the virus provides protein or glycoprotein. These viruses are assembled near the plasma membrane of the host cell and become surrounded by membrane as they are released.

11. Release of the mature virus particles is achieved by extrusion as described above or following lysis of the infected cell.

12. The temperate or lysogenic bacteriophages enter a special relationship with their host cell. The virus DNA becomes integrated into the chromosome of the bacterial host entering the prophage state. Many copies of prophage are made as the host cell divides and all its progeny carry the prophage. The lysogenic condition can be ended by various treatments and then the virus DNA replicates in the normal way quite independently of the host chromosome. Proteins are synthesised and following assembly of virus particles the host cell lyses.

CHAPTER FIVE

SPORE FORMATION IN BACTERIA

FOUR TYPES OF SPORES ARE PRODUCED BY A NUMBER OF REPRESENTATIVE groups of bacteria. The most widely studied are the endospores, which are found in three genera—*Bacillus*, *Clostridium* and *Sporosarcina*. Endospores are essentially dormant or resting cells and their formation does not represent a reproductive process. The same is true for cysts, although a cell producing cysts in fact gives rise to two. Cyst formation is a characteristic of the genus *Azotobacter*. Myxospores, produced by members of the Myxobacterates, are also resting cells. In contrast, their formation involves the differentiation of specialised spore-bearing structures but, even so, each spore is a product of a single bacterial cell. The only true spores, i.e. reproductive structures produced for dissemination and multiplication of the species, are the conidia, or arthrospores, produced by the Actinomycetes.

The development of spores represents a distinct morphological change and provides an example of altered gene activity. The switch from vegetative growth to sporulation is invariably a response to changes in the environmental situation and the development that ensues represents the interaction of these changes with the genome of the organism. In most of these cases of spore development the nature of this interaction is still unknown, but in recent years our knowledge of the molecular events associated with endospore formation has proceeded to the extent that hypotheses, with reasonable experimental support, can now be put forward.

Endospore development

Endospores are typically found in cultures of *Bacillus* and *Clostridium* at the end of the exponential phase of growth when the generation time of the cells is gradually increasing in response to depletion of the carbon or nitrogen, and sometimes phosphate, source. Two methods are used to induce sporulation in laboratory cultures. In one the starvation effect is applied by using a carbon or nitrogen limited medium and allowing the cells to deplete the particular nutrient concerned. The difficulty with this method is the lack of control which can be achieved over the initiation step. The second method is more amenable in this respect and involves the transfer of exponentially growing cells from a rich to a nutritionally poor medium. Sporulation then begins in a more synchronous manner. The development of a mature spore takes 7–8 hours. The end of logarithmic growth and the initiation of sporulation is conventionally designated T_0 with subsequent timings T_1, T_2, T_3 etc.

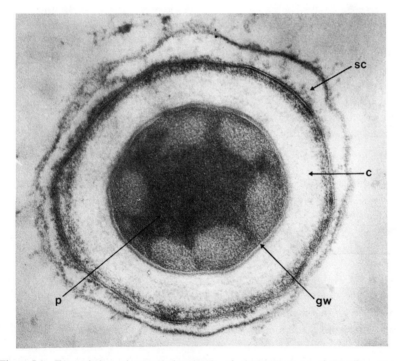

Figure 5.1 Transmission electron micrograph of the endospore of *Bacillus cereus* ($\times$ 90 000). From Dring, G. J. and Gould, G. W. (1976) in *Microbial Ultrastructure: the use of the electron microscope* (ed. R. Fuller and D. W. Lovelock) Academic Press, London, 147–159. Reproduced by kind permission of Dr G. J. Dring and the Society for Applied Bacteriology.
sc, spore coats; c, cortex; gw, germ wall; p, spore protoplast.

Spore structure

The endospore is characterised by the presence of a multilayered envelope or spore coats, which encloses the spore (figure 5.1). The number of coats in this envelope is a characteristic feature within a species but differs between species. The outer coat is known as the exosporium and this forms either a tight or a loose outer cover. In many species the exosporium gives the spore surface a characteristic morphology by the presence of patterned ridges. The chemical profile of the exosporium includes lipid and protein with the latter characteristically having a low cysteine-methionine content. The protein component is also highly resistant to proteases, a feature that is of undoubted significance in the survival of spores in nature. The inner spore coats are more complex in composition containing glycopeptide as well as lipid and protein. The inner spore coat proteins are highly specific molecules with a high sulphur content. They are unique to spores and not present in vegetative cells. The spore coats make up some 30–60 per cent of the spore dry weight and the spore coat protein can account for up to 80 per cent of the total spore protein.

Inside the spore coats is a readily distinguishable region, bounded by membranes on both outer and inner surfaces, called the cortex. Several components have been isolated from the cortex including dipicolinic acid (DPA), peptidoglycan and Ca^{2+} ions. The DPA component is of some importance in spore physiology; evidence for this is seen in the isolation of several mutants of *Bacillus* which cannot synthesise DPA and these cells will only produce spores when DPA is added as a medium constituent. The cortex peptidoglycan is very similar to the polymer found in the wall of vegetative cells (figure 5.2). In fact the biosynthesis of the two polymers involves a common pathway with a split in the final stages.

The germ cell of the endospore, the part that grows out to form the vegetative cell, is enclosed with the cortical layer forming the central region of the spore. The germ cell is surrounded by a lysozyme sensitive wall and is therefore assumed to contain peptidoglycan. Teichoic acids are absent from the germ cell wall thus distinguishing it from the wall of the vegetative cell. The spore protoplast, enclosed within the germ cell wall, is very similar to its counterpart in the vegetative cell. The cytoplasm includes DNA, RNA and protein, part of which is enzymatic. Many of the enzymes in the spore protoplast also occur in the vegetative cells, but some are spore specific. Elucidation of specificity can be difficult because enzymes which appear to be synthesised *de novo* may be de-repressed enzymes of the vegetative cell incorporated into the spore as it is formed.

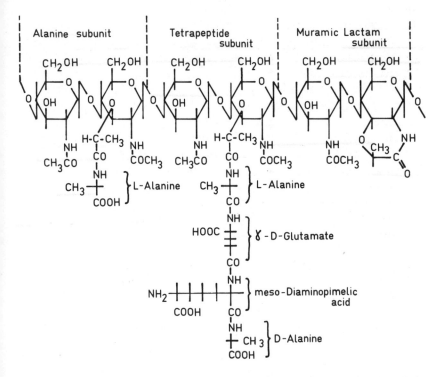

Figure 5.2 Repeating units of the peptidoglycan from the cortex of *Bacillus subtilis* endospores.

Despite the universal occurrence of certain enzymes in spores and vegetative cells those present in the former are normally more heat resistant than their counterparts in vegetative cells and frequently the kinetic properties of the two corresponding enzymes are also different.

An important characteristic of bacterial endospores is the high level of resistance to heat, chemicals, desiccation and irradiation they exhibit. Several theories have been proposed relating these properties to various aspects of spore structure. The more recent suggestions assume a single mechanism is involved in the control of structure and other spore properties, such as their ametabolic state and their non-stainability. Central to these ideas is the role of the cortex in bringing about dehydration of the spore protoplast. Evidence for this theory again rests

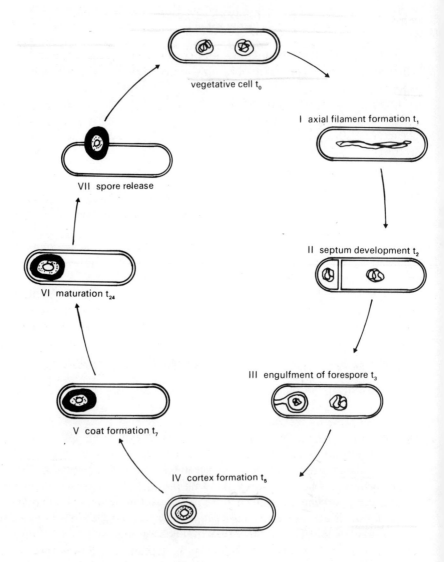

Figure 5.3 Schematic representation of the morphological changes associated with bacterial sporulation.

on studies with DPA-lacking mutants of *Bacillus* referred to earlier. If the cells of this strain are grown in the presence of varying concentrations of DPA the amount of cortex produced can be varied. Spores produced in this controlled way with a high cortex content, are more resistant and refractile than spores containing less cortex. Subsequent experiments showed that the cortex is involved in the dehydration processes during spore formation.

Endospores are also produced by Actinomycete species belonging to the genera *Thermoactinomyces*. They are very similar in morphology and structure to the spores of *Bacillus* and *Clostridium*, and also have similar properties.

Morphological stages of endospore development

Endospore development is a process of continuous morphological change starting from the vegetative cell and culminating in the release of a mature spore. Within this overall process of change seven distinct morphological stages, designated with Roman numerals (I–VII), can be recognised (figure 5.3) and these are used as reference points to which the many other metabolic and physiological changes can be related.

The transition from vegetative growth to endospore formation involves a major ultrastructural change associated with the DNA of the cell. Vegetative cells in logarithmic growth normally have two chromosomes, although the number can vary and is a function of growth rate. Stage I in endospore development is identified as the time when the two chromosomes have become joined to form a single body, called the axial filament. This lies centrally in the cytoplasm and almost traverses the whole length of the cell. This change in the nuclear material is independent of both DNA and protein synthesis. The process is completed at $T_{1.4}$. The spore-forming cell is then designated a mother cell.

The next stage (II) involves the formation of a septum transversely across, and near to one end of the cell giving rise to the prespore. This stage lasts for 0.9 hours. Part of the DNA (it must be at least one copy of the genome) becomes included in the smaller protoplast before the septum is finally completed. Electron micrographs of spore-mother cells between stages I and II clearly show the presence of mesosomes and their association with the developing fore-spore septum. An attachment between the chromosome and the mesosome is also visible. The mesosomes arise *de novo* rather than by transportation from some other site on the plasma membrane.

In stage III the prespore becomes totally engulfed by the protoplast of the spore-mother cell, giving rise to the forespore. This is achieved by growth of the plasma membrane of the spore-mother cell in the periplasmic space between what is now the forespore plasma membrane and the cell wall. Eventually the forespore becomes enclosed as a double-membraned structure.

What then follows is the deposition of additional layers of spore material between the two membranes. A layer of peptidoglycan is laid down as the germ cell wall on the surface of the inner membrane and to the outside of this the cortex is formed, constituting stage IV of the development sequence. The peptidoglycan component of the cortex is believed to be synthesised in association with both the forespore membranes, but the DPA component of the cortex is synthesised by the mother cell and then transported across the outer forespore membrane and deposited in the region between the two membranes. Stage V represents the period of coat formation and during this time the outer forespore membrane becomes lost. Stage VI is an ill-defined period of maturation that appears to be necessary before the spore can be released from the mother cell as a result of lysis (stage VII).

The initial stages of endospore development, i.e. stages I and II have been described as a modification of cell division. There are two distinct differences which are put forward to discount this idea. In the first place the prespore septum is displaced from the central location as is typical for cell division, and secondly, septum development is not accompanied by obvious wall formation. In fact the evidence from electron micrographs of some species suggests that a limited amount of wall synthesis does occur. It has been argued that this is necessary to give some direction to the synthesis of the prespore membrane. The inclusion of axial filament formation, at the end of the logarithmic growth phase, as a stage in endospore formation, has also been challenged with the suggestion that septum development be designated stage I.

Initiation of endospore formation

Experiments on *Bacillus subtilis* have demonstrated that initiation of sporulation occurs at a specific point in the cell cycle but the process will only occur if the inducing conditions, e.g. nutrient starvation, exist at that time (Szulmajster, 1973; Sonnensheim and Campbell, 1978). Other environmental changes that induce sporulation, e.g. presence of slowly metabolised carbon sources, can be readily identified, but how do these interact with the control mechanisms operating inside the cells? The genome of spore producing cells is comprised of a vegetative component and genes associated with spore development. During vegetative growth the activity of the sporulation genes is blocked by some repression mechanism. An original view, that the blockage was mediated through catabolite repression caused by the presence of glucose, is now losing favour. The transition from vegetative growth to sporulation will therefore involve de-repression events associated with the spore genes and the simultaneous repression of the vegetative genome. Whether the latter is a partial or total effect is not yet clear.

One suggestion for the repression of sporulation during vegetative growth implicates a nitrogen containing metabolite or metabolites which at specific concentrations exert their effect. The intracellular concentration of such a molecule or molecules would be controlled by the availability and rate of metabolism of the carbon and nitrogen sources. To explain induction of sporulation by phosphate limitation, it is concluded that the metabolite(s) in question is a phosphorylated molecule. Several attempts have been made to define an initiation molecule for sporulation. In one approach mutants were investigated which exhibit both suppressed sporulation and restricted metabolism of the carbon and nitrogen sources resulting in the accumulation of specific metabolic intermediates. Several metabolites were identified including α-glycerol phosphate and glucose-6-phosphate, which are normally found at low concentrations in logarithmically growing cells. The inference drawn from these experiments was that initiation was a function of the depletion of certain metabolites during vegetative growth. This view has been questioned on the basis of its simplicity and it is now suggested that initiation probably involves several metabolic steps.

A role for ATP in initiation has also been put forward. This idea stems from findings with *Bacillus subtilis* where the level of ATP falls at the end of exponential growth. It is argued that depletion is the signal for initiation mediated through a phosphorylated protein functioning as an aporepressor. When ATP is maintained at a high level, as in growing cells, sporulation is blocked. Despite the depletion in ATP referred to above, sporulation is itself a highly energy dependent process with the active synthesis of ATP being necessary. This need is fulfilled by the de-repressed TCA cycle.

A contrasting view suggests that the initiator molecule could be an intracellular compound that is synthesised in a large quantity at the start of sporulation. Such a compound is 3′5′-cyclic guanosine 5′-monophosphate and this could function in a similar manner to cyclic AMP which is involved in catabolite repression of inducible enzyme synthesis in Gram negative bacteria. An interaction of c-GMP with glucose could then provide the repression mechanism for sporulation.

Once sporulation begins to what extent is the cell committed to producing a mature spore? Is the process reversible and if so at what stage does this property change? Information on this point remains controversial, even from experiments on the same organism. In experiments with *Bacillus subtilis* it was shown that spore development was not affected by the addition of glucose to cultures at any time after T_0. In contrast other workers showed that if spore-forming cells were transferred to fresh medium then stage II of the development process appeared to be a transition point. Thus cells at a pre-stage II underwent reversion, but those at post-stage II did not. Further conflicting observations stemmed from experiments in which cultures of spore-forming cells were diluted with fresh medium. In this case it was found that reversion to vegetative growth occurred up to the time of stage IV.

One possible cause for this variation in findings is the fact that the cultures used were not synchronised to any great extent. Later workers attempted to introduce synchrony, with a fair degree of success—80 per cent of the population attaining stage I almost simultaneously. Samples were taken from the sporulating cultures at intervals and inoculated into fresh growth medium. As a measure of reversion samples from these cultures were tested for heat resistance at intervals of time after transfer. Samples taken from sporulation cultures up to T_2 showed a high degree of reversion but later samples continued spore development even after transfer.

Biochemical changes during sporulation

A number of biochemical changes have been detected in spore-forming cells, the significance of the changes in relation to the developmental events in most instances remains to be established. Undoubtedly many are of no consequence, but some may be. Four types of change can be identified:

1. Enzyme activities which increase in spore-forming cells.
2. Synthesis of specific molecules by spore-forming cells.
3. Formation of spore specific components.
4. Components of vegetative cells that are either absent from spores or present in small amounts.

In the first category of change are the enzymes of the tricarboxylic acid cycle (TCA) (Szulmajster, 1973). Several enzymes of the cycle have been reported to be present in vegetative cells, e.g. aconitase, fumarase and succinate dehydrogenase, but others would appear to be absent. The appearance of a fully functional cycle, at about stage II in the development process, has been correlated with the utilisation of the presence of acetate and derived from the metabolism of glucose during vegetative growth. An obvious role for the TCA cycle during sporulation is the provision of ATP. Some idea as to the relationship between the TCA cycle and the spore-forming process can be obtained from studies on various mutant strains which are asporogenous, i.e. do not sporulate. Certain of these mutants of *Bacillus subtilis* are deficient for the TCA enzyme aconitase and are unable to synthesise glutamate. Transformation experiments using DNA from wild-type strains have shown very clearly that these mutants have a complete genome for sporulation. Their apparent asporogenous condition could therefore be the result of a physiological block in the metabolism involved in spore formation, steming from the absence of a functional TCA cycle.

Several other enzymes included in this category are present in vegetative cells at very low activities or may be completely undetectable and of

Table 5.1 Antibiotics produced by some *Bacillus* species.

Organism	Antibiotic
Bacillus subtilis	bacillin
	bacillomycin
	subtilin
	mycobacillin
	fungistatin
	subsporin
	neocidin
	eumycin
Bacillus licheniformis	bacitracin
	licheniformin
	proticin
Bacillus cereus	biocerin
	cerexin
	thiocillin
Bacillus brevis	gramicidin S
	tyrocidine
	edeine
	brevin
	brevistin
	eseine

these the extracellular proteases have been implicated as having a function in sporulation. In *Bacillus subtilis* there are two enzymes, a serine protease and a metalloprotease which have alkaline and neutral pH optima, respectively. Evidence has been put forward to suggest that the serine protease is involved in the modification of RNA polymerase that occurs prior to the transcription of sporulation genes (see later). Work on other species of *Bacillus* contradicts this view with the finding that several do not secrete protease yet sporulate quite normally.

Considerable interest has been shown in the various antibiotics produced by sporulating cells—Table 5.1 (Sadoff, 1972); the production of these metabolites is an example of the second category of change listed above. *Bacillus subtilis* produces several known antibiotics mostly with antibacterial activity, but at least one that is active against fungi. The antibacterial agents are thought to be associated with spore formation because loss of synthetic ability and an asporogenous condition are often associated. An example of this is the similar response of cells, in regard to spore formation and antibiotic production, to inhibitors and changes in the cultural conditions. What might the role of these antibiotics be? Several have been shown to be highly effective growth inhibitors—thus Tyrothricin (synthesised by *Bacillus brevis*), when added to actively growing cultures of the producer bacterium prevents growth by inhibiting RNA polymerase. This observation gave rise to a hypothesis which suggested that the antibiotic has a function in the selective repression of the transcription of vegetative genes during sporulation. This could be achieved by blocking the interaction between the RNA polymerase and the promoter, necessary for the transcription of the vegetative genome. *Bacillus brevis* produces another antibiotic called Edeine A which causes the reversible inhibition of DNA synthesis (figure 5.4). A role for this metabolite is seen in the blocking of DNA replication early in the differentiation process. A universal role for the antibiotics, produced at the commencement of sporulation, must remain controversial for the present because of the conflicting evidence from other studies. Thus mutants of *Bacillus licheniformis*, deficient in antibiotic biosynthesis, sporulate quite normally and wild-type, normal-sporulation strains of *Clostridium pasteurianum* do not produce antibiotics.

A number of spore specific components have been described including the peptidoglycans, DPA, spore antigens and spore coat proteins. The synthesis of peptidoglycan represents an important step in the development of the endospore. Synthesis of the polymer in the cell wall ends at the time of investigation of the prespore by the cytoplasmic membrane but

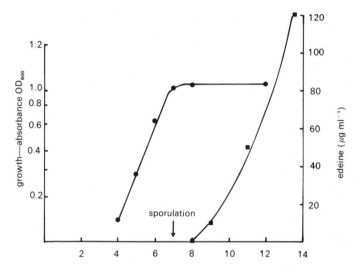

Figure 5.4 Growth of *Bacillus brevis* (●) and edeine production (■) at the onset of sporulation. Adapted from Sadoff, H. L. (1972) *Spores V* (ed. H. O. Halvorson, R. Hanson and L. L. Campbell) American Society for Microbiology, Washington DC, 157–166.

deposition of the spore polymers soon follows. In *Bacillus cereus* cells grown on ^{14}C diaminopimelic acid, two periods of peptidoglycan synthesis were found, resulting in the formation of two different molecular structures. The first period of synthesis coincides with the timing of formation of the germ cell wall and the second is associated with the formation of the cortex and occurs simultaneously with the synthesis of DPA.

Differences between the two peptidoglycans are reflected in their hydrolysis and turnover during germination and in the effect of penicillin on their synthesis. With regard to lysozyme induced hydrolysis, the cortical polymer is rapidly broken down but the germ cell wall is more resistant to attack and is hydrolysed more slowly. Penicillin has no effect on the formation of germ wall peptidoglycan but cross-linking, and therefore final polymerisation of the cortical molecule, is markedly inhibited. Under normal circumstances the synthesis of both peptidoglycans is a *de novo* process, there being no detectable incorporation of precursors from the wall of the spore-mother cell.

As implied above the Ca^{2+} ions and DPA found in bacterial spores are closely associated with the cortical peptidoglycan. The spores of *Bacillus*

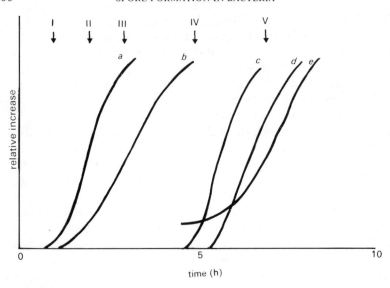

Figure 5.5 Synopsis of the molecular and physical changes during sporulation; (*a*) antibiotic production, (*b*) protein turnover, (*c*) dipicolinic acid content, (*d*) heat resistance, (*e*) core and coat proteins.

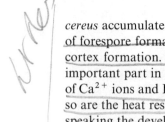

cereus accumulate Ca^{2+} ions very early in development, around the time of forespore formation. The DPA appears at stages IV–V at the time of cortex formation. These two spore components are believed to play an important part in the heat resistance property of spores. Where the levels of Ca^{2+} ions and DPA in spores are reduced by the presence of inhibitors so are the heat resistance properties of the spores also reduced. Generally speaking the development of heat resistance in spores is paralleled by the synthesis of DPA although it has been demonstrated, e.g. in *Bacillus cereus*, that a minimal level of the spore component, equivalent to one-third of the final amount, has to be present before thermoresistance can be detected in the developing spores.

The unique cysteine-rich coat proteins are synthesised early in the sporulation process at stage II in the morphological sequence. The site of synthesis of these proteins is thought to be the cytoplasmic membrane of the spore-mother cell on polysomes with bound, stable, mRNA. The oxidation of the sulphydryl groups to form disulphide bridges is an integral step in the synthesis of these proteins. As spore development progresses, so the disulphide/sulphydryl ratio increases.

The significance of the disulphide bridges might relate to spore morphology and possibly other properties, e.g. spore permeability, which was found to be changed when the disulphide content of the proteins was reduced. A role for the coat protein may be in the provision of protection against ionising radiations because the development of resistance to UV light has been shown to follow a similar timing and pattern as the deposition of these spore components.

Several of the enzymes extracted from spores are identical to those obtained from vegetative cells. The use of molecules with identical primary structures clearly aids the efficiency of the organism preventing excessive turnover of proteins. If enzymes are the same in both vegetative cells and in mature spores how does the resistance manifest by spores affect the enzymes. For many enzymes it is known that heat resistance is the result of stabilisation within the spore structure and not because the molecules are thermostable. Stabilisation sites have been found to be located in the spore wall in the case of alanine racemase in *Bacillus cereus*. Other enzymes are stabilised by Ca^{2+} ions where the spore enzyme and the vegetative cell enzyme are different, e.g. catalase, the spore form is found to be a heat-resistant molecule.

The relationship between the appearance of specific components and properties of spores and the morphological development is summarised in figure 5.5.

Macromolecular synthesis during endospore formation
DNA synthesis is terminated in spore forming cells with the completion of the rounds of replication that are in progress at the time of induction. This is achieved by stage I in the development cycle and the DNA copies are ultimately segregated between the developing spore and the spore-mother cell. DNA synthesis was found to be essential for the induction of sporulation in *Bacillus subtilis*. Thymine starvation of a mutant, having a requirement for the nutrient, resulted in the blockage of sporulation at stage II with the prevention of septum formation. In cells growing on a nutritionally poor medium a correlation was found between the timing of induction of sporulation and the replication of a specific region of the chromosome. Induction coincided with the time at which DNA replication was one-third completed.

The synthesis of enzymes and proteins not present in vegetative cells requires the transcription of hitherto dormant genes and the production of new species of mRNA. Continued transcription is an essential feature of sporulation as indicated by the inhibiting effects of antibiotics, that affect

RNA polymerase, on sporulation. The mRNA synthesised during sporulation has a short half-life.

The evidence for changes in the transcription machinery in spore-producing cells stems from four lines of experimental investigation; an examination of changes occurring early in the sporulation process, an analysis of mRNA, a comparison of the RNA polymerases present in vegetative and sporulating cells, and finally from a study of mutants with altered RNA polymerases (Doi, 1977a, b).

The occurrence of changes at the transcriptional level very early on in the spore-forming process was demonstrated in experiments in which vegetative and sporulating cells were compared in respect of bacteriophage infection and replication. The DNA of certain phages, that successfully infect log phase vegetative cells, is replicated only to a limited degree in sporulating cells and copies of the molecule are incorporated into the developing spore. In other phages normal, but slow, replication of the particles occur after a prolonged latent period. The host cell is eventually lysed and a small yield of particles is released. In the first situation no phage RNA is produced suggesting marked changes in the transcription machinery. The reduced replication of phage as found in the second instance might be interpreted in terms of similarity of promoter regions between the phage DNA and the host vegetative DNA that is transcribed during sporulation.

An analysis of the rate of RNA synthesis in sporulating cells reveals a pattern of peaks and troughs. As logarithmic phase growth ends and sporulation begins a dramatic decrease in RNA synthesis occurs to a level about 10 per cent of that in the vegetative phase cells. During sporulation the rate picks up and changes several times. How does the mRNA produced at these times compare with that found in vegetative cells and to what extent is new mRNA required for sporulation? An interesting situation was revealed using DNA–RNA hybridisation techniques in that even in the later stages of spore development about 60 per cent of the mRNA was of the type also present in vegetative cells. Despite this situation sporulation has to be regarded as a more complex process than vegetative growth simply because more forms of mRNA are necessary for the process to be completed, i.e. products of sporulation genes are superimposed on the existing and newly formed proteins derived from the vegetative genome. However, the specificity of the so-called sporulation mRNA in relation to functions related to spore formation still requires experimental evidence.

Arising from these two areas of investigation is the implication that two forms of transcriptional machinery, i.e. RNA polymerases specific for the vegetative and sporulation components of the genome, are present. A major problem in elucidating an answer to these questions, which indeed in the earlier studies gave rise to misleading data, relates to the activities of endogenous proteases in the cell extracts causing changes to the enzyme molecules under consideration. However, by using modified procedures for the elimination of the proteases more meaningful studies have been carried out. The RNA polymerase from vegetative cells has a core of three protein sub-units designated $\alpha_2\beta\beta^1$ which are associated with another core sub-unit σ to form the holoenzyme. Other small polypeptides are found in association with the core giving a variety of enzyme molecules. Extracts from cells at stages III and IV of spore formation contain two new forms of the enzyme which differ with respect to the core associate sub-unit. Cells at stage III have a specific core associate peptide δ^1, i.e. total enzyme $\alpha_2\beta\beta^1\delta^1$, which has a molecular weight of 27 000 and those at stage IV have an associated peptide of molecular weight of 20 000, called δ^2, i.e. $\alpha_2\beta\beta^1\delta^2$. The σ factor is therefore absent in both forms of the enzyme. The significance of the δ units in relation to RNA polymerase function is still speculative but not surprising is the suggestion that these sub-units play a key role in transcription by their recognition of specific promoters in the sporulation genome. This view is not totally lacking in experimental support, because cells treated with low doses of the antibiotic Netropsin that do not stop vegetative growth, are blocked in sporulation. The antibiotic binds to regions of DNA rich in adenine-thymidine bases and in experiments comparing its effect on RNA polymerases, the enzyme isolated from cells at stage III of spore development is inhibited more than the enzyme from vegetative cells. It was concluded from these observations that the two polymerases differ in their promoter regions and the regions recognised by the sporulation enzyme are richer in A–T regions and it is possible that the difference in the core associated polypeptide could be significant in this respect.

RNA polymerases are subject to inhibition by rifampicin which binds specifically to the sub-unit of the enzyme core. Mutants which exhibit resistance to the antibiotic can be isolated and these produce enzymes with modified sub-units. The study of these mutants is still in its early stages but their diversity, which is an expression of differences in the form the mutation takes at the molecular level, promises that future investigations should be profitable. The mutants obtained so far fall into four phenotypic groups which range from types with normal behaviour to types which exhibit a temperature sensitive mutation and are normal at the permissive temperature but fail to sporulate at the non-permissive temperature. Within this latter group the strains isolated differ with respect to the timing of the block in sporulation in the morphological stages sequence 0 to IV. The altered RNA polymerase core functions normally during vegetative growth at the non-permissive temperature but distinct changes in RNA synthesis occurs during sporulation particularly in cells which have developed as far as the morphological block. Continued RNA synthesis is found in these cells suggesting that only part of the transcriptional part of the machinery is affected.

It is interesting to consider whether the transcription process is the only mechanism of control of development in sporulating cells (Sonenshein and Campbell, 1978). Messenger RNA of bacterial cells has a short half-life (about 2 minutes) so it is clear that rapid changes in gene expression can be accommodated by transcription. However, several examples of stable mRNA have been described associated with specific functions and this had led to speculation of the role of stable mRNA in spore development. The evidence for the presence of these molecules is not strongly convincing in view of technical problems in the experiments. Thus in some cases the occurrence of RNA synthesis in the system could not be ruled out and for other experiments very high concentrations of inhibitors had to be used, but claims have been made for the occurrence of stable mRNA's for at least three spore specific proteins; dipicolinic acid synthetase in *Bacillus subtilis*, parasporal protein in *Bacillus thurigiensis* and the enterotroxin of *Clostridium perfringens*. However, experiments involving the use of temperature sensitive RNA polymerase mutants, as described above, failed to reveal any stable molecules.

Structural and functional changes in the ribosomes of spore-forming cells have been described by several workers but again the data is controversial. Differences in electrophoretic mobilities of ribosomes from vegetative and sporulating cells have been described from some laboratories but others have failed to find these differences. However, differences in structure may exist that cannot be detected by electrophoretic methods. A number of functional differences have been described for the two populations of ribosomes, differences in antibiotic sensitivity, differences in the nature of nucleotides synthesised by ribosomes and variation in ability of ribosomes to translate the message of synthetic nucleotides. In view of the continued transcription of part of the vegetative genome in sporulating cells provision must be made for the translation of these messengers. This again raises the question regarding structural alterations that occur to the ribosomes and which might be expected to completely modify their function. Two possibilities therefore exist, firstly the ribosomal population is mixed furnishing the needs of the two components of the genome or alternatively the ribosomes relate to mRNA's transcribed from both parts of the genome.

The diversity of studies described strongly support the view that during sporulation modifications to the core of RNA polymerase are necessary to allow transcription of the genes having functions geared to spore formation. In the spore-forming cells transcription of part of vegetative genome continues simultaneously with transcription of the newly derepressed sporulation genes. The significance of translational processes in the control of sporulation is less clear cut, but undoubtedly many of the questions will be answered in the not too distant future.

Genetic aspects of sporulation

A large number of mutants blocked in spore formation have been isolated in several *Bacillus* species (Piggot and Coote, 1976). These fall into two groups, the asporogenous types where spore production is totally blocked and the oligosporous types which form spores only at very low frequencies, i.e. 1 in 10^5 or 10^6 cells. The asporogenous mutants can be differentiated in relation to the morphological stage to which they can develop under the conditions that induce sporulation in wild strains. Phenotypically the mutants are designated spo O, spo I, etc. Genetic analysis using transformation and transduction has resulted in the mapping of several different loci for the various phenotypes. Stage O mutants (spo O) involve nine loci which are genotypically designated *spo OA*, *spo OB*, etc. Some *spo O* mutations are pleiotropic, i.e. have several effects, involving loss of antibiotic production and loss of extracellular protease production. Investigations on some of these mutants suggest that the cell membrane and certain of its functions are affected by the activity of the mutated gene. However, many of these mutants recover these lost properties if cultured under specific conditions but they remain asporogenous suggesting that the *spo O* genes control sporulation factors as their prime effect. Mutants with blocks at the later stage of development have also been obtained but the functions of the mutations involved have not been identified. Included in this group are mutants that produce spores with reduced levels of DPA in the cortex. The loci for both the early and late gene functions are found scattered throughout the chromosome (figure 5.6) although genes associated with stages II and III tend to be clustered in particular regions.

It is not possible, at present, to relate developmental stages of spore

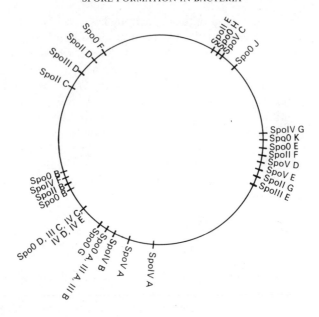

Figure 5.6   Genetic map of sporulation genes of *Bacillus subtilis*.

formation to a sequential expression of those genes associated with the morphological events which identify with those stages. In fact sequential transcription may not occur in view of the finding that certain events realised late in sporulation are the result of the early transcription and translation of genes.

This is so for some of the spore coat proteins which first appear at stages I–II although the coat structure is not organised until much later in the development.

Cyst formation in *Azotobacter*

Properties and morphology of cysts

Cysts are resting cells produced characteristically by members of the genus *Azotobacter* (Sadoff *et al.*, 1975). Like endospores they exhibit low metabolic activity and they show a higher degree of resistance to toxic chemicals than do the vegetative cells of this bacterium. They also contain high levels of Ca^{2+}. Unlike endospores, cysts are not heat resistant and do not contain DPA.

Cysts are vegetative cells which have been modified in three respects;

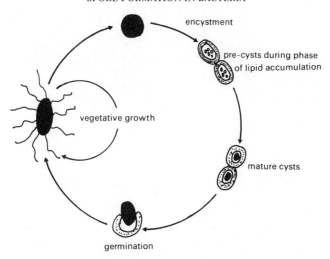

Figure 5.7   The life cycle of *Azotobacter vinelandii*.

they cease to be motile, their shape is changed from a bacillary form to an oblate spheroid, i.e. more rounded and shorter than the vegetative cell, and they have multilayered coats. Encystment begins with division of the cell into two parts called pre-cysts (figure 5.7). Each pre-cyst contains one copy of the chromosome. As the cyst matures it has a thin wall made of peptidoglycan around which are two coats, the inner, or intine, which is electron transparent and contains lipid and carbohydrate and the outer, or exine, which is multilayered and comprised of lipoprotein and lipopolysaccharide (figure 5.8).

Physiology of encystment
Encystment takes 36 hours but unlike endospore development is not so readily sub-divided into definable morphological steps. The growth medium used to culture the *Azotobacter* cells has an important effect on encystment. The process is generally associated with poor growth performance and thus can be induced if ethanol or butanol are used as the carbon source. In the presence of glucose or sucrose growth is greatly enhanced and encystment is very restricted. The medium must also be free of nitrogen in a bound form because this also inhibits cyst formation.

A characteristic feature of metabolism in *Azotobacter* species is the accumulation of the lipid reserve poly-β-hydroxybutyrate (**PHB**) and a close relationship has been found between a cell's ability to produce this

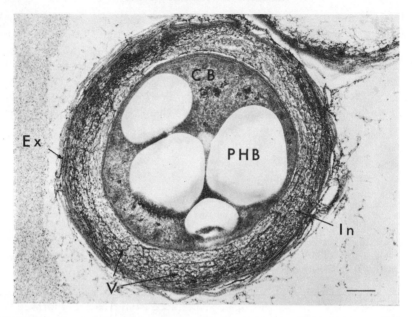

Figure 5.8 Transmission electron micrograph of a mature cyst of *Azotobacter vinelandii*. Ex, exine; In, intine; CB, central body; PHB, polyhydroxybutyrate granules; V, vesicles (bar marker 0.2 m). From Lin, L. P., *et al.* (1978) *J. Bact.*, **135**, 641–646. Reproduced by kind permission of Dr L. P. Lin.

reserve and to form cysts. This relationship is thought to involve the utilisation of the reserve for encystment. A breakdown product of PHB, beta-hydroxybutyrate (BHB), has been shown to induce encystment when supplied exogenously. When labelled BHB is fed to cells during encystment about 50 per cent of the substrate is incorporated into membrane phospholipid, mainly phosphatidyl ethanolanine, indicating that changes in the plasma membrane might be associated with the encystment process. Confirmation of the role of BHB *in vivo* must await experimentation but demonstration of an inducer function might be expected.

Biochemical changes associated with encystment
Carbohydrate metabolism in vegetative cells of *Azotobacter vinelandii* utilises the Entner–Duodoroff pathway with a minor involvement of the pentose phosphate pathway. Acetate can also be used as a substrate for growth demonstrating the presence of a functional TCA cycle. Following the induction of encystment, e.g. with BHB, changes in the level of activity

of enzymes in the Entner–Duodoroff pathway, TCA cycle and in enzymes involved in gluconeogenesis and the glyoxylate shunt are detectable. The key enzymes that have been investigated as indicators of metabolic change are: glucose-6-phosphate dehydrogenase (Entner–Duodoroff pathway) which becomes undetectable after induction, isocitrate dehydrogenase (TCA cycle) which shows two peaks of increased activity during encystment, isocitrate lyase and malate dehydrogenase (glyoxylate shunt) which are low in activity in vegetative cells and increase dramatically during encystment, and aldolase and fructose 1, 6-diphosphatase (gluconeogenesis) which are detectable during encystment. The implication of these changes in enzyme activities, which are not detectable in stationary phase cells and do not therefore represent responses to medium changes in relation to growth, is the requirement for enhanced activity of the TCA cycle and glyoxylate shunt to provide the additional ATP required to promote gluconeogenesis and polysaccharide biosynthesis.

DNA synthesis ceases following the induction of encystment. As in endospore formation, the rounds of DNA replication in progress at the time of induction, are completed and copies of the chromosome are dispersed to the two pre-cysts. DNA synthesis is normally completed three hours after induction.

Information on RNA synthesis during encystment is limited. The increases in enzyme activities and the appearance of new enzymes during encystment implies the need for stable mRNA transcribed during vegetative growth or *de novo* synthesis of new message. There is no net increase in RNA in encysting cells so new molecules must arise through turnover and resynthesis.

Myxospore formation

Morphology

Myxospores are produced by the fruiting myxobacteria, so-called because spore formation involves a defined cycle of development culminating in the formation of a fruiting body—figure 5.9 (White, 1975). During vegetative growth the cells in a colony maintain a loose association by a slime layer. Spore formation commences with the aggregation of cells into tight clusters. This is brought about by the cells gliding over the surface of the substratum probably responding to some chemotactic material. The cells in these aggregates differentiate into fruiting bodies with some of the cells changing from a cylindrical form into the spherical resting spores. Laboratory investigations have resulted in the isolation of mutants in

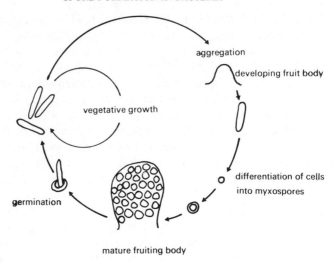

Figure 5.9   The life cycle of *Myxococcus xanthus.*

which spore formation occurs without fruiting body development. It has also been shown that inducing agents, e.g. glycerol, stimulate myxospore formation in cultures by-passing the normal developmental cycle.

Myxospores contrast from endospores and cysts in having 3 or 4 copies of the chromosome. This is because they develop directly from the vegetative cell without any prior division of the genetic material. The spore protoplast is enclosed in a wall which corresponds to the Gram negative nature of the vegetative cell and this in turn is covered by a capsule layer. The complete developmental cycle takes 50 hours but when glycerol induction is used the spores are formed within 2 hours.

Initiation of myxospore formation
The developmental cycle of *Myxococcus xanthus*, the species most extensively studied, can be achieved in laboratory cultures when the organism is grown on a medium containing heat-killed cells of *Escherichia coli*. In an attempt to identify nutrients that might be involved in the initiation of the developmental cycle a minimal medium was formulated which contained 17 amino acids. Using such a medium it was shown that starvation of certain amino acids, including phenylalanine, tryptophane and methonine, induced sporulation. Subsequent experiments with auxo-trophic mutants demonstrated a requirement for the same plus an additional number of amino acids for growth on a defined medium.

Limiting the availability of these nutrients impaired growth and induced spore development.

Metabolic activities during sporulation
The metabolism of vegetative cells and developing spores is apparently very similar. One difference reported in glycerol-induced sporulating cells is the presence of enzymes involved in the glyoxylate shunt pathway.

The patterns of nucleic acid metabolism resemble those described for endospores and cysts. New rounds of DNA replication are blocked once spore development commences. This has interesting consequences arising out of the fact that the two chromosomes in the vegetative cells replicate in sequence and not simultaneously. Thus cells induced to sporulate may complete replication of only one chromosome giving rise to a spore with three copies, others which are induced during replication of the second chromosome will give rise to spores having four copies.

RNA synthesis continues during spore development with turnover of pre-existing RNA providing the source of nucleotides. rRNA is common to vegetative cells and sporulating cells but new mRNA is produced.

Actinomycete spores

A variety of types of spore are produced by the Actinomycetes, however, the following discussion will concentrate on the spores produced characteristically by *Streptomyces* species, called arthrospores or conidia.

Morphology of arthrospore formation
These spores are produced as chains, 50–100 spores long on aerial hyphae that grow up from the spreading vegetative mycelium (figure 5.10). These hyphae are characterised by a sheath, which, as the spores are formed, encloses them and confers a distinctive surface appearance. Electron microscope studies have been carried out on several species showing differences in development especially in relation to septum formation. Three basic patterns of septation have been recognised.

In *Streptomyces coelicolor* six developmental stages have been recognised. The aerial hyphae become coiled and synchronous septum formation then occurs. The septa are formed at 1–2 μm intervals by centripetal growth of two rings of material originating from the inner hyphal wall. As the septa grow so the nuclear material in the hyphae becomes constricted and divided prior to septum completion. Next follows a period when new wall material is added to the septa and also to an inner wall layer to give a

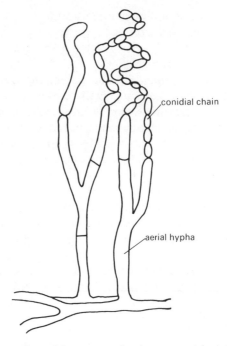

Figure 5.10 Aerial mycelium of *Streptomyces* bearing spores. Adapted from Wildermuth, H. (1970) *J. Gen. Microbiol.*, **60**, 43–50.

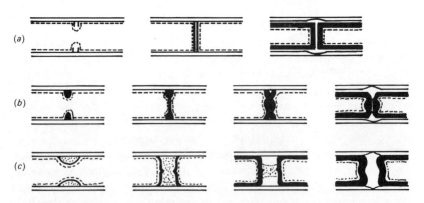

Figure 5.11 Stages in spore formation in *Streptomyces*; (*a*) *Streptomyces coelicolor*, (*b*) *Streptomyces antibioticus*, (*c*) *Streptomyces cinnamonensis*. Adapted from Hardisson, C. and Manazanal, M-B. (1978) in *Spores VII* (ed. G. Chambliss and J. C. Vary) American Society for Microbiology, Washington DC, 327–334.

thick spore wall. Eventually the connection between the two septal layers breaks down leaving the spores enclosed in the hyphal sheath (figure 5.11). The second type of septation is exemplified by *Streptomyces antibioticus* and commences with the deposition of a ring of dense amorphous material around the inner side of the hyphal wall. From this is synthesised a double-layered septum. New wall material is then laid down as described above (figure 5.8). *Streptomyces cinnamonensis* is an example of the third type of septum development and here a complete, thick disc of dense material grows centripetally across the hypha. Septal material is then formed on each side of the disc on the surface of the plasma membrane. This is followed by the deposition of new wall material (figure 5.8).

The arthrospores are very hydrophobic as a result of the lipid material present in the sheath enclosing them. The spore wall, which is laid down as described above, is similar to the hyphal wall, being rich in peptidoglycan. Unlike the hyphal wall the spore wall is not affected by lysozyme suggesting a difference possibly in the fabric of the wall or the association of the peptidoglycan with other wall components.

SUMMARY

1. Four different types of spore are produced by particular groups of bacteria. These are endospores, cysts, myxospores and arthrospores; the latter are the only true reproductive structures being produced in large numbers and widely disseminated to continue the species. The other types are resting spores and enable the organism to withstand extreme environmental conditions.

2. Endospores are produced by species of *Bacillus*, *Clostridium* and *Sporosarcina*. One spore is produced per cell. The endospore has a distinctive structure and organisation. The centrally located germ cell is enclosed in several layers, the cortex, the spore coats and the outer exosporium. Several of the chemical components of these structures are unique to spores.

3. Seven morphological stages are identified in endospore formation and are used as reference points for metabolic and physiological events.

4. The initiation of endospore development marks a switch in gene activity in the cell. During vegetative growth the sporulation genes are subject to repression and then the situation is reversed when spore formation occurs.

5. Many biochemical changes have been identified in sporulating cells and can be classified into four types: (i) increase in activity of certain enzymes, (ii) synthesis of new compounds not found in vegetative cells, (iii) formation of spore specific components and (iv) components specific to vegetative cells. The significance if any of many of the identifiable changes to endospore formation still requires elucidation.

6. Macromolecule synthesis in endospore forming cells is restricted to mRNA and protein. DNA synthesis ceases with the rounds of replication in progress when sporulation is induced. New mRNA is produced during the transcription of sporulation genes at the expense of turnover of existing RNA. The protein formed includes many enzymes, and also structural components.

7. The selective transcription of the sporulation genome is thought to be mediated by RNA polymerase produced in vegetative cells, but having a structural modification which changes its template specificity.

8. Mutants lacking sporulation capability can be isolated. The asporogenous types, in which sporulation is totally blocked, have lesions that can be related to the specific developmental stages. The biochemical defect(s) present in these mutants which are responsible for the lack of spore-forming ability still require identification.

9. Cysts are resting cells produced by species of *Azotobacter*. A cell produces two cysts and these share many features in common with endospores. Cyst development is generally correlated with restricted growth of a culture brought about by the particular carbon source supplied. Growth on glucose containing media is good and cyst formation is very limited. Media containing poorly metabolised substrates, e.g. ethanol, support restricted growth and cyst formation is prolific. Cells grown on these nutritionally poor media synthesise high levels of a lipid reserve called polyhydroxybutyrate and this is probably utilised during the encystment process. Some obvious biochemical shifts have been identified in cells forming cysts, these relate to the development of the TCA and glyoxylate shunt and of the gluconeogenic pathway.

10. Myxospores are resting spores formed by Myxobacteria. These organisms have a life cycle that culminates in the development of fruit bodies in which the spores are found. The switch from vegetative development to fruit body formation involves the development of close aggregates of cells which ultimately differentiate into the fructification with some of the cells forming spores.

11. Unlike the other types of bacterial spores the arthrospores or conidia are produced in large numbers by Streptomycetes. The bacteria have a mycelial organisation with the spores developing on aerial hyphae.

CHAPTER SIX

DEVELOPMENT IN SLIME MOULDS

THE SLIME MOULDS OR MYCETOZOA ARE A UNIQUE GROUP OF EUKARYOTIC microorganisms whose usual life cycle is comprised of an animal-like (protozoan) feeding stage and a spore-producing stage which bears resemblances to fungi. The group includes a large number of species which are placed in four distinct groups (Lechevalier, 1978). The life cycles of all types show basic similarities with the vegetative stage represented by an amoebal form, or myxamoeba which then develops into a multinucleate or multicellular stage depending on the organism (figure 6.1). The truly reproductive stage involves the formation of a fruit body bearing spores which provide the start of a new cycle. Two species have been the centre of very intensive research; *Physarum polycephalum* which is an acellular slime mould or Myxomycete, and *Dictyostelium discoideum* a cellular slime mould and thus a representative of the Acrasiales. These two organisms are used extensively by cell biologists and developmental biologists exploiting some of their individual features as model systems. As a consequence microbiologists interested in developmental processes in other types of organisms can benefit from this broad area of research utilising the knowledge in an understanding of their own systems. Although this chapter will deal primarily with the developmental cycles of *Physarum polycephalum* and *Dictyostelium discoideum*, it should be realised that other species of these genera and other slime moulds are now being studied more widely.

Development in the Myxomycete *Physarum polycephalum*

Spore germination and the Myxamoebal stage
The life cycle of *Physarum polycephalum* begins with the germination of the haploid spore which takes place in winter. Biflagellate swarmers are

115

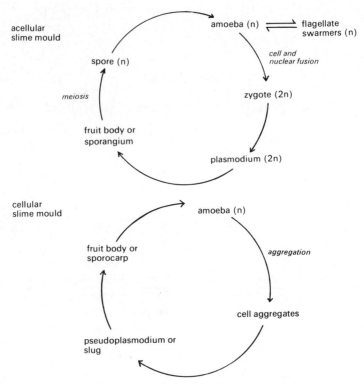

Figure 6.1 Generalised life cycles of acellular and cellular slime moulds.

released from each spore and transfer to an agar plate induces the swarmers to assume an amoeboid form (myxamoeba), the flagella being absorbed by the cells. The myxamoebae feed on bacteria ingesting them by phagocytosis (figure 6.2). The myxamoebae are small uninucleate cells, about 10 μm diameter, and having a large central vacuole. With a continual supply of living or dead bacteria the myxamoebae grow and divide following a typically eukaryotic cell cycle with recognisable G1, S, G2 and M phases. For many years our knowledge of the cell biology and biochemistry of the myxamoebae was limited by the need to cultivate the myxamoebae in the presence of bacteria. However, a few years ago (McCullogh and Dee, 1976) defined media were devised for the axenic culture of these cells (i.e. pure culture) providing opportunities for studies on the biochemistry and genetics of this vegetative stage in the *Physarum* life cycle.

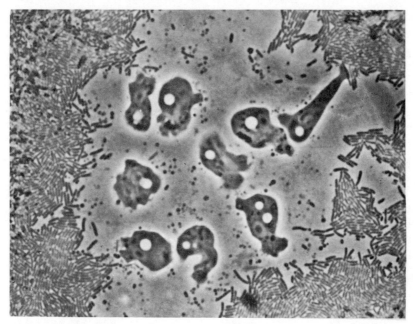

Figure 6.2 Myxamaoebae of *Physarum polycephalum* feeding on *Escherichia coli*. The nucleus with nucleolus and contractile vacuole can be seen. Phase contrast microscopy (× 2000). From Dee, J. (1975) *Sci. Prog. Oxf.*, **62**, 523–542. Reproduced by kind permission of Dr J. Dee.

The plasmodium

Following a period of active growth and division myxamoebae may fuse in pairs to give cells which represent the commencement of the plasmodial phase—a diploid vegetative phase (figures 6.3 and 6.4). Cell fusion occurs between genetically compatible strains; in *Physarum polycephalum* and in other species the mating type control is mediated by a multi-allele system designated mt_1, mt_2, etc. Genetic analysis has shown that the two alleles involved in a compatible pairing ultimately segregate in equal ratios when the spores are formed.

Myxamoebal fusion does not occur in plasmodium formation in every species of acellular slime mould. Thus in *Didynium iridis* plasmodia develop in cultures of single strains of myxamoebae. The myxamoebae and plasmodia are of the same ploidy and further investigation revealed that the latter arose following repeated nuclear divisions within the individual amoebae, i.e. apogamous development. Interestingly, nuclear division in these myxamoebae occurs without the breakdown of the nuclear membrane (as in some fungi) a feature that is typical of the plasmodium stage but not normally of the myxamoebae. A mutant strain of *Physarum polycephalum* called colonia has a similar pattern of development although the origin of the haploid plasmodia by apogamy or by fusion of haploid cells without nuclear fusion, is unknown. This strain developed as a result of a mutation at the mating type locus and if myxamoebae of this and a normal heterothallic strain are mixed diploid plasmodia develop which again show the 1:1 segregation of the alleles in the spores.

Evidence of plasmodium development in a myxamoebal culture is the development of clear areas in the lawn of growth that covers the agar medium. The clear areas are the result of predation by the plasmodium on its neighbouring amoebae. The plasmodium is a syncytium or multi-nucleate cell that develops from the diploid cell, formed after myxamoebal fusion. The multinucleate state—there may be millions of nuclei in a large

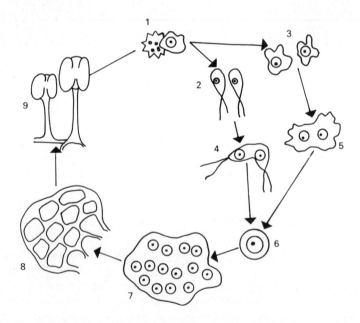

Figure 6.3 Life cycle of *Physarum polycephalum*: (1) germinating spore, (2) biflagellate swarmers, (3) myxamoebae, (4) fusion of biflagellate amoeba of compatible mating types, (5) fusion of compatible myxamoeba, (6) zygote, (7) developing plasmodium, (8) plasmodium with reticulate venation, (9) sorocarps.

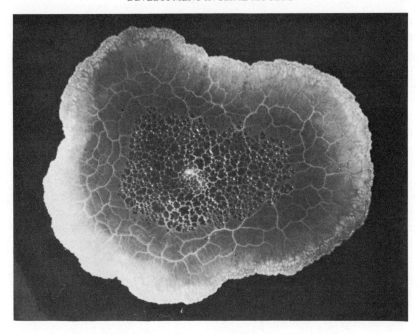

Figure 6.4 A plasmodium of *Physarum polycephalum* on agar medium (× 1.5). From Dee, J. (1975) *Sci. Prog. Oxf.*, **62**, 523–542. Reproduced by kind permission of Dr J. Dee.

plasmodium—results from the uncoupling of mitosis from cell division. The nuclear divisions occur synchronously at a frequency of 8 to 10 hours depending on the strain. This feature of the plasmodium has attracted cell biologists interested in cell cycle studies, although other aspects of the plasmodium make it atypical, e.g. intranuclear mitosis, the absence of cytokinesis and the absence of a G1 phase (Sauer, 1978).

The cytoplasm of the plasmodium is permeated by a network of veins in which continuously moving particles occur. The walls of the veins include fibrillar materials and there is evidence to suggest these may include contractile proteins similar to those occurring in vertebrate muscle. Further support for this view has come from the isolation of actin and myosin from plasmodia. This protein complex was found to have contractile properties which were stimulated by ATP. Addition of ATP to plasmodial cultures stimulates streaming in the veins suggesting an involvement for the contractile proteins in this process.

The plasmodium is also a migrating structure. In the presence of an adequate food supply its entire margin spreads evenly over the substrate. In the absence of food, e.g. on water agar, the individual plasmodia move in a more co-ordinated manner searching the dish for further food sources. Under these circumstances the migration paths can be traced by slime tracks, the slime being a polymer of galactose. During migration plasmodia may come into contact with each other and may fuse. As in the myxamoebal stage, fusion is subject to compatability controls involving several genes. Where incompatible fusions occur, and this is rare, a lethal reaction results with one or both of the plasmodia succumbing.

Plasmodia are readily cultured on laboratory media and techniques for doing this have been available for some time. When grown in shaken liquid cultures the plasmodia break up into smaller units called microplasmodia. These display mitotic synchrony only within the individual cells but when transferred back to a solid medium they fuse to form a large macroplasmodium and synchrony in nuclear division is re-established. The method of culture involving liquid medium has provided a convenient form for maintaining stocks of strains in the laboratory.

Differentiation of the plasmodium
The growing plasmodium can undergo two possible forms of differenti-

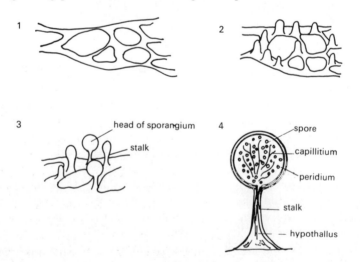

Figure 6.5 Development of the sporangium in *Physarum polycephalum*; (1) plasmodium with veins, (2) development of papillae from plasmodial veins, (3) development of sporangia, (4) mature sporangium.

ation that are morphologically and physiologically distinct. Macroplasmodia grown on a solid substratum, e.g. filter paper saturated with nutrients, and then transferred to a medium free of nutrients and incubated in darkness for 4 to 7 hours, then exposed to light, become transformed into aerial sporangia. The second form of differentiation occurs if the macroplasmodia are desiccated or if microplasmodia are subjected to nutrient starvation. In the case of the macroplasmodium, the structure becomes sub-divided into units containing up to 5 nuclei which then form thick walled cells, or spherules. Many spherules are formed from a single macroplasmodium. The process of spherule formation from a microplasmodium involves the formation of a thick wall around each structure. Spherulation can be induced synchronously and easily in microplasmodial cultures and as a consequence has been studied to a much greater extent than sporulation. Germination of the spherules leads to plasmodium formation.

Sporulation

The events associated with sporulation fall into five phases:

(i) A period starvation of nutrients, except for the vitamin nicotinic acid, when the plasmodia develop competence to the light stimulus.
(ii) The illumination phase during which sporulation is induced.
(iii) A period when the plasmodium is committed to produce spores, the so-called determination phase.
(iv) The differentiation phase during which the plasmodia are finally programmed for sporulation.
(v) The morphogenesis phase during which structural changes occur leading to the development of complete sporangia.

The first evidence of sporulation by a plasmodium is the development of small protruberances or papillae on its surface (figure 6.5). Continued development of the papillae in the vertical axis gives rise to the stalk, which is made rigid by the deposition of granular material, and a head region. Two independent processes occur in the latter, the development of a network of non-living threads called the capillitium and the cleavage of the cytoplasm to form uninucleate cells which develop into thick walled spores. The capillitium provides support for the spore mass. The spores are uninucleate and haploid indicating the occurrence of meiotic division during their formation. The sporangia have a characteristic appearance (figure 6.6) which varies widely in form and pigmentation in different species.

The effects of environmental factors controlling sporulation have been

Figure 6.6   Sporangia of *Physarum polycephalum* (× 40). From Dee, J. (1975) *Sci. Prog. Oxf.*, **62**, 523–542. Reproduced by kind permission of Dr J. Dee.

studied in many laboratory experiments. The requirement for nicotinic acid during starvation is interesting in view of the fact that it is not required for vegetative development of the plasmodia. A possible significance of this requirement is the switching of metabolic pathways leading to the production of pyrimidine nucleotides and increasing the sensitivity of the plasmodia to illumination. Glucose in the medium overrides the effect of nicotinic acid repressing sporulation. The role of illumination in inducing sporulation remains to be elucidated. *Physarum polycephalum* plasmodia have a yellow pigment, a conjugated polyene, which is assumed to be a photoreceptor. Species occur that lack pigments and do not require illumination to induce sporulation.

Differentiation of the plasmodium is assumed to involve a range of gene activities not found in the growing vegetative form. Unlike spherulation (see later), and undoubtedly for technical reasons involved in handling the system, biochemical studies on the sporulation process are restricted (Sauer, 1973). New species of RNA are synthesised during the starvation period but this is not translated immediately. Thus protein synthesis which follows is not dependent upon concomitant RNA synthesis. Selective RNA synthesis also occurred during illumination and in the 2–3 h period following—several lines of evidence support this view. Sporulation was inhibited by the addition of actinomycin D to illuminated plasmodia and ^{3}H-uridine fed to illuminated plasmodia was incorporated into RNA. In DNA–RNA hybridisation experiments the saturation values with RNA from sporulating plasmodia were higher than for vegetative plasmodia suggesting the RNA composition to be more heterogeneous. The sporulation process is reversible up to 3 h following the illumination period despite what might be regarded as evidence for a change in the transcription programme possibly involving selective gene activation. After the time of commitment to sporulation had passed no further major RNA synthesis appeared to be required. This was not the case with protein synthesis which appeared to be necessary at all stages of sporulation. As stated previously protein synthesis during starvation was not dependent on concomitant RNA synthesis and a similar situation pertained after the period of commitment. However, inhibition of RNA synthesis during the 2 hour post-illumination period also caused a block in protein synthesis. These observations indicate possible differences in the stability of messengers transcribed at different periods in the development sequence. A comparison of starved plasmodia exposed to illumination with non-illuminated plasmodia showed that although the total protein content of induced plasmodia decreased the synthesis of specific proteins increased, these were primarily larger polypeptides. Likewise the histone content of sporulating plasmodia was some 30 per cent less than that of the non-illuminated plasmodia, and furthermore histone synthesis had ceased. This might be expected if the nuclei in the illuminated plasmodia were still synchronised and were in G2 prior to the final mitosis that occurs 13 h after illumination. Information on specific gene products having a function in differentiation or morphogenesis is lacking. However, the extensive production of mutants showing blocks at specific stages in sporulation should make the elucidation of specific biochemical markers possible.

Spherulation
Spherule formation is readily induced in laboratory cultures either by starvation of the plasmodia or by addition of 0.5 M mannitol to the growth medium. In the former case clusters of spherules are formed and isolated spherules in the latter. During spherulation the plasmodia

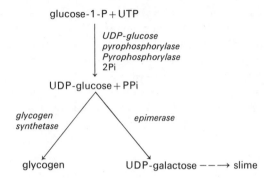

glucose-1-P+UTP

UDP-glucose
pyrophosphorylase
Pyrophosphorylase
2Pi

UDP-glucose+PPi

glycogen
synthetase   *epimerase*

glycogen   UDP-galactose − − → slime

Figure 6.7   Pathways of glycogen and slime biosynthesis.

undergo a defined and time-ordered sequence of cytological changes (Zaar and Kleinig, 1975). The first change is the rapid disappearance of glycogen granules, which are a major feature in the cytoplasm, accounting for up to 70 per cent of the total glycogen during the first 15 h of starvation. At this same time period golgi apparatus is formed only to disappear again at 21 h after starvation. This is the only time that these organelles are seen in the plasmodia. During the time that golgi apparatus is present the developing plasmodia show maximal slime production and this has led to the suggestion that the golgi apparatus is involved in slime secretion. At 24 h after the onset of starvation the cytoplasm is cleaved by the fusion of vesicle-like structures, cell wall formation then begins and the spherules attain their final shape.

As in the case of sporulation, the plasmodial nuclei undergo a further mitosis following transfer to the starvation conditions but there is evidence for a change in the plasmodial cell cycle following starvation. The nuclei of the spherules have only half the DNA content of vegetative plasmodia during G2. The vegetative cycle excludes a G1 phase and DNA synthesis follows immediately after mitosis. The lowered DNA content of spherule nuclei suggests the situation here is different and it is suggested that these nuclei are in a G1 phase. Support for this view is found from two lines of evidence. In the first place there is evidence for DNA synthesis, measured by thymidine incorporation during germination and before the first mitoses occur, and secondly the absence of an S phase following the mitosis in the starved plasmodia. The occurrence of the delayed S phase is further supported by studies on two enzymes, ornithine decarboxylase and 5-adenosyl-L-methionine decarboxylase, that are

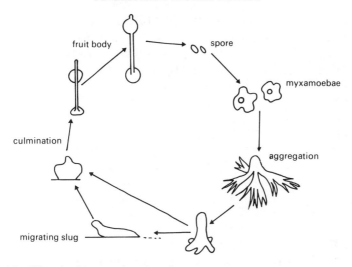

Figure 6.8   Life cycle of *Dictyostelium discoideum.*

known to be associated with this specific phase of the *Physarum* cell cycle. The activity of both enzymes declines very rapidly during spherulation but their re-synthesis occurs several hours before mitosis in the germinating spherules confirming the occurrence of an S phase.

A number of gross changes in metabolism have been described in spherulating plasmodia. The most pronounced are associated with carbohydrate metabolism (Hutterman, 1973). The high level of glycogen utilisation has already been referred to and associated with this is the production of slime. The other aspect of carbohydrate metabolism that is significant at this time is the formation of the spherule cell wall. The slime is a branched galactan polymer with β-1, 3-, β-1, 4- and β-1, 6-linkages. The spherule wall is a complex of galactosamine, amino acids and phosphate. The biosynthesis of glycogen and the galactan slime are linked and involve four key enzymes as shown in figure 6.7. Following starvation the UDP-glucose pyrophosphorylase and glycogen synthetase first increase in activity and then decrease rapidly. Simultaneously the activity of UDP-glucose-4-epimerase increases at least two-fold. The regulation of these enzymes at this time has still to be verified but there is evidence that changes in enzyme location may be involved.

Spherulation is also characterised by a high degree of nucleic acid and protein turnover. Significant amounts of DNA, RNA and protein in the vegetative plasmodia are degraded following starvation but new RNA and protein molecules are also being actively synthesised (Wendelberger–Schieweg and Hutterman, 1978). Many of these proteins are undoubtedly enzymes but reports of differential enzyme synthesis are still limited. Using density gradient separation techniques on isotopically labelled enzymes at least two enzymes, glutamate dehydrogenase and phosphodiesterase I, were found to be synthesised *de novo* during spherule development. The patterns of synthesis were different—the glutamate dehydrogenase was produced 16–24 h after starvation and the phosphodiesterase I was synthesised continuously after starvation. In recent years studies have also been made on several isoenzyme series using gel electrophoretic techniques. So far none of the enzymes examined have shown significant changes in isoenzyme pattern during development ruling out any possible significance in terms of regulatory functions. However, these studies have revealed differences in activity patterns during spherulation induced by different procedures. Thus phosphodiesterase II which in spherules is induced by starvation procedures disappears some 12 h after starvation, remains throughout development in spherules induced by mannitol. Clearly the effects resulting from induction of spherulation are multiple and it is still impossible to distinguish the key events that are significant to the differentiation process. This task is not going to be made easier if the various methods of induction used cause different effects.

Development in the cellular slime mould *Dictyostelium discoideum*

The life cycle
Dictyostelium discoideum is a uninucleate amoeba that lives in soil feeding on bacteria and organic detritus. The cells grow and divide whilst adequate food is available setting up individual territories and repelling each other, but when this is depleted they embark on a developmental sequence that terminates in the formation of spores (figure 6.8). In the laboratory this sequence can be demonstrated in cultures transferred from a growth medium to another solid substratum lacking nutrients. After 8 h in these conditions the amoebae become mutually attractive and form into groups that continue to increase in size fed by radial, randomly branched streams of cells.

As the groups increase in cell number they take the form of hemispherical mounds and a slime sheath is then secreted that constrains the aggregate into a vertical cylindrical structure the apex of which is elastic. The finger-like structures that develop, known as pseudoplasmodia or

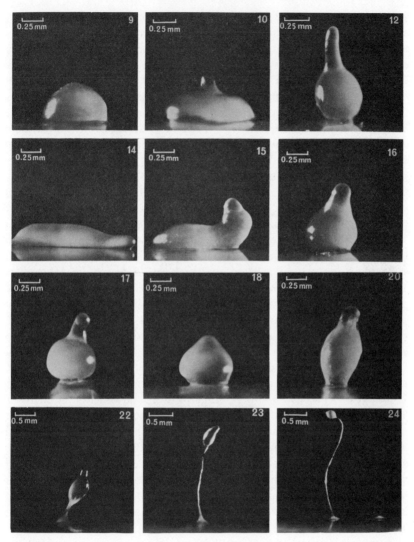

Figure 6.9   Slug and fruiting body development in *Dictyostelium discoideum*. From Loomis, W. F., *Dictyostelium discoideum: a developmental system*. Reproduced by kind permission of Dr W. F. Loomis and Academic Press.

slugs, contain variable numbers of cells. The number of cells in a slug is a function of the number of cells in the aggregation territory. The slime sheath is composed of polysaccharide of which about 80 per cent is cellulose, other sugars found in hydrolysed slime preparations are mannose, galactose and N-acetylglucosamine. There are suggestions that the cellulose fibrils account for the strength of the sheath.

At this stage the finger-like aggregate can develop directly into a fruiting body, or sorocarp, or develop into a migrating slug (figure 6.9). The pattern of development is determined by different environmental conditions. The migrating slug moves over the surface of the substratum for variable periods of time which may last for several days. Migration is stimulated by high humidity and low ionic concentrations and the slugs are positively phototactic. As a slug moves the slime sheath is continuously synthesised by the cells at the anterior tip. The sheath itself is immobile and the cells move in relation to it. The sheath behind the slug collapses and remains as a trail marking the slug's movements.

When migration stops the slug rounds up and constructs a fruiting body—this is called the culmination stage. A vertical cellulosic tube is produced by the culminating slug and a proportion of the cells enter the tube, these are the stalk cells, they become vacuolate and die. Most of the remainder move up to the top of the stalk, produce a wall and become spores. Those left at the base of the stalk form a basal disc and provide a means of attachment for the fruiting body or sorocarp.

Several features of this life cycle have attracted the interest of developmental biologists and as a consequence a very extensive literature on the organism is available. Central to this interest is assembly of a multicellular structure from individual cells. Related questions concern the communication between cells resulting in aggregation, the differentiation of individual cells to specific functions and the associated pattern formation whereby the proportional and spatial relationships of cells are established. The distinct stages of development exhibited by the organism also provide a situation that lends itself to a study of the molecular basis of the whole process. Much of the progress made in understanding the behaviour of this organism stems from the availability of mutant strains, the amoebal stage of which can be grown in axenic culture on defined media.

The control of aggregation of amoebae

The pattern of aggregation of the amoebae following starvation has been studied using time-lapse cinemicrography. These observations have shown the movement of the amoebae is complex in both spatial and temporal terms. Centres of aggregation become established and the individual cells approach these by pulsatile movements involving directional pseudopodial extensions. A rhythm of movement is established for

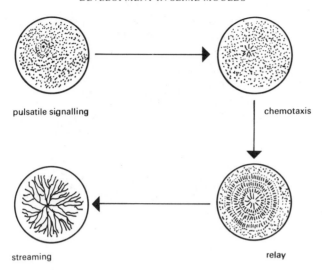

pulsatile signalling

chemotaxis

streaming

relay

Figure 6.10 The aggregation phase in *Dictyostelium discoideum*. Adapted from Newell, P. C. (1978) *J. Gen. Microbiol.*, **104**, 1–13.

each cell, once per 2 to 10 min, but the activities of all the cells are co-ordinated and are seen as periodic waves of movement radiating from the aggregation centre (Newell, 1978).

Following extensive studies it was demonstrated that aggregation of the amoebae is caused by a chemotactic response to cAMP (Konjin *et al.*, 1968). Some of the cells in the population begin spontaneous secretion of the nucleotide and so establish the aggregation centres (figure 6.10). The cAMP is released in rhythmic pulses rather than continuously. Evidence for this stems from observations on the bands of cells around the aggregation centres which appear as light and dark concentric rings. At the macroscopic level these bands move outwards from the centre through the mass of aggregating cells. From microscopic observations the light bands are thought to be the cells that have received the chemotactic signal and are moving and the dark bands are cells that are stationary and awaiting the signal (figure 6.11). The cells in the two bands differ in shape; in the light bands the cells are elongated and those in the dark band are rounded. The elongated shape is a transitory form and is believed to be a response to cAMP. After receiving the signal the cells become insensitive to another one for a period of time known as the refractory period. The basis for the pulsed release of cAMP from cells in the aggregation centres is unknown. The enzyme concerned in its synthesis, adenylate cyclase, is

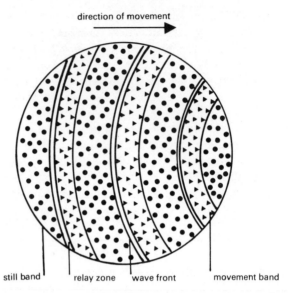

Figure 6.11 Diagrammatic representation of part of an aggregating complex. Adapted from Newell, P. C. (1978) *J. Gen. Microbiol.*, **104**, 1–13.

located on the inner surface of the plasma membrane, but how it is regulated to produce cAMP pulses is not known.

Reception of the cAMP signal by an amoeba involves specific molecules on the cell surface. The binding characteristics of cAMP to its receptors resembles the binding of hormones to cell surfaces in higher animals and because of this the study of aggregation of *Dictyostelium* amoebae could give leads to our general understanding of cell communication. The operation of the pulsatile system requires a mechanism for the destruction of the signal, were this not to happen the concentration of cAMP would increase and so produce a continuous gradient.

Dictyostelium discoideum produces two phosphodiesterases that degrade cAMP, one is bound to the plasma membrane and the other is a soluble enzyme secreted by the cells. The two enzymes exhibit different properties; the extracellular enzyme is inhibited by a protein also secreted by the cells but the membrane enzyme is unaffected. Synthesis of the phosphodiesterase is induced by cAMP and inhibitor synthesis is blocked by cAMP pulses. The interaction of the extracellular phosphodiesterase and the inhibitor has led some workers to cast doubt on the role of the enzyme in the destruction of the cAMP signal. Recent studies with mutants that fail to produce aggregates suggests, however, that the extracellular enzyme has this function (Darmon *et al.*, 1978). Mutants defective in the production of extracellular phosphodiesterase, and therefore unable to form aggregates, were found to behave normally in the presence of the enzyme prepared from other *Dictyostelium* strains. Direct contact between the enzyme and the plasma membrane of the mutant amoebae was not required. It was concluded that the role of the extracellular phosphodiesterase was to maintain the concentration of cAMP at a minimal level so that the signal pulses of the nucleotide could be recognised, i.e. it controls the signal to noise ratio.

Cells receiving the signal respond in two ways, they exhibit the chemotactic response moving towards its source and they relay the signal to other amoebae. The chemotactic response lasts for about 100 seconds in which time a cell moves $20\,\mu m$. The chemotactic sensitivity of cells has been determined by applying calibrated pulses of cAMP to monolayers of cells on agar by electrophoresis using a glass microelectrode. The cAMP diffuses from the electrode and is depleted at a known rate by phosphodiesterase. These experiments have shown that the cells are fully sensitive to cAMP at 4 h after starvation. The cells within a defined radius of the electrode are attracted, the size of the zone of attraction being a function of pulse size. The calculated maximum cAMP concentration, following a pulse, at the chemotactic radius is between $1–4 \times 10^{-9}\,M\,cAMP$ and this is assumed to be the threshold signal.

An important feature of the aggregation process is the relay of the signal perceived by an amoeba, to its neighbouring cells. The waves of movement seen during aggregation do not decrease in either amplitude or velocity implying a signal relay system rather than a response of the whole aggregating mass to the aggregation centre. In fact the pulse of cAMP emitted from the aggregating centre is short lived and diffuses only a short distance, about $100\,\mu m$, from its source before it is broken down by the phosphodiesterase. The cells to which cAMP binds are induced to produce more of the nucleotide and so the signal is relayed. Studies on cell extracts have shown that the activity of adenylate cyclase increases some 5 to 8 fold for a brief period following stimulation with cAMP. The activation of the enzyme by cAMP occurred only *in vivo*, as cell extracts were completely insensitive to the nucleotide. Some recent research (Wurster *et al.*, 1977) suggested that the enzyme guanylate cyclase was involved as an intermediary between the cAMP binding on the plasma membrane and the activation of adenylate cyclase. Within 9 seconds of a cAMP pulse the concentration of cGMP in the cells increased and this molecule could initiate the synthesis of the new pulse of cAMP by the receiver cell. It was further proposed that guanine cyclase could be an effector molecule in the membrane with which the cAMP receptor binds. Cyclic AMP is now also thought to have another effect on aggregating amoebae in controlling the formation of cell surface receptors called contact sites A. These are proteins which are involved in the cohesion of cells in a head to tail fashion in the streams moving to the aggregation centre and within the slug when it develops. A protein has been obtained from amoebae that causes the agglutination of red blood cells and it is this molecule that is believed to be involved in the linking of cells because it accumulates in them as their cohesiveness increases.

Cell differentiation in the slug and pattern formation
The development of the fruiting body in the cellular slime moulds provides a primitive example of pattern formation in a multicellular system with the stalk and spore cells differentiating in specific proportions and exhibiting a spatial relationship. There is now clear evidence from several lines of experimentation to show that cell differentiation and the initiation of the fruit body pattern occurs in the slug.

One line of study has involved grafting experiments. Slugs were allowed to develop in separate *Dictyostelium* cultures that had been fed on colourless bacteria and on *Serratia marcescens*, a red-pigmented bacterium. The slugs that developed on the latter organism were also red coloured due to the accumulation of the pigment in vacuoles. The anterior ends, equivalent to one-third, of the colourless and red slugs were then exchanged by making grafts. During migration of the slugs the line of the graft was seen to be maintained and at fruiting the distribution of cells to specific functions was always constant, the cells at the anterior end formed stalks and those at the rear formed spores. Observations on slugs derived from amoebae stained with dyes confirmed these observations. Comparison of the cells from the anterior and posterior regions of slugs revealed several differences of an ultrastructural, biochemical and physical nature. A conspicuous feature of the pre-spore cells, i.e. posterior cells, is the presence of a large vacuole which is not found in cells from the front end. The development of more refined techniques has enabled the pre-stalk and pre-spore cells to be separated on density gradients (Oohata and Takeuchi, 1977). The cells were examined for several enzymes known to be developmentally regulated. Thus the hydrolases β-glucosidase, β-galactosidase, acetylglucosaminidase and alkaline phosphatase were higher in activity in pre-stalk cells a feature consistent with the presence of autophagic vacuoles in these cells. In contrast UDP-galactose poly-saccharide transferase was found only in pre-spore cells. Other differences between the two groups of cells relate to their density and adhesiveness. The first cells to aggregate are believed to form the anterior region of the slug although considerable sorting can take place as aggregation continues. The cells which initiate aggregation by autonomous secretion of cAMP are probably more active metabolically.

The differentiation of a specific function does not appear to be irreversibly fixed in the slug cells. Slugs can be disaggregated by mechanical disruption to give individual cells which re-aggregate and re-capitulate to their original form if placed on a solid substratum (Newell *et al.*, 1972). Also slugs cut into three pieces give rise to three fruiting bodies each with similar ratios of spore and stalk cells if the pieces are allowed to develop and migrate as separate entities. If migration is prevented the slugs develop into structures comprised mostly of stalk cells. Excision of the tip blocks development of the slug until a new tip is formed. The apex is therefore seen to have a major role as an organiser of the slug controlling its ultimate development into a fruit body.

A model for the regulation of fruit body development has been proposed by Sussman and Schindler (1978) which resulted from a re-examination of the transformation of the multicellular aggregate either directly to a fruiting body or into a migrating slug prior to fruit body formation. Slug formation was shown to depend on a localised accumulation of a metabolite secreted by the cell aggregate. When this metabolite was removed a switch to fruit body formation occurred. Subsequent experiments showed the metabolite to be ammonia and implicated three factors which controlled its presence or absence in the cell aggregate:

(i)   The rate of production from the degradation of proteins.
(ii) The rate of loss from the aggregate by diffusion and evaporation.
(iii) The ratio of NH_3 to NH_4^+ which is controlled by the pH of the environment.

The model implicates an interaction between cAMP and NH_3. (Earlier work had implicated cAMP in controlling slug migration and the maintenance of polarity and apical dominance in both the migrating slug and the developing fruiting body.) Four assumptions, as yet without extensive experimental support, were made in proposing the model:

(i)   The synthesis and/or release of cAMP is affected by NH_3.
(ii) cAMP serves as chemotactic attractant to cells within the aggregate as well as during aggregation.

16 hours aggregation—fruit body development or slug?

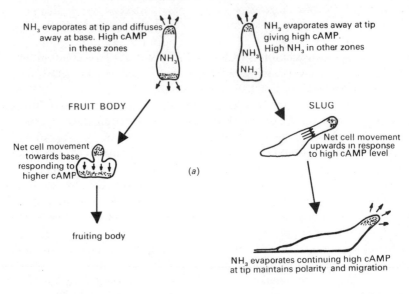

(a)

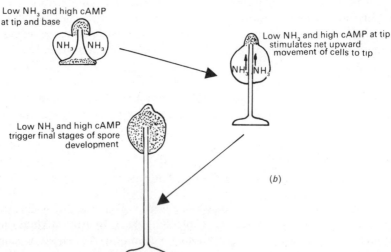

(b)

Figure 6.12 Model for the control of fruiting body and slug development in *Dictyostelium discoideum*.
(a) The first decision stage.
(b) The transition from slug to fruiting body.
Adapted from Sussman, M. and Schindler, J. (1978) *Differentiation*, **10**, 1–5.

(iii) high and low concentrations of cAMP determine the differentiation of stalk and spore cells respectively.

(iv) cAMP initiates the release of various inclusions, e.g. vacuoles, vesicles and fibrils by the cells.

The mechanism of control of development of the cell aggregate along its two possible pathways is shown in figure 6.12. The immediate initiation of fruiting body formation is the result of the loss of NH_3 from two zones of the erect cell aggregate. This could occur by evaporation through the tip where there is no slime sheath and by diffusion from the base of the aggregate into the substratum where a high $NH_4^+ : NH_3$ ratio would be favoured by a low pH. Provided cAMP is still functioning as a chemotactic attractant a transiently higher level of the nucleotide at the base would induce the cells in the middle of the aggregate to move to its base and so form the culminating structure. Conversely the prevention of NH_3 diffusion at the base of the aggregate would create conditions where a high cAMP concentration occurs only at the tip of the aggregate stimulating an upward movement of the cells causing an elongation and development of the finger-like slug. Maintenance of polarity in the slug and its migration can also be explained on the basis of the cAMP : NH_3 model. Evaporation of NH_3 from the sheath-free tip will maintain a high cAMP in this zone (figure 6.12a). This condition would be maintained until the NH_3 concentration in the posterior region decreased allowing an increase in cAMP at the base with concomitant fruiting body development.

The changes in NH_3 and cAMP and the mechanics of fruiting body formation are shown in figure 6.12b. The cells with high cAMP levels at the apex and base of the culminating structure are induced to produce and then to release the materials required for the formation of the stalk and the basal disc, e.g. the cellulose fibrils. As these two components of the fruiting body develop the pre-spore cells in the region with high NH_3 accumulate spore-specific components, e.g. pre-spore vacuoles, spore coat and enzymes. These cells are then attracted to the apex of the stalk by cAMP, as they move up NH_3 evaporates from the cells and they also start to make cAMP. In the presence of high concentrations of cAMP the pre-spore cells release and secrete the necessary materials to form the wall and complete differentiation.

Molecular aspects of development

Cell differentiation during fruiting body formation involves synthesis of molecules and structures not produced or present in the amoebae. These changes are brought about by the catalytic actions of newly synthesised proteins. At the gross molecular level changes in RNA and proteins occur with a turnover in both cell components being a characteristic feature. A notable feature is a 50 per cent decrease in the protein content of cells when exogenous nutrients are no longer available. The changes in RNA are associated mainly with mRNA—the rRNA of vegetative cells is stable for at least two cell generations during the following developmental phase when newly synthesised ribosomes are found. The first reports suggested these were recruited immediately into the functional polysomes as the vegetative ribosomes were eliminated. Subsequent studies failed to confirm this observation indicating that the developing cells do not discriminate between vegetative and developmental ribosomes during degradation.

In a gel electrophoretic study of cellular proteins at the different developmental stages some 400 different types were detected. The majority were synthesised continuously during differentiation and about 100 showed changes in their relative rates of synthesis. During aggregation 10 vegetative cell proteins and their associated mRNA's were subject to degradation, but 40 new proteins appeared. Major changes in the relative roles of synthesis occurred during the culmination phase but no new proteins were detected at this time.

The activities of a number of enzymes has been studied during development in *Dictyostelium* and several have been shown to be stage specific (Loomis *et al.*, 1977). The patterns of activity fit broadly into three groups, enzymes present only in growing cells, enzymes in growing and differentiating cells and enzymes only in differentiating cells. Enzymes associated with the growth phase disappear rapidly after development is initiated through nutrient starvation. Trehalase is a key enzyme in the germinating spore mobilising the stored trehalase, after germination the enzyme is no longer required and is secreted. Amino acid metabolism plays an important role in the overall metabolism of growth and development. The demand for amino acids during growth is reflected in high levels of activity of enzymes involved in synthesis. During cell differentiation amino acids are subject to catabolism and used as an energy source. This switch in amino acid metabolism is reflected in changes in threonine deaminases; threonine deaminase I involved in the conversion of threonine to leucine is present in growing cells and is then lost, threonine deaminase II appears in differentiating cells.

Enzymes associated with growth and development include adenyl cyclase, amylase, glycogen synthetase and the enzymes of the Embden

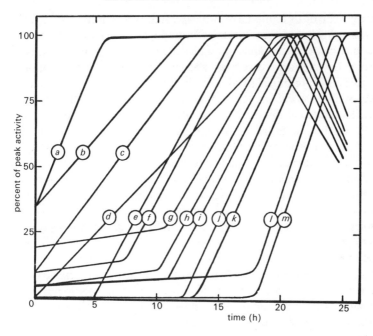

Figure 6.13 Stage specific enzymes in *Dictyostelium discoideum* showing the kinetics of synthesis: (*a*) leucine aminopeptidase, (*b*) alanine transaminase, (*c*) acetylglucosaminidase, (*d*) mannosidase, (*e*) trehalose phosphate synthetase, (*f*) threonine deaminase 2, (*g*) tyrosine transaminase, (*h*) UDPG pyrophosphorylase, (*i*) UDP galactose epimerase, (*j*) UDP galactose transferase, (*k*) glycogen phosphorylase, (*l*) alkaline phosphatase, (*m*) glucosidase 2. Adapted from Loomis, W. F., Dimond, R. L., Free, S. J. and White, S. S. (1977) in *Eucaryotic microbes as model developmental systems* (ed. D. H. O'Day and P. A. Horgen) Marcel Dekker Inc., New York, 177–194.

Meyerhof Parnas pathway. These enzymes are present at all stages and at the same specific activity.

More than twelve enzymes have been described as developmental enzymes and as showing stage specificity (figure 6.13). Evidence from inhibitor experiments indicate that the enzymes arise from *de novo* synthesis rather than a selective degradation of other enzymes and proteins. A period of RNA synthesis is required before the enzymes are produced. A technique used extensively in these experiments involved pulse labelling and radioimmunoprecipitation. An enzyme studied by these techniques was UDP glucose pyrophosphorylase which is required for the synthesis of UDP glucose. The enzyme was found to exist at a low but constant level during aggregation and increasing by 10-fold during the slug state.

A number of mutants have been isolated which have lesions affecting the various stage specific enzymes. Mutants lacking N-acetylglucosaminidase produced aggregates but failed to develop into migrating slugs. Normal development occurred if the aggregates were kept under conditions favouring direct fruiting body development. Mutants that fail to produce mannosidase develop normally. Strains lacking the capability to produce UDP pyrophosphorylase developed slugs under appropriate conditions but these failed to culminate and develop normally. Despite the absence of this enzyme and the failure to normal development, several enzymes synthesised later in the programme were produced as normal albeit at lower specific activities. This and similar observations with other mutants, suggests that the enzymes accumulate independently of each other and consequently raises significant questions in relation to the underlying control mechanism. Two alternatives would be possible, a process of multiple timing or possibly a single timing system based on a developmental sequence.

A similar approach to the question of the relationship between enzymes and development has involved the isolation of morphological mutants with blocks at specific stages in development. These strains were examined for the various enzymes shown to be stage specific (figure 6.13). Generally

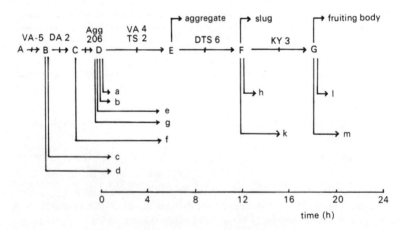

Figure 6.14 Dependent sequence of events during fruiting body development in *Dictyostelium discoideum*. Seven steps are defined according to the pattern of accumulation of enzymes as shown in figure 6.12. Mutants blocked at different stages in the sequence are designated by letter and number codes. Redrawn from Loomis, W. F., Dimond, R. L., Free, S. J. and White, S. S. (1977) in *Eucaryotic microbes as model developmental systems* (ed. D. H. O'Day and P. A. Horgen) Marcel Dekker Inc., New York, 177–194.

speaking where a mutant failed to produce an enzyme early in the sequence so later enzymes were not synthesised, i.e. synthesis of later enzymes showed some dependence on synthesis of early enzymes. In this case it was found that the sequence of dependent enzymes differed from the timed sequence of stage specific enzymes. Thus Loomis *et al.* (1977) suggest a dependent sequence of events involving seven discrete steps which relate to the blocks in morphological development (figure 6.14). A number of criticisms have been voiced regarding this approach in some of the work of stage specific enzymes and the use of developmental mutants (Wright and Thomas, 1977) making the point that further study is required before a true understanding of the molecular basis of differentiation is possible.

SUMMARY

1. The slime moulds are a unique group of eukaryotic microorganisms having an unusual life cycle comprised of animal-like feeding stage and a fungal-like spore producing stage.

2. The free-living animal-like stage takes the form of an amoeba, or myxamoeba, that exists by feeding on bacteria. The amoebae ultimately develop into either a multi-nucleate form or a multicellular form, depending on the species, from which the spore-producing stage develops.

3. The two most studied representatives of the slime moulds are *Physarum polycephalum*, an acellular type, and *Dictyostelium discoideum*, a cellular type. Several features of their biology have made these organisms attractive models for cell biologists and developmental biologists.

4. *Physarum polycephalum.* The amoeba of *Physarum* following active growth fuse in pairs to give a diploid cell that represents the commencement of the plasmodium stage of the life cycle. This develops into a multinucleate cell or syncytium. Cell fusion to form the plasmodium is controlled genetically by mating type factors.

5. The plasmodium is also a feeding stage that predates on the amoebal cells as well as bacteria. The plasmodium can grow to a very large size covering several square centimetres. During this growth period the nuclei divide many times to give a structure with several million nuclei. Nuclear divisions are synchronous, occurring every 8 h in ideal growth conditions. The plasmodium has a eukaryotic type of cell cycle but there is no G1 phase.

6. The plasmodium is characterised by the presence of a network of veins. The walls of the veins are thought to contain contractile proteins which are probably involved in the movement particles that can be observed in the veins.

7. In conditions unfavourable for growth the plasmodium will differentiate in one of two ways. Plasmodia that are starved of nutrients, except for nicotinic acid, and then exposed to light for a short period will produce spore bearing structures called sporangia. Plasmodia that are starved or transferred to a medium containing mannitol differentiate into thick-walled cells called spherules.

8. Biochemical studies on sporangia development are restricted in comparison to spherule development. However, the synthesis of new RNA and protein molecules has been shown to be an integral feature of sporulation. Protein synthesis is not dependent on concomitant RNA synthesis at all stages of sporangium development. Information on specific gene products involved in the differentiation process is lacking.

9. Spherule development involves a number of clearly defined ultrastructural changes including the formation of a golgi apparatus for a period 6 h during the process. This structure is believed to be associated with the secretion of slime that occurs actively.

10. Several biochemical and molecular changes have been described during spherulation. Glycogen, which is synthesised by growing plasmodia is rapidly broken down, the glucose residues presumably being utilised to manufacture the slime and the cell wall. Active protein and RNA turnover also occurs. Some of the new proteins have been identified and the patterns of their synthesis, during spherule development, described.

11. *Dictyostelium discoideum.* The life cycle commences with the germination of spores to give an amoebal stage which feeds on bacteria. When their food supply is depleted they form aggregates which may develop directly into fruiting bodies or into a migrating, non-feeding slug stage which ultimately develops into a fruiting body.

12. During aggregation the cells become congregated in discrete masses. This results from four competences developing in the cells following starvation; (i) in a minority of cells a competence for the autonomous secretion of pulses of cAMP, (ii) in the large body of cells a competence for chemotaxis to cAMP, (iii) a competence to relay the cAMP signal when stimulated by the nucleotide from an exogenous source and (iv) a competence to develop cohesion sites resulting in a head to tail configuration of the cells.

13. Reception of the cAMP stimulus by aggregating cells involves specific molecules on their surface and involves a binding reaction, the characteristics of which resemble hormone binding to cells of animals.

14. The pulsatile nature of the signal during aggregation is believed to be controlled by an extracellular phosphodiesterase.

15. The climax of aggregation is the formation of finger-like masses of cells raised vertically from the substratum. The cell mass is bounded by a sheath.

16. The cell mass then develops directly into a fruiting body or a migrating slug and then a fruiting body. The pattern of development is under environmental control.

17. Cell differentiation, as reflected in the stalk and spore components of the fruiting body, commences in the migrating slug. The front end of the slug, which controls its

movement and acts as an organiser during the climax stage of development, is the region destined to become the stalk and the posterior end the spores. This has been demonstrated by grafting experiments and in studies in which cells were stained with vital dyes.

18. Differences in ultrastructure and enzymic complement occur between pre-stalk and pre-spore cells, however, the pattern of differentiation is not irreversible. Removal of the stalk region initiates the differentiation of more pre-stalk cells from the remainder of the slug.

19. The regulation of fruiting body development could be controlled by differential levels of NH_3 and cAMP. Cells where NH_3 level is high, have low cAMP levels and vice versa. It is suggested that NH_3 is generated by the cells during the degradation of proteins. NH_3 can evaporate from the apex of the aggregate and diffuse from basal cells if substratum is suitably porous. High levels of cAMP are generated and stimulate development of the fruiting body, first the stalk and later the spores. Where basal diffusion of NH_3 is prevented the migrating slug develops. Polarity of slug could be maintained by high cAMP at the tip.

20. Molecular changes associated with development at the gross level involve turnover of both RNA and protein. New proteins are produced during development of the fruiting body, many of these are enzymes which undoubtedly have a role in terminal differentiation. Temporal sequence of enzymes has been shown to follow the developmental sequence. Attempts have been made to relate the appearance of specific enzymes to specific stages in development.

CHAPTER SEVEN

ASEXUAL REPRODUCTION IN FUNGI

THE FORMATION OF ASEXUAL SPORES BY FUNGI FULFILS TWO PURPOSES :

(i)   The production (normally) of vast numbers of propagating units which ensure that the organism can be widely and quickly disseminated.
(ii) To provide a mechanism of resistance to unfavourable environmental conditions.

The diversity in type and morphology of spores (figure 7.1), and the structures that bear them, is enormous and adds to the fascination of the fundamental question regarding the processes that control and are involved in their formation. Studies on the environmental parameters

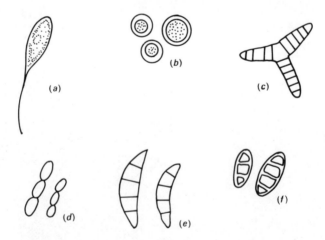

Figure 7.1   Some examples of the diversity in morphology found in asexual spores. (*a*) Zoospore of *Allomyces*. (*b*) Sporangiospores of *Pilobolus*. (*c–f*) Conidia of an aquatic Hyphomycete, *Penicillium*, *Fusarium* and *Helminthosporium*, respectively.

affecting asexual spore production are found from the earliest days of fungal physiology. More recently observers have taken advantage of electron microscopic techniques and advanced culture techniques to provide some answers to aspects of this basic question.

Types of asexual spore

Two main types of asexual spore are produced by fungi, sporangiospores and conidia. They are distinguished by the morphology of the structure (sporophore) that produces them and by the mechanisms by which they are formed.

Sporangiospores are produced and retained within a sporangium (figure 7.2). This structure normally develops at the tip of an aerial hypha but may also arise at an intercalary site. During its development the sporangial wall develops from the hyphal wall and the cytoplasm within it becomes cleaved into the individual spores. The latter may or may not have a wall—walled spores are non-motile and called aplanospores, naked spores are motile zoospores. Release of the spores from the sporangium may involve a variety of mechanisms.

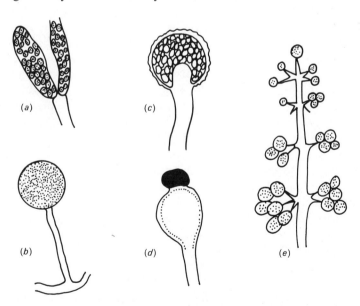

Figure 7.2   Diversity in morphology of the sporangium; (a) *Saprolegnia*, (b) *Pythium*, (c) *Rhizopus*, (d) *Pilobolus*, (e) *Mortierella*.

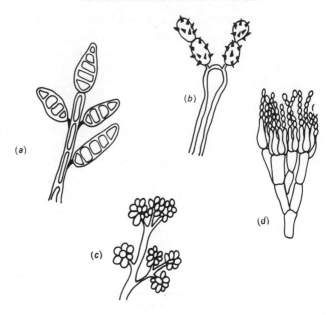

Figure 7.3   Morphology of conidiophores; (*a*) *Alternaria*, (*b*) *Cladosporium*, (*c*) *Botrytis*, (*d*) *Penicillium*.

The term conidium is used by some mycologists to describe all other types of asexual spore produced by fungi. At least four major types of conidium are recognised arthrospores, blastospores, porospores and phialoconidia. These different types are recognised by the mechanisms by which they are formed (see p. 147). With the exception of the arthrospores, these spores may be formed on specialised hyphae called conidiophores. In some species these structures are very simple showing little difference from somatic hyphae but in other species the structure is very complex. This diversity in spore types and spore bearing structures are important taxonomic criteria (figure 7.3).

Two further spore types are the chlamydospore and the oidium. Both arise from vegetative hyphae at either intercalary or terminal sites. Part of their development involves the thickening of the hyphal wall and expansion of the segment giving rise to the spore.

The biological roles of these different spores may be considered in relation to the way in which they are produced and the number of spores involved. Sporangiospores and conidia are formed in large numbers and are used to spread the fungus and allow it to colonise new environments.

Chlamydospores and oidia are generally more resistant, lacking a mechanism for liberation or dispersal, and have a role in maintenance of the species under adverse environmental conditions.

Patterns of spore formation

Our knowledge of the events that occur in the differentiation of sporangiospores and conidiospores is now quite extensive and stems from many detailed studies using the scanning and transmission electron microscopes. Undoubtedly the information regarding changes at the ultrastructural level will be of even greater interest in the future as we learn more of the associated biochemical changes.

Development of zoosporangiospores

The differentiation of sporangiospores has been investigated in several Phycomycete fungi and in all of them the cleavage of sporangial cytoplasm into the individual spore units is brought about by the activity of vesicles. What is different in spore development in these species is the origin of the vesicles involved in the cleavage process.

In Oomycete species, which produce zoospores, sporangium development begins with an expansion of the sporangial initial hypha caused by an inflow of cytoplasm from neighbouring hyphae (Bartnicki–Garcia and Hemmes, 1976). The extent of this expansion varies in different species. As the sporangium develops secondary wall thickening also occurs, however, the biochemical changes associated with this are unknown. Other notable events in the formation of the sporangium are the differentiation of a basal plug which separates the sporangium from the support hypha and an apical papilla, which is the site of spore discharge.

Differentiation of zoospores has been examined in detail in four Oomycete species. In *Phytopthora*, *Pythium* and *Saprolegnia* cytoplasmic cleavage is achieved by vesicle fusion (figure 7.4), but *Aphanomyces* is an exception and no *de novo* membrane synthesis is found. In *Phytopthora* and *Pythium* the cleavage vesicles arise from activity of golgi and dictyosomes, but their origin is unknown in the case of *Saprolegnia*. Fusion of the vesicles with themselves and with vacuolar membranes results in the establishment of furrows dividing the cytoplasm. Cleavage of spore units in the sporangium of *Aphanomyces* is achieved by activity of the plasma membrane and tonoplast of the hyphae present prior to sporogenesis.

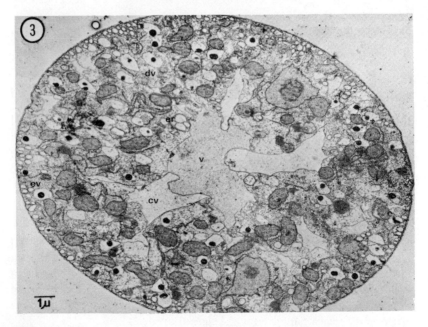

Figure 7.4 Ultrastructure of the developing sporangium of *Saprolegnia ferax*, transmission electron micrograph (× 65 000). Various membranous profiles are prominent in this section: cleft vesicles (cv) that make contact with centrally located vesicle (v), smaller vesicles with dense contents (dv) and empty vesicles (ev) underlying the plasma membrane, endoplasmic reticulum (er) is also prominent. From Gay, J. L. and Greenwood, A. D. (1966) in *The Fungus Spore* (ed. M. F. Madelin), Butterworths, London, 95–110. Reproduced by kind permission of Dr J. L. Gay.

Development of sporangiospores

Our knowledge of the ultrastructure of sporangiospore development stems from some elegant studies on *Gilbertella persicaria* (Bracker, 1966), a member of the Mucorales. The sporangium initial is very similar in ultrastructure to a normal hypha; it contains many nuclei but there is no evidence of nuclear division occurring before cytoplasmic cleavage. A unique feature is the interconnection of nuclei by endoplasmic reticulum with up to seven nuclei in a group. As pre-cleavage development ensues, small peripheral vesicles develop from the cisternae. As the sporangium develops, the vesicles apparently disappear and become replaced by larger so-called cleavage vesicles. The larger vesicles are identified by the presence of granules around the inner surface of the vesicle membrane.

The origin of the cleavage vesicles is unknown but they may represent a changed form of the peripheral vesicles.

Another important pre-cleavage change in the developing sporangium concerns the mitochondria which become associated with a double membrane which appears densely stained in electron micrographs. Eventually the mitochondria become totally engulfed by these membranes and later they are seen to disintegrate. Up to one third of the mitochondria may be lost at this time. The reasons for this mitochondrial degeneration are unknown and as yet there is no biochemical data to amplify the cytological change.

The division of the cytoplasm into the individual spore units commences with the grouping and eventual fusion of the cleavage vesicles. The fusion events result in a system of membrane-bounded tubes that ramifies the cytoplasm of the sporangial protoplast. *Gilbertella persicaria* is typical of many Mucorales species having a columella as part of its sporangial structure. The columella is a cap-shaped membranous structure that delimits the spores from the sporangial stalk. Cleavage of the columella from the sporangium appears to be effected in a similar manner to the spores, i.e. by the activity of cleavage vesicles.

Following the cleavage the sporangium is filled with wall-less spore protoplasts with the membrane surrounding them originating from the membrane tubes derived from the cleavage vesicles. The granules first seen inside the vesicle are now apparent on the outer surface of the spore membrane. The granules eventually become fused into a network of irregular rods which then become part of one of the spore wall layers. As the spores continue to develop, the cytoplasm becomes denser, membrane contrast is lost and additional wall material is laid down.

Development of conidia

Production of conidia is a feature of Ascomycete and Deuteromycete fungi. Conidia have three distinctive features, they are non-motile, not formed by cleavage and thus not enclosed within a spore-bearing structure. Three patterns of conidium development are recognised, fragmentation, fission and extrusion, and these provide useful taxonomic criteria.

Arthrospores, blastospores and porospores are types of conidia formed by relatively simple mechanisms. During the formation of arthrospores the differentiating hyphal apex becomes expanded and meristematic, producing a chain of cells in basipetal sequence. Blastospores and porospores develop by extrusion methods from either somatic hyphae or from specialised spore-bearing hyphae called conidiophores. Blastospores are produced at apical or lateral sites of either hyphae or conidiophores by a budding process. Porospores develop as extrusions through pores formed in the outer wall layer of the conidiophore by enzymatic digestion. The inner wall layer is pushed out to form the spore wall. In many instances the mechanism of spore formation is not so clear cut, e.g. macroconidia formation in *Neurospora crassa*. The first stage of spore development is undoubtedly a blastic process or extrusion involving the enlargement of the conidium initial. Subsequent septa production and separation of the spores has been described as an arthic or fragmentation process.

Phialoconidia, typical of the genera *Aspergillus* and *Penicillium*, are characterised by their formation from a specialised conidiophore cell called the phialide. These are single cells produced as lateral branches of aerial conidiophores or in clusters at the apices of conidiophores. The spores arise as apical extrusions of these cells and in many fungi a chain of spores is produced in basipetal sequence.

Ultrastructural aspects of the development of the conidiophore and conidia have been investigated in various Aspergilli. Distinct stages in differentiation of the mature conidiophore can be recognised starting with the transformation of a hyphal segment into the foot cell of the conidiophore. The conidiophore stalk grows from the foot cell as an aerial branch and it can be distinguished from a somatic hypha by its greater diameter and thicker wall. In *Aspergillus niger* as many as eight wall layers have been reported in the basal region of the conidiophore stalk. In other species the conidiophore wall is composed of two layers.

The intracellular structure of the young conidiophore is reminiscent of the vegetative hypha, the cytoplasm is rich in ribosomes and other organelles, with vesicles at the apex. As the stalk of the conidiophore lengthens the basal regions become vacuolated.

A characteristic feature of the *Aspergillus* conidiophore is the vesicle which represents the swollen apex of the stalk. As the vesicle forms so the stalk wall becomes thickened. Internally the spatial distribution of organelles, characteristic of the elongated hypha, becomes disrupted as the organelles become uniformly distributed throughout the vesicular cytoplasm. Another notable change is seen as the shape of nuclei and mitochondria change from an elongated form in the stalk region, to ellipsoidal and spherical forms.

The next stage of differentiation involves the development of numerous cells, called sterigmata, over the surface of the vesicle. They begin as

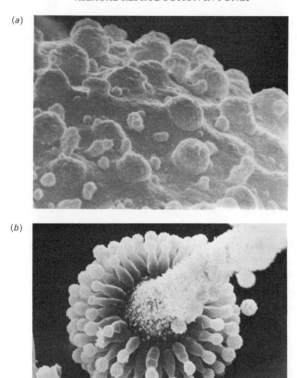

Figure 7.5 Conidiogenesis in *Aspergillus flavus* as seen by scanning electron microscopy.
(*a*) The vesicle at an early stage of phialide development (× 8640).
(*b*) Mature conidiophore showing phialides bearing conidia (× 1464).
Crown copyright: From Kozakiewicz, Z. (1978) *Trans. Brit. Mycol. Soc.*, **70**, 175–186.
Reproduced by kind permission of Miss Z. Kozakiewicz.

spherical protrusions, forming in a fairly synchronous manner. Up to 500 sterigmata have been observed in *Aspergillus niger*. These cells become elongated and cylindrical in shape and eventually are separated from the vesicle by the formation of septa. In some species the sterigmata become phialides each producing a chain of conidia, but in others the sterigmata produce another elongated cell which functions as the phialide. The phialides are uninucleate, in most species, and contain other organelles.

The phialides give rise to spores in rapid succession by basipetal budding (figure 7.5). This must involve continuous synthesis of wall materials, repeated nuclear divisions and synthesis of RNA and protein to be packaged in the spore. The site of these latter syntheses is unknown and could be the vesicle with subsequent transport of the product to the spores.

Environmental control of sporulation

In fungi having the genetical competence for asexual reproduction the switch from vegetative growth to reproductive development is generally greatly influenced by environmental factors. The period of vegetative growth following the colonisation of a new substrate or medium, is variable but ultimately the exhaustion of a nutrient, particularly assimilable carbon and/or nitrogen, may act as a trigger to initiate reproduction. There are some exceptions to this general situation, however, e.g. *Aspergillus nidulans*, where surface colonies derived from single spores will produce conidiophores and conidia after only 20 hours at 36°C. Depletion of nutrients is unlikely in this short period of growth so an alternative explanation is necessary. One interesting view suggests that conidiophore induction depends on gene controlled initiation and that it takes up to 20 hours for this event to be brought about.

Our knowledge of the environmental conditions influencing asexual reproduction in fungi is now very extensive and although much of the earlier work was of a descriptive nature, it is possible to formulate some generalised statements about the interactions:

1. The environmental conditions that favour vegetative growth may not favour asexual reproduction.
2. The range of conditions that promote asexual reproduction is normally narrower than the conditions that promote vegetative growth.
3. Environmental conditions that influence the initiation of asexual sporulation may differ from the conditions that favour development and maturation of the spore-bearing structures.

In some fungi physical factors are important in the control of asexual sporulation and particular interest has been paid to the role of light which may be either stimulatory or inhibitory—figure 7.6 (Tan, 1978). The major features of light controlled development are the wavelength and dose of light and the physiological status of the mycelium receiving the stimulus. In many of the light-sensitive fungi near-UV light is a common promoter and blue light also in other species, however, there are no reports of red photoresponses. Interestingly several of the species exhibit-

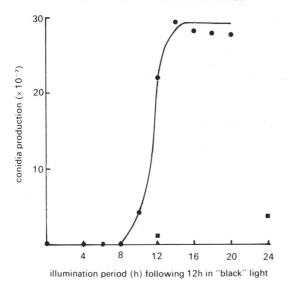

Figure 7.6 The effect of light on conidiation in *Botrytis cinerea*. The organism was grown in liquid culture in darkness for $3\frac{1}{2}$ days before irradiation. Spore counts were then made on cultures exposed to near UV light (●), blue light (▲) and kept in total darkness (■). Adapted from Tan, K. K. (1976) *J. Gen. Microbiol.*, **93**, 278–282.

ing near-UV controlled sporulation also show blue light inhibition but this effect is reversible following further exposure to near-UV. A photo-receptor system based on a pigment called mycochrome (M) has been proposed to explain this reversibility. The pigment exists in two forms, one absorbing near-UV (M_{NUV}) and the other, blue light (M_B).

$$M_{NUV} \underset{\text{blue}}{\overset{\text{near-UV}}{\rightleftharpoons}} M_B$$

Constituents of cell extracts having these light absorbing properties have been reported. The so-called M_{NUV} exists either as a soluble component in the cytoplasm or in a form loosely bound to the particulate fraction. The M_B is found tightly bound to the particulate fraction. The chemical nature of mycochrome is unknown as is the nature of its interaction with the metabolic processes associated with sporulation.

In recent years the shift in interest to the biochemical basis of asexual reproduction has resulted in a more critical examination of the interaction between the environment and the organism. It is generally recognised that fungi grown in surface culture, typical of the earlier studies, do not

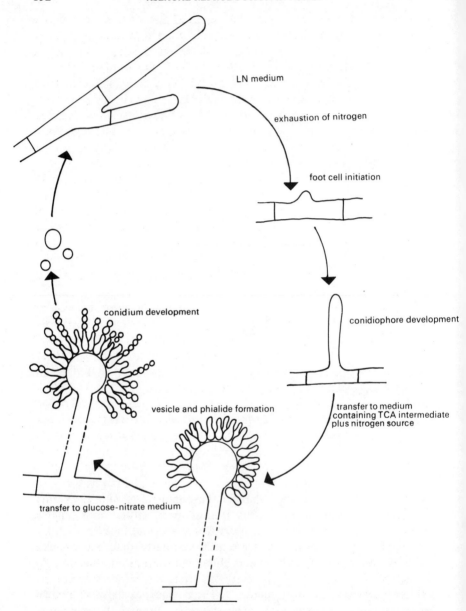

Figure 7.7   Nutritional control of conidiogenesis in *Aspergillus niger*. Adapted from Smith, J. E. and Anderson, J. G. (1973) *Symp. Soc. Gen. Microbiol.*, **23**, 295–337.

provide the homogeneous material required for analysis of specific enzymes or cell constituents. The consequent use of liquid cultures, grown in shake flasks or fermenters, has resulted in a reappraisal of the physiological control of asexual sporulation. The number of fungi studied with these methods is as yet limited and generalised statements are therefore not possible. *Aspergillus niger* has proved particularly useful in this area of experimentation (Smith, 1978). As stated previously exhaustion of the carbon source is a stimulus to sporulation and although this is an important factor in this fungus, however, the nature of the nitrogen source is also critical; conidia production occurs if nitrate is used but does not if the nitrogen source is an ammonium salt. The inhibition caused by excess ammonium ions can be reversed by the addition of acetate, pyruvate, tricarboxylic acid intermediates and amino acids to the medium. Inhibition of conidiogenesis in *Neurospora crassa* is also caused by the presence of ammonium nitrogen in a medium containing citrate as carbon source. Substitution of the ammonium salt with nitrate again stimulates spore formation. In this fungus the effect of ammonium ions can be overcome by aeration of the cultures.

The outcome of the research on the nutritional control of conidiation was the development of a nutritional replacement technique whereby the development of conidiophores and conidia could be controlled as a staged process (figure 7.7). Spores are germinated in a nitrogen-limited medium containing glucose (LN medium), and during the development of the mycelium foot cells arise (stage 1), from which conidiophores (stage 2) ultimately grow as the nitrogen becomes exhausted. The initiation of foot cells does not occur if both carbon and nitrogen are exhausted simultaneously or if the oxygen supply is reduced to cultures growing in the nitrogen-limited medium. After conidiophore elongation no further development occurs in the LN medium, but replacement with a fresh medium containing nitrate and a tricarboxylic acid intermediate, e.g. citrate, induces vesicle and phialide development (stage 3). A final replacement with a glucose-nitrate medium induces the final stage of differentiation, the formation of conidiophores (stage 4).

Microcyclic conidiation (chapter 8) also provides a useful experimental system for the study of the biochemical basis of sporulation. Increasingly, the use of chemostats is also providing a useful technique whereby the influences of environmental control can be manipulated and studied. However, there are possible disadvantages in the use of these varied techniques and the results should be interpreted with some caution. For example when nutrient replacement techniques are used it is necessary to establish that the observed biochemical changes are causes and part of the reproductive development, not effects brought about by the nutritional changes. Despite this, these various methods and approaches have been greatly advantageous and have provided some interesting observations which are considered in the next section.

Biochemical changes associated with asexual sporulation

Energy metabolism
The significance of nutrient exhaustion in the initiation of asexual reproduction was discussed in the previous section. Depletion of a key nutrient will result in a metabolic shift in the organism which in some way

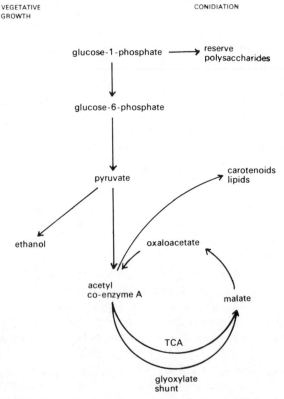

Figure 7.8 Changes in carbon metabolism associated with conidiation in *Neurospora crassa*. Adapted from Turian, G. and Bianchi, D. (1972) *Bot. Rev.*, **38**, 119–154.

is probably associated with the new pattern of development. Observations on standing cultures of *Neurospora crassa* support this hypothesis. When plentiful supplies of carbon and nitrogen (glucose and nitrate) are available active hyphal growth occurs. Cytochemical studies have shown that the energy metabolism at the hyphal apices is fermentative and this is substantiated by the detection of ethanol in the culture medium (Turian, 1975). The high concentration of glucose causes the repression of oxidative metabolism and restricts mitochondrial development. As aerial branches grow up from the mycelium the glucose effect is gradually reduced, probably because of reduced translocation of the sugar, and oxidative metabolism can be demonstrated. Thus reduction in available glucose brings about depression and a metabolic shift in favour of the tricarboxylic acid (TCA) cycle. The aerial hyphae then go on to produce macro-conidia (figure 7.8). The possible significance of this metabolic shift is a need for a greater energy supply for macromolecule synthesis in the developing spore. Investigations on *Aspergillus niger* have also demonstrated the functioning of the TCA cycle in cultures undergoing conidiation.

Another detectable change recorded in several fungi undergoing conidiation is a switch in importance in the pathway of glucose metabolism. In vegetative hyphae the Embden Meyerhof Parnas (EMP) pathway pre-

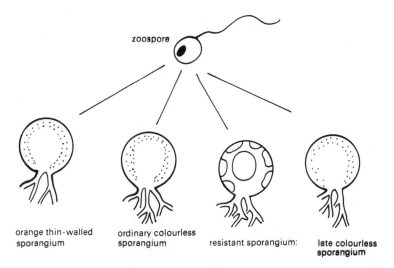

zoospore

orange thin-walled sporangium

ordinary colourless sporangium

resistant sporangium:

late colourless sporangium

Figure 7.9 Patterns of sporangium development in *Blastocladiella emersonii*. Adapted from Cantino, E. C. (1961) *Symp. Soc. Gen. Microbiol.*, **11**, 234–271.

dominates to provide pyruvate, which may be converted to ethanol as described previously. During conidiophore formation the pentose phosphate (PP) pathway becomes more significant. The significance of this metabolic switch is not understood, but clearly the PP pathway will provide an enhanced supply of precursors for the biosynthesis of the materials required for spore formation.

Experiments on two taxonomically very different fungi, *Blastocladiella emersonii* and *Aspergillus niger*, have shown that the enzymes isocitrate dehydrogenase and isocitrate lyase may have some role is asexual reproductive development. The former organism provides a fascinating developmental system whereby the vegetative cell (thallus) can differentiate sporangia which show morphological differences (figure 7.9). The normal pattern involves the development of so-called ordinary colourless (OC) sporangia, but in the presence of bicarbonate a thick walled resistant sporangium (RS) is formed. Amongst the many analyses of enzymes and cell constituents made on cultures during the development of these two distinct pathways the enzymes, NADP dependent isocitrate dehydrogenase and isocitrate lyase appeared to have higher activities in the RS culture. The former enzyme was found to operate in reverse of its normal role in the TCA cycle yielding isocitrate from α-oxoglutarate by reductive carboxylation. Isocitrate lyase then brings about the cleavage of isocitrate to glyoxylate and succinate (figure 7.10). The significance of this

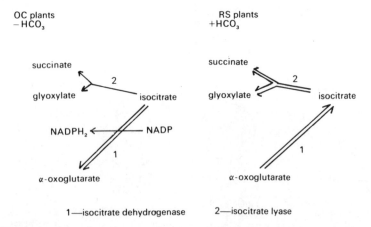

Figure 7.10 The effect of bicarbonate on metabolism of *Blastocladiella emersonii*. Double arrows indicate major enzyme activities. Adapted from Cantino, E. C. (1961) *Symp. Soc. Gen. Microbiol.*, **11**, 234–271.

metabolic switch, it is claimed, is in the utilisation of glyoxylate in amino acid and subsequent RNA synthesis that occurs during differentiation of the RS sporangium. These conclusions were later challenged when comparisons were made between OC and RS developing cultures during the period of exponential growth. In the OC cultures this lasts for the whole developmental period, but in the RS cultures exponential growth occurs for only part of the developmental cycle. Using, it was argued, more comparable material for these analyses, the differences described previously were not found in these later experiments. This controversy again raises the question as to whether the changes in enzyme activity were casual in the development process, or the effect of a changed environment.

Further support for a role for these two enzymes in asexual development can be found in experiments with *Aspergillus niger*. The induction of conidiation in batch cultures, chemostat cultures or in cultures subjected to the nutrient replacement procedures, resulted in an increase in isocitrate dehydrogenase and isocitrate lyase in every case. Enhanced isocitrate lyase activity has also been described in conidiating cultures of *Neurospora crassa*.

Macromolecule synthesis

Spore development clearly depends on the synthesis of a spectrum of macromolecules including polysaccharides for the spore walls, membrane lipids, proteins and nucleic acids, however, it is in this broad area that our knowledge is very sparse. Ultrastructural investigations considered in a previous section have shown the involvement of the hyphal walls during spore development involving budding and membrane activity was seen to be greatly significant in the cleavage of endogenously produced spores. Spore formation involves repeated nuclear division, at some stage, indicating a need for extensive DNA replication.

The most extensive investigations on macromolecule biosynthesis during asexual sporulation have been made on some of the more primitive fungi belonging to the Phycomycete group. In both *Achlya bisexualis* and *Allomyces arbuscula* active RNA and protein synthesis occur during spore development. From isotopic count determinations made of three parameters in studies on *Achlya*, i.e. rate of amino acid incorporation, specific activities of amino acid pools and the release of amino acids from pre-labelled proteins, protein turnover values of 75 per cent were obtained. A large proportion of the amino acids released were re-utilised in *de novo* protein synthesis during zoospore differentiation.

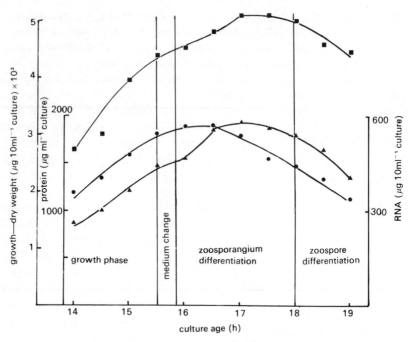

Figure 7.11   Changes in dry weight and macromolecular composition of cells of *Blastocladiella emersonii* during growth and zoospore formation: (■) dry weight, (▲) protein, (●) RNA. Adapted from Murphy, M. N. and Lovett, J. S. (1966) *Dev. Biol.*, **14**, 68–95.

The occurrence of macromolecule synthesis during zoospore formation in *Blastocladiella emersonii* has proved more difficult to demonstrate (Lovett, 1975). The transition from vegetative growth to zoosporangium formation is characterised by a marked decline in the rate of synthesis of DNA, RNA and protein (figure 7.11) and under these conditions the determination of *de novo* synthesis is not easy. A requirement for mRNA and protein for this development step is a reasonable assumption but this requirement could be fulfilled by synthesis of the specific molecules at a time prior to spore differentiation, i.e. the later phase of vegetative growth or during the early period of zoosporangium development.

Experiments on *Trichoderma viride*, a fungus that requires a light stimulus for the induction of conidiation, have shown that RNA is produced continuously during critical periods of the light induction period. However, DNA/RNA hybridisation failed to show differences in the RNA transcribed during photo-induction. Even so it was suggested that new species of RNA were being transcribed but could not be detected because the amounts produced were very small with respect to the total RNA in the culture. Incorporation studies have been made with a few fungi and provide general evidence for RNA and protein synthesis during sporulation, but details regarding the specificity of the macromolecules are not yet available.

Genetic control of asexual sporulation

Study of the genetical control of asexual reproduction has been restricted to two fungi, *Neurospora crassa* and *Aspergillus nidulans*. This is not unexpected in view of the broader genetical knowledge of these two organisms. In general many of the mutations which affect conidiation in these fungi also cause other unrelated defects, i.e. they are pleiotropic mutations. In *Neurospora*, however, mutants have recently been isolated in which only conidiation has been affected; these mutants affect the developmental steps shown in figure 7.12. So far only mapping work and limited biochemical experiments have been carried out with these mutants (the gene loci involved are located on separate chromosomes), but they obviously provide interesting subjects for detailed biochemical investigations (Mishra, 1977).

The more complex conidiophore apparatus of *Aspergillus nidulans* provides a wider scope for possible deformities through mutation (Clutterbuck, 1978). Some of the earliest known mutants involved the colour of the spores. Wild strains produce green spores, but white and yellowed spored mutants are easily isolated. The mutant spores are deficient in at least one enzyme, laccase (p-diphenol oxidase), which is involved in pigment biosynthesis.

Several different types of mutant with altered conidiophore morphology have also been isolated (figure 7.13): the *bristle* mutant develops conidiophore stalks which grow indefinitely but does not produce spores;

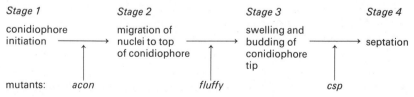

Figure 7.12   Phase-specific mutations affecting conidiation in *Neurospora crassa*.

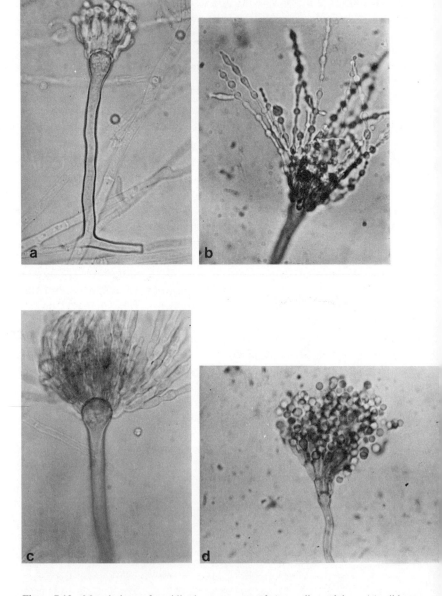

Figure 7.13 Morphology of conidiophore mutants of *Aspergillus nidulans*; (*a*) wild-type, (*b*) abacus mutant, (*c*) leaky bristle mutant, (*d*) medusa mutant (× 1000). From Clutterbuck, A. J. (1969) *Genetics*, **63**, 317–327. Reproduced by kind permission of Dr A. J. Clutterbuck.

abacus produces a normal conidiophore but instead of conidia it form root-like structures with swellings at intervals; *medusa* produces conidia but has at least two sterigmata supporting the chain, and finally *stunted* produces very short conidiophores. Some of these mutations are pleiotropic, e.g. sexual development may also be affected, and some exist also in temperature sensitive form, i.e. the mutation is expressed only at a higher temperature (permissive temperature) than the normal growth temperature. The *bristle* mutant is an example of a tactical or morphogenetic mutant in which the abnormal morphology results from the developmental process failing to move from one stage to the next. There is repetition of the final stage, thus in this mutant very long conidiophore stalks are formed. The *abacus* mutant is similar, the abnormal structure of the conidiophore probably being the result of repeated phialide formation. The *medusa* and *stunted* types are mutations which affect auxiliary loci, that is they affect functions that are supplementary to the conidiation process. Both these mutants produce conidia but in smaller numbers than the wild strain because of modifications to the conidiophore.

Both the *Neurospora* and *Aspergillus* mutants have been investigated for conidiation-specific enzymes, but none of those considered so far fulfils such a function. The occurrence of the enzymes, associated with pigmentation of conidiophores and conidia of *Aspergillus nidulans*, in the abnormal mutants has been investigated. Cresolase, the enzyme concerned in the synthesis of a pigment in the conidiophores and sterigmata, and laccase are both absent from *bristle* mutants, but *abacus* does produce cresolase. The interrelationship between the activities of these two genes still has to be resolved, however, it is likely that the *bristle* locus plays a key role in the regulation of conidiophore development.

SUMMARY

1. Asexual reproduction in fungi is concerned with the production of spores which are diverse in type. Two broad groups of spores are recognised, those produced endogenously within a specialised structure the sporangium and thus called sporangiospores, and those produced exogenously on specialised hyphae and called conidia. Generally speaking particular spore types are produced by the different taxonomic forms. Some fungi produce other types of asexual spores called chlamydospores and oidia. These are

resistant cells and their major role is that of maintenance of the species under extreme environmental conditions.

2. The endogenous development of sporangiospores is brought about by the cleavage of the sporangial cytoplasm into discrete uni- or multi-nucleate masses. In most of those fungi studied so far cytoplasmic cleavage results from the activity of vesicles which fuse to form furrows and channels that ramify the cytoplasm. Each cytoplasmic unit develops into a spore.

3. Conidia develop by one of three mechanisms; hyphal fragmentation, hyphal fission and extrusion. In the former a hypha becomes divided by septation. In the fission process the hyphal tip forms chains of cells by repeated nuclear division and septation, in many fungi this occurs in the terminal cells of branches of specialised hyphae called conidiospores. Extrusion of spores is achieved by a pore forming in the outer layer of the hyphal wall and the inner layer bulging out to form the spore.

4. Asexual reproduction is controlled by a diverse range of environmental factors both nutritional and physical.

5. Environmental control of asexual development can be used to induce synchrony and regulation of the developmental sequence of sporulation in a few fungi. Such control is highly necessary for meaningful biochemical studies to be carried out.

6. The transition from vegetative growth to asexual reproduction is accompanied by changes in carbon metabolism. In *Neurospora crassa* the vegetative hyphal tips are fermentative whereas the aerial reproductive hyphae are oxidative in their metabolism. This switch is related to the depletion of the available glucose which is thought to cause the depression of the TCA cycle and other related pathways. In several fungi an increase in the activities of isocitrate dehydrogenase and isocitrate lyase have been found. The significance of these enzymes is believed to relate to the production of glyoxylate which can be utilised to produce glycine and ultimately RNA.

7. The formation of RNA and protein is an integral part of spore development. In most spores much of the mRNA required at germination is transcribed during spore development and to a lesser extent proteins are also produced.

8. The underlying genetic control of asexual development is demonstrated by the isolation of mutants which have deformities in the reproductive structure or are unable to produce spores.

CHAPTER EIGHT

SEXUAL REPRODUCTION IN FUNGI

SEXUAL REPRODUCTION IN FUNGI IS CHARACTERISED BY A WIDE VARIETY OF
mechanisms and controlling factors. The underlying feature, typical of all
sexually reproducing organisms, is a fusion event involving two compatible nuclei. However, fungi are mostly haploid, and meiotic division
occurs after nuclear fusion. In this respect the fungi differ from most other
eukaryotes. The bringing together of the compatible nuclei is achieved in
a variety of ways, ranging from the exogenous fusion of gametes, through
mechanisms which involve the production of distinct sex organs, to the
situation in many fungi where gametes and sexual structures are not
produced but where "mating" involves the fusion or anastomosis of
somatic or vegetative cells.

Genetic control of sexual reproduction operates at two levels in relation
to mating and in the developmental sequence leading to the formation of
sex organs or associated structures. Sexual development, along with
asexual development and vegetative growth, is subject to environmental
influences and in some fungi the involvement of hormones is also a major
feature of the overall control mechanism.

Morphology of sexual reproduction

The sexual reproductive cycle involves three distinct phases, plasmogamy,
karyogamy and meiosis. An overall survey of the cycle in different fungi
reveals several patterns which vary in relation to the duration of the
particular stages (figure 8.1). Plasmogamy involves fusion of two cells
resulting in a common cytoplasm and the bringing together of two or
more compatible nuclei. At some stage, sooner or later, karyogamy
(nuclear fusion) occurs, to be followed by meiosis. The products of meiosis

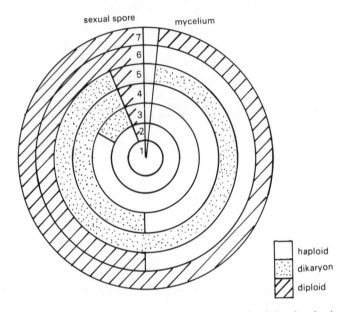

Figure 8.1   Diagrammatic representation of sexual cycles in fungi showing the duration of the three nuclear phases, haploid, dikaryon and diploid. Adapted from Raper, J. R. (1966) in *The Fungi*, Vol. 2 (ed. G. C. Ainsworth and A. S. Sussman) Academic Press, New York, 473–511.

are ultimately incorporated into sexual spores and so provide the start for a new cycle of development. In some fungi nuclear fusion may occur as a rare event in somatic cells, and the diploid nucleus can be perpetuated for varying lengths of time through the formation of asexual spores. Such diploid strains vary in their stability and may slowly loose chromosomal material giving rise to aneuploids and ultimately haploids. Mitotic recombination can also occur as a rare event in these diploids and genetically altered progeny may be recovered following haploidisation. This sequence of events involving somatic diploidy and haploidisation is called the parasexual cycle.

Mechanisms of plasmogamy
Five different mechanisms of plasmogamy have been recognised; gametic conjugation, gametangial contact, gametangial conjugation, spermatisation and somatic cell fusion (figure 8.2). Gametic conjugation, found in the Chytridiomycetes, is the simplest mechanism involving fusion of two

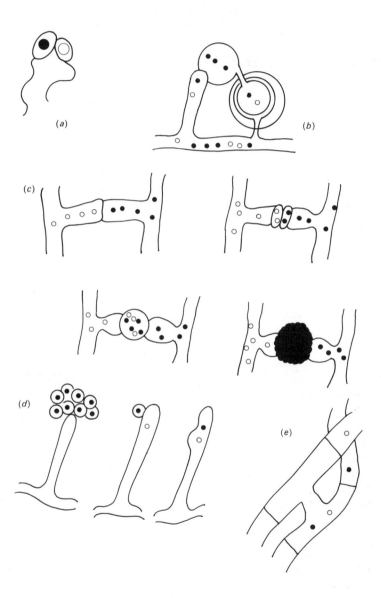

Figure 8.2   Mechanisms of plasmogamy in fungi; (*a*) gametic conjugation, (*b*) gametangial contact, (*c*) gametangial fusion, (*d*) spermatisation, (*e*) somatic cell fusion.

gametes. The gametes involved may be similar in size and are frequently motile. In some fungi behavioural differences occur and this may be a reflection of differences in the gametangia that produced them. In *Blastocladiella variabilis* fusion of gametes, which are themselves identical but arise from morphologically different thalli, is controlled by environmental factors. Gamete fusion is not an essential event. Under conditions that prevent fusion the gametes can germinate directly giving thalli of the two morphological types.

Increasing complexity in the organisation of sex organs is reflected in the mechanism of plasmogamy. Oomycete fungi produce distinct male (antherdia) and female (oogonia) sex organs or gametangia, however, gametes of both sexes are non-motile and plasmogamy is achieved by gametangial contact. A channel of communication between the organs is required and this is achieved either by the formation of a continuous pore through their walls, presumably by enzyme degredation, or by the development of a fertilisation tube.

Gametangial conjugation is the mechanism of plasmogamy found in some of the Chytridiomycetes, the Zygomycetes and the yeasts. In the former, distinct male and female gametangia develop and following fusion the cytoplasmic contents of the male cross over to the female gametangium. In the Zygomycetes the gametangia show no morphological differences although in many species fusion will only occur between compatible structures produced on two different mycelia. In the rest, gametangia produced by a single mycelium will fuse. Following gametangial fusion a cell is formed between the two gametangia at the point of contact and the contents of the two organs pass into it. In the yeasts conjugation of two compatible cells first involves the growth of a tube or channel between the cells. The nucleus from each cell passes into this and they fuse. This stimulates the development of a bud from the conjugation tube and the nucleus migrates into it (figure 8.3). The diploid cell may reproduce for many generations, by budding, before further development takes place.

Spermatisation is the mechanism of plasmogamy found in some of the Ascomycetes and Basidiomycetes. The functional units are a uninucleate male cell or spermatium (which resembles the asexual conidium but lacks the ability to germinate) which fuse with a female gametangium. The nature of the latter is variable ranging from a highly developed sex organ, the structure of which varies in different species, to a vegetative hypha which takes on this specialised reproductive function. The product of plasmogamy is a cell containing the two compatible nuclei, i.e. a

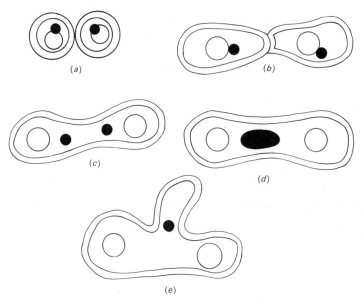

Figure 8.3 Schematic representation of cell conjugation in yeast; (*a*) cell contact, (*b*) elongation of the conjugation tube, (*c*) breakdown of the cell wall, (*d*) nuclear fusion, (*e*) development of the diploid bud.

dikaryotic cell. The subsequent pattern of development varies in different fungi, in some the dikaryotic phase is short whereas in others it can persist as a vegetative form for a considerable time.

The fusion of somatic cells, or somatogamy, as a mechanism of plasmogamy gives a similar result to spermatisation. In the filamentous fungi the somatic structures are hyphae and their nuclear status following fusion depends very much on the particular organism. In some Ascomycetes a heterokaryon develops, i.e. a mycelium which carries several copies of two genetically distinct nuclei, in this case sexually compatible nuclei. This situation arises as a result of the hyphal organisation of these fungi. Eventually at the pre-karyogamy stage a cell develops which contains only one copy of each type of nucleus. In other Ascomycetes and in some Basidiomycetes this binucleate condition develops from the outset. In the latter group, cells of the two compatible mycelia fuse and there is a reciprocal exchange of nuclei. Then follows a migration of the exchanged nuclei up to the apical cells of the hyphae of the respective mycelia which thus become binucleate. Nuclear migration

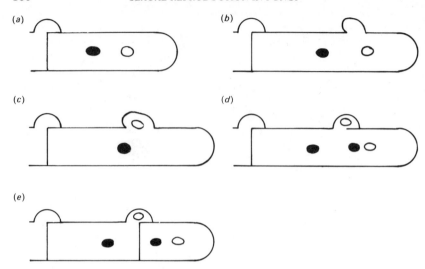

Figure 8.4   Cell division in a basidiomycete dikaryon involving the formation of clamp connections; (*a*) binucleate terminal cell, (*b*) development of new clamp, (*c*) migration of nucleus into clamp, (*d*) nuclear division, completion of clamp and beginning of septum formation, (*e*) completion of clamp.

involves the dissolution of the complex dolipore septa characteristic of these fungi. The binucleate apical cells are the foundation of the dikaryotic mycelium which can in some cases exist for indefinite periods. A characteristic of the dikaryon in many of the Basidiomycetes is conjugate division of the two nuclei which is achieved by the formation of clamp connections (figure 8.4). This pattern of development is not typical of all Basidiomycetes, with *Agaricus bisporus*, the commercial mushroom, being one of the notable exceptions.

Karyogamy and meiosis
These events occur immediately or shortly after plasmogamy in some fungi, but in many a period of vegetative growth, e.g. dikaryotic phase in Basidiomycetes, intervenes. In the former situation nuclear fusion occurs in the fused gametes or in the cell formed by gametangia or in the female organ where these are produced. Meiotic division is presumed to follow, immediately restoring the haploid state (or diploid state as in the Oomycete genera, *Pythium* and *Phytopthora*) which is the condition of the vegetative growth stage. In the Ascomycete and Basidiomycete fungi, where a period of vegetative development intervenes, karyogamy occurs

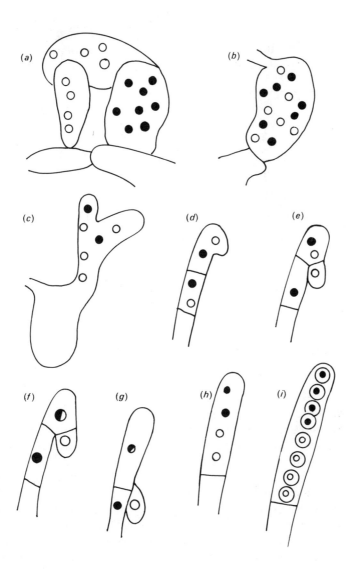

Figure 8.5 Generalised pattern of ascus development; (a) male and female organs, (b) fertilised ascogonium, (c) development of ascogenous hyphae from the ascogonium, (d) formation of the crozier apical cell on an ascogenous hyphae, (e) nuclear division in the crozier apical cell, (f) nuclear fusion to form the ascus mother cell, (g) elongation of the ascus mother cell, (h) first meiotic division in the ascus, (i) ascus with eight ascospores.

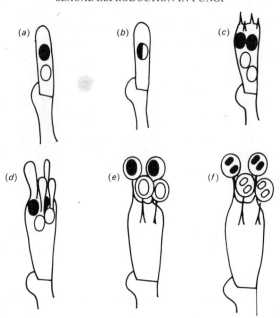

Figure 8.6 Development of the basidium; (a) binucleate basidium mother cell, (b) nuclear fusion in the basidium, (c) meiotic division and sterigmata formation, (d) early stage of spore formation, (e) uninucleate spore stage, (f) nuclear division in the spores and maturation.

in a specially developed cell. These are of two types, the ascus (Ascomycetes) and the basidium (Basidiomycetes). In the normal development of the ascus the two daughter nuclei fuse and the diploid nucleus divides immediately first meiotically and then by mitosis, to give eight daughter nuclei which become incorporated into an equivalent number of ascospores. These spores develop endogenously within the walls of the ascus. Development of the basidium differs in two major respects, firstly the diploid nucleus that results from karyogamy divides only meiotically and the four products of the division are involved in the development of four basidiospores which are borne exogenously on sterigmata. The development of the ascus and the basidium is shown in figures 8.5 and 8.6.

Sexual spores, the products of sexual reproduction

Sexual reproduction is concerned with the production of a cell or spore which, on subsequent germination (see next chapter), gives rise to a new generation of the fungus. The mechanisms of sexual reproduction and the nature of the sexual spores are central to fungal taxonomy providing the basis for several groupings.

Spore types

Five main types of sexual spore can be identified, the motile zygote, the oospore, the zygospore, the ascospore and the basidiospore.

Motile zygotes are found in fungi that produce motile gametes that fuse exogenously. The product after a period of motility develops into a thallus which bears either a sporangium with diploid zoospores or a thick-walled resting sporangium in which haploid zoospores arise by meiotic division. The latter germinate to give a new generation of gametangial bearing thalli.

Oospores arise following the fertilisation of stationary oospheres within the female oogonium by antherozooids. On germination the oospore may give rise to a sporangium or to a vegetative germtube.

Zygospores are produced where the sexual mechanism involves gametangial conjugation. Diversity of zygospore morphology is reflected in the texture of the spore surface and in the presence or absence of appendanges that develop from the suspensor cells which support the zygospore.

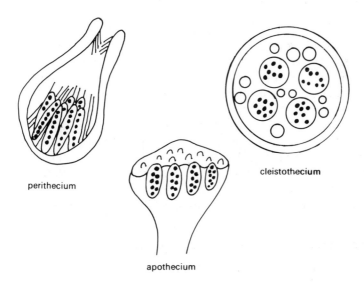

perithecium

apothecium

cleistothecium

Figure 8.7 Morphology of ascocarps.

A characteristic of the majority of the Ascomycete and Basidiomycete fungi is that a single event of plasmogamy results in the development of many spore producing structures, i.e. asci and basidia respectively. The

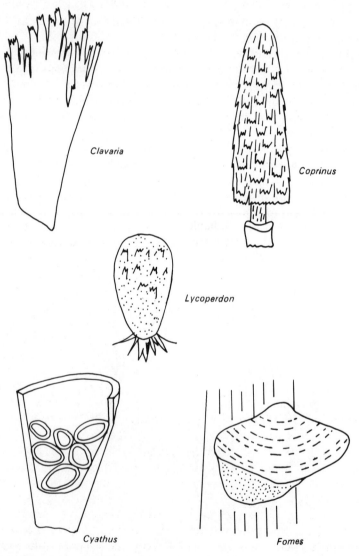

Figure 8.8   Morphology of basidiocarps.

yeasts provide the major exception to this rule in that the diploid bud which develops following conjugation of two compatible cells may differentiate immediately into an ascus producing ascospores. However, under certain environmental conditions the diploid cell may bud to give a diploid clone with each cell having the ultimate capability of producing an ascus. In this respect yeasts may correspond in behaviour to the majority of the Ascomycetes.

With a few exceptions the many asci and basidia, as described above, are borne in or on specialised structures called fruiting bodies, ascocarps and basidiocarps respectively. Several forms of ascocarp are produced which differ in a number of respects, e.g. whether the structure is open or closed and if closed whether it is completely closed or has a pore, and whether the asci are produced in a regular layer or hymenium or are irregularly distributed within the ascocarp (figure 8.7). Ascus morphology is also a variable feature in the group as a whole with wall structure being a major distinguishable feature. Ascospores also show variation in several features namely shape, size, ornamentation and pigmentation.

The basidiocarp is also a diverse structure in terms of morphology. In those groups with the common names mushrooms, brackets, puffballs, earthstars, etc., the basidiocarp is a distinctly recognisable macroscopic structure (figure 8.8). In such structures, the basidia are formed in a layer, the hymenium, covering the external surface of gills, e.g. *Agaricus* (figure 8.9), or tubular chambers, e.g. *Boletus*, which form part of the pileus region of the basidiocarp or is part of the internal structure of the fruit body, as in the puffballs and earthstars. In the club-like or clavaroid form of fruit body the hymenium covers the surface of the upper regions, but in the cup-shaped or cyphelloid fruit body the hymenium forms the lining of the inner part of the cup. Some basidiomycetes, e.g. the plant pathogenic rusts and smuts, do not produce such recognisable fruit bodies. In these fungi the basidia are produced at the germination of an earlier spore stage, the teleutospores, in the life cycle. The latter are produced in a structure called a sorus which develops in the superficial tissues of the leaves of infected plants. Basidium morphology and development also varies. In one type, the holobasidia, four basidiospores are normally produced on sterigmata which develop at the basidium apex and in the phragmo-basidia. Each basidium is divided into four uninucleate cells by either horizontal or vertical septa with each producing a sterigma and a basidiospore. Basidiospores show few distinctive features, they are generally small, smooth and colourless showing one surface feature, the hilum, that marks the point of attachment to the basidium.

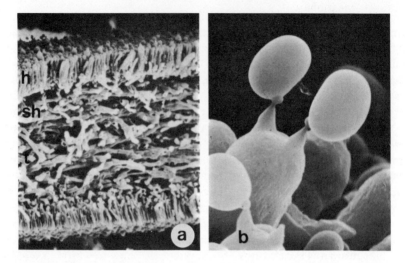

Figure 8.9 (*a*)   Scanning electron micrograph of gill section of *Agaricus bisporus* showing the three layers, (h) hymenium, (sh) sub-hymenium and (t) trama (× 300).
(*b*)   Scanning electron micrograph of a mature basidium of *Agaricus bisporus* bearing two basidiospores (× 2900). From Craig, G. D., *PhD Thesis*, University of Kent. Reproduced by kind permission of Dr G. D. Craig.

Spore ultrastructure

In common with asexual spores interest in spore structure has centred on the nature of the spore wall and special features found in the spore protoplast. Many sexual spores function as resting spores and this property is reflected in their structure. As stated above, the surface texture is very variable extending from smooth surfaces to surfaces that are warty or bear spines. The texture may be related to the chemistry of the wall, which in many instances is more complex than the hyphal wall of the particular organism. Thus the wall of *Mucor mucedo* zygospores, with their characteristic warty texture, contain melanin and sporopollenin along with chitin and chitosan.

The wall of all types of sexual spore is multilayered, in some cases up to six layers have been identified. Identification of the chemical composition of these different layers has been achieved in only a few species, e.g. *Mucor mucedo*. The cytoplasm of the spore includes all the organelles expected in a eukaryotic cell. A characteristic feature of most spores is the presence of reserve materials, usually in the form of lipid bodies.

Sexual compatibility

In sexual reproduction the gene pool of a species can be continuously mixed and so provide variability which may be used to advantage in differing environmental situations. In many fungi the reproductive mechanism is organised or controlled in a manner to promote outbreeding but there are exceptions to this where inbreeding occurs, as well as examples where an intermediate situation may exist. In the more primitive types, e.g. *Blastocladiella* species, virtually no differentiation into sexual types is found. In the related genus *Allomyces*, distinct male and female gametangia and their respective gametes are produced. There is no mechanism to ensure fusion of gametes from different thalli and this is therefore a chance event when it does occur. Male and female sex organs are also a feature of the Oomycetes and in some species both are produced on one thallus, in others on separate thalli. In the latter instance possibilities clearly exist for variation to be increased through sexual reproduction, however, in none of these instances is the genetic basis for sex understood.

The Mucorales includes self-fertile or homothallic or homomictic species, and self-sterile or heterothallic or dimictic species. In the former, gametangial fusion occurs within a single colony or mycelium but sexual development in the self-sterile strains requires fusion between gametangia of two compatible strains. These are designated + and − strains because no obvious sexual differences exist. In the homothallic strains experiments involving the use of sex hormones suggest that individual gametangia behave as either + or −.

Homothallic and heterothallic species are also found in the Ascomycetes. In some species sex organs or distinct male and female gametes are produced. *Neurospora crassa* provides a classic example with the existence of two compatible strains designated *A* and *a*. The female structure in this fungus, is a protoperithecium that has finely branched receptive hyphae called trichogynes. These fuse with the male gametes that are either the micro or macroconidia. The fusion pattern involves the male gamete from the *A* strain and a trichogyne from the *a* strain or vice versa. This relatively simple mating system is genetically controlled by two alleles, but the biochemical expression of these and the mechanism of compatibility is unknown. A similar mechanism of genetic control of compatibility is found in yeasts, e.g. *Hansenula wingei* and *Saccharomyces cerevisiae*, and in the latter species mating type specific cell surface recognition molecules, in the form of glycoprotein, have been identified (Crandall, 1976).

Several deviations from these mating systems have been identified in other Ascomycetes. In *Aspergillus nidulans*, a homothallic species, outbreeding can be forced using genetic selection methods. This involves the incubation of a mixed spore suspension derived from two mutant strains that have different nutritional requirements, e.g. specific amino acids. These requirements can be compensated in a balanced heterokaryon which arises through anastomosis of the germ tubes derived from the spores which will therefore grow on an unsupplemented minimal nutrient medium. The situation in the fission yeast, *Schizosaccharomyces pombe*, also deviates from the standard pattern. Three strains have been identified with respect to mating behaviour. Two of these behave in a conventional manner and are designated h^+ and h^-, the third called h^{90} is self-fertile and produces ascospores. The origin of the latter has caused some controversy and the matter still requires resolution. One argument suggests that the h^+ and h^- loci are comprised of two closely linked components, thus the h^+ locus might be h^+h^+ or h^+h^0 and the h^- would be h^-h^0. Crossing over within the locus would give the recombinant h^+h^- which it is suggested is the h^{90} strain. A second suggestion implicates a particular modifier gene s^h which specifically affects the h^- strain with the h^{90} resulting from the combination h^-s^h.

The most complex compatibility control systems are found in some of the Basidiomycetes and result in obligate outbreeding. Two systems are identified, the unifactorial and the bifactorial with A and AB mating type factors respectively (Casselton, 1978). Each factor occurs in multiple allelic form with compatible matings resulting from crosses such as $A_1 \times A_2$ and $A_1B_1 \times A_2B_2$. In the bifactorial types the two factors have been found to be located in different linkage groups resulting in the segregation of the factors into parental and non-parental associations. Detailed investigations in recent years have shown that both the A and B factors are made up by two genes α and β which, although closely linked, can be separated by crossing-over. Thus an A_1 factor would be equivalent to $A\alpha_1\beta_1$ and $A\alpha_2\beta_2$ equivalent to A_2, etc. In the cross $A_1 \times A_2$, two recombinant types $A\alpha_1\beta_2$ and $A\alpha_2\beta_1$ could arise. These discoveries helped our understanding as to how the multiple allele system could arise. In *Schizophyllum commune*, a bifactorial species, the $A\alpha$ gene has 9 alleles and the $A\beta$ has 32 alleles giving 288 possible A factors. The B factor has 9 alleles for both the α and β genes with the possibility of 81 different factors. Through experiment some 96 A factors and 56 B factors have so far been identified.

A further indication of the increased complexity of these compatibility systems arises from the regulatory functions which these factors also have. Heterokaryotic matings can be made in which the two nuclei carry either common *A*, common *B* or both common *A* and *B* alleles. A study of the development of these three types of heterokaryon has furthered our knowledge of these functions. Matings between strains with common *A* factors exhibit hyphal fusion with nuclear exchange and migration. The nuclei fail to pair, however, and as a consequence conjugate division does not take place either. In heterokaryons derived from common *B* factor matings nuclear migration is blocked, but where fusion involves two apical cells conjugate nuclear division occurs, but normal nuclear separation is prevented because of the failure of the clamp cell to fuse with the sub-apical cell. Septa are produced across the hypha and the clamp cell giving a uninucleate terminal cell. In common *A* and *B* heterokaryons no development is observed. The observation made on these heterokaryons led to the suggestion that the *A* factor controls conjugate division of the nuclei and initiates the formation of the clamp cells and the *B* factor controls nuclear migration and fusion of the clamp cell and the parent hypha.

Physiology of sexual reproduction

Environmental factors
Sexual development, in line with other developmental processes is subject to environmental influences. There are many reports on the influence of specific nutritional or physical factors on sexual reproduction but few are extensive in relation to a single organism. In part this is a reflection of technical problems associated with quantification of developmental events and consequently much of the work is of a descriptive nature. The diverse factors that influence sexual development include the nature and availability of the carbon source, concentration of nitrogen source, a requirement for vitamins and various minerals. Physical agents include pH, aeration, and in some cases light is an important stimulus.

Sex hormones
The involvement of chemical attractants or hormones in fungal sexual reproduction has been known for many years (Bu'Lock, 1976). The hormones so far identified have one of two functions, acting as sexual attractants, i.e. one gamete to another, or they induce sexual differentiation. The realisation of these two functions has led to a recent suggestion that these compounds be called pheromones.

The only known example of a sexual attractant occurs in the Chytridio-mycete genus *Allomyces*. The motile female gamete secretes a hormone, called sirenin (figure 8.10), that is an attractant for the male gametes. The concentration of hormone required for attraction is extremely low at 10^{-10} M. The male gametes converge on the female gamete in large numbers, but only one is involved in plasmogamy and when this occurs

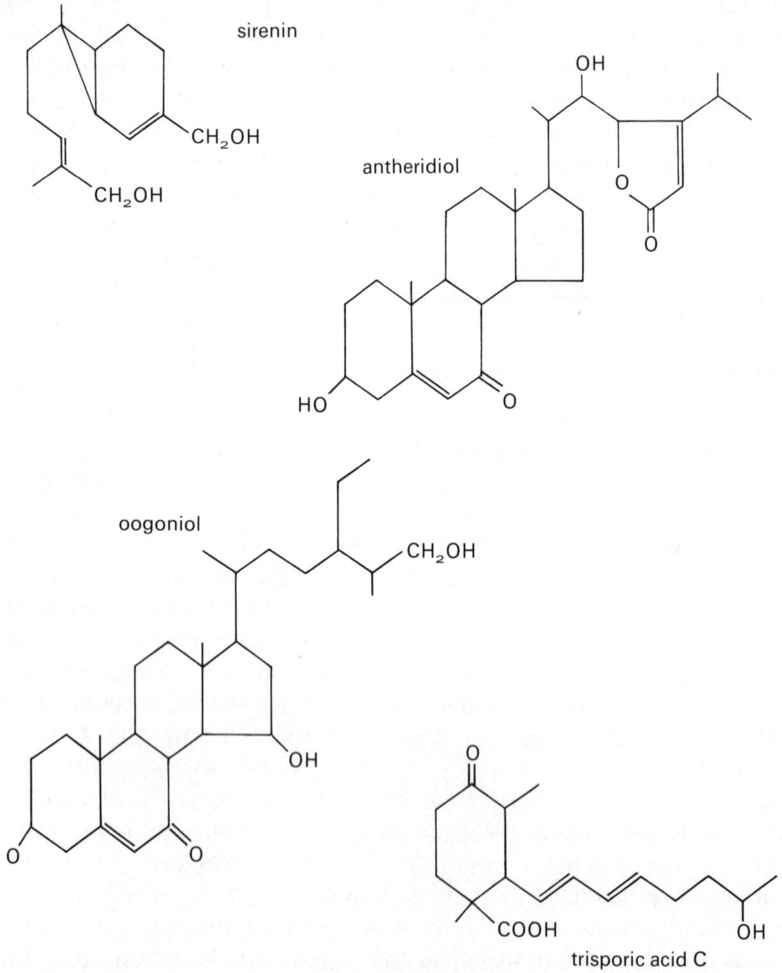

Figure 8.10 Hormones involved in sexual reproduction.

secretion of the hormone, by that female gamete, stops. Sirenin was the first fungal sex hormone to be chemically analysed and characterised. To produce the large quantities of hormone required it was necessary to devise specialised culture conditions because normal wild strains, in producing both male and female gametes simultaneously, synthesise very small amounts of the hormone. The problem was overcome by the use of an *Allomyces* hybrid, which produces strains that are almost 100 per cent male or female. Analysis showed the hormone to be a bicyclic sesquiter-penediol with a molecular weight 236. The mode of action of the hormone remains unknown, it is taken up by, or bound to, the male gametes and cannot be re-extracted. This suggests that the molecule might be rapidly metabolised to some inactive product. With prolonged exposure to the hormone the gametes become saturated and fail to maintain the chemo-tactic response. This state may last for up to 45 minutes.

Achlya is a fungus that produces hormones which are involved in the initiation of and control of the development of sex organs. Most species are bisexual, but two, *Achlya bisexualis* and *Achlya ambisexualis*, are single sexed and these are known to produce hormones (Barksdale and Lasure, 1973). The female strain constitutively produces hormone A, or antheridiol (figure 8.10), which stimulates the male strain to embark on the differentiation of the male sex organs, the antheridia. The developing antheridial branches grow towards the source of hormone, i.e. the female thallus, and simultaneously begin to produce and secrete a second hormone B_1 or oogoniol, which initiates the development of oogonia. A third hormone, C, was proposed with the role of causing differentiation of the antheridia on the antheridial branches, however, the demonstration that antheridiol can also induce the same effect disposed of the need for hormone C. A further hormone (D) has been proposed to control the delimitation of oogonia and differentiation of the oospheres. Antheridiol was found to be a sterol, and oogoniol is believed to be a variant of the molecular form. Several biochemical changes have been described in the male strain after exposure to antheridiol. These include glucan degrad-ation and the production of a cellulase enzyme. The latter may be of significance in relation to changes in the cell wall required for initiation of the male sex organs. Observations on *Achlya ambisexualis* suggest that the action of hormone A might be augmented or retarded by three other hormones designated A_1, A_2 and A_3 (figure 8.11).

The hormones found in Mucorales species provided an unusual ex-ample of initiation control. The first suggestions that hormonal inter-action between compatible mating strains came from experiments

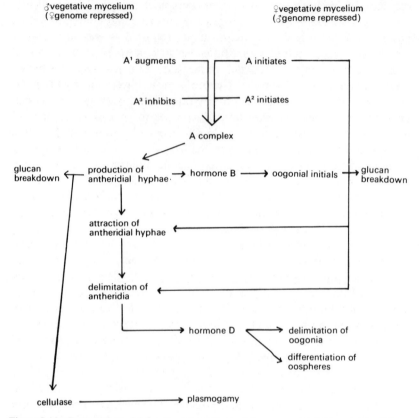

Figure 8.11 Proposed model for the interactions of hormones in *Achlya*. Adapted from Bu'Lock, J. D. (1976) *The Filamentous Fungi*, Vol. II (ed. J. E. Smith and D. R. Berry) Arnold, London, 345–368.

performed over 50 years ago. The two strains were separated by a colloidon membrane but the development of zygophores still occurred, implicating a possible low molecular weight diffusable molecule as the controlling mechanism. Some years later these ideas were substantiated by more experiments, with the conclusion that each strain produced a hormone which influenced the opposite strain. An obvious conclusion was that two hormones were involved, however, only one compound was isolated which induced zygophore development in both strains. How could one hormone function in a supposedly differential manner affecting the development of two strains? The possible answer to this question followed the identification of the hormone as a trisporic acid which is derived as a degradation product from β-carotene. Thus trisporic acids induce the formation of zygophores in both $+$ and $-$ strains of *Mucor mucedo* (van den Ende, 1978). When $+$ and $-$ strains are grown in mixed culture *cis-trans* trisporic acid B is synthesised, but not when the strains grown individually. The reason for this was realised following the discovery of two mating strain specific precursors produced in very small quantities in *Mucor mucedo* and *Blakeslea trispora*. The compound produced by the $+$ strain is a 4-hydroxymethyl trisporate and that from the $-$ strain is trisporal. Each precursor induces zygophore development in the opposite strain and when taken into the hyphae of that strain the precursor is converted to trisporic acid (figure 8.12). As trisporic acid is produced, so more of the precursor is synthesised. The precursor molecules are also thought to be involved in the zygotropic response of the developing zygophores as they grow towards each other.

It is interesting to note that the homothallic strains of *Mucor* and other related genera also produce trisporic acid. When matings are set up between heterothallic and homothallic species sexual development occurs in both and the zygophores of the heterothallic strain grow towards those of the other but fusion does not occur. Cytochemical studies on a homothallic species of *Zygorrhynchus* related to the localisation of enzymes involved in the synthesis of trisporic acid precursors indicated that differentiation into $+$ and $-$ zygophores occurs. In these species it also seems that gametangial fusion is controlled to some degree.

The involvement of hormones in sexual reproduction in the higher fungi, i.e. Ascomycetes and Basidiomycetes, is not so well known. The α mating strain of *Saccharomyces cerevisiae* has been shown to secrete a peptide called α-factor which induces two identifiable changes in cells of the *a* strain. The latter became arrested at the G_1 stage of the cell cycle and deformities in cell shape, thought to be associated with alterations in the cell wall.

This was clarified in a more recent study by Schekman and Brawley (1979) in which *a* mating cells exposed to α-factor deposited chitin over a much larger area of their surface than during budding (see chapter 2). The hormone caused activation of plasma membrane-bound chitin synthase zymogen. These results imply a role for chitin during conjugation which could be as an anchor for cell adhesion and fusion factors or could represent a site rich in mating factors and thereby control the number of cells involved in a conjugation event.

A hormonal system is also thought to exist in another Ascomycete,

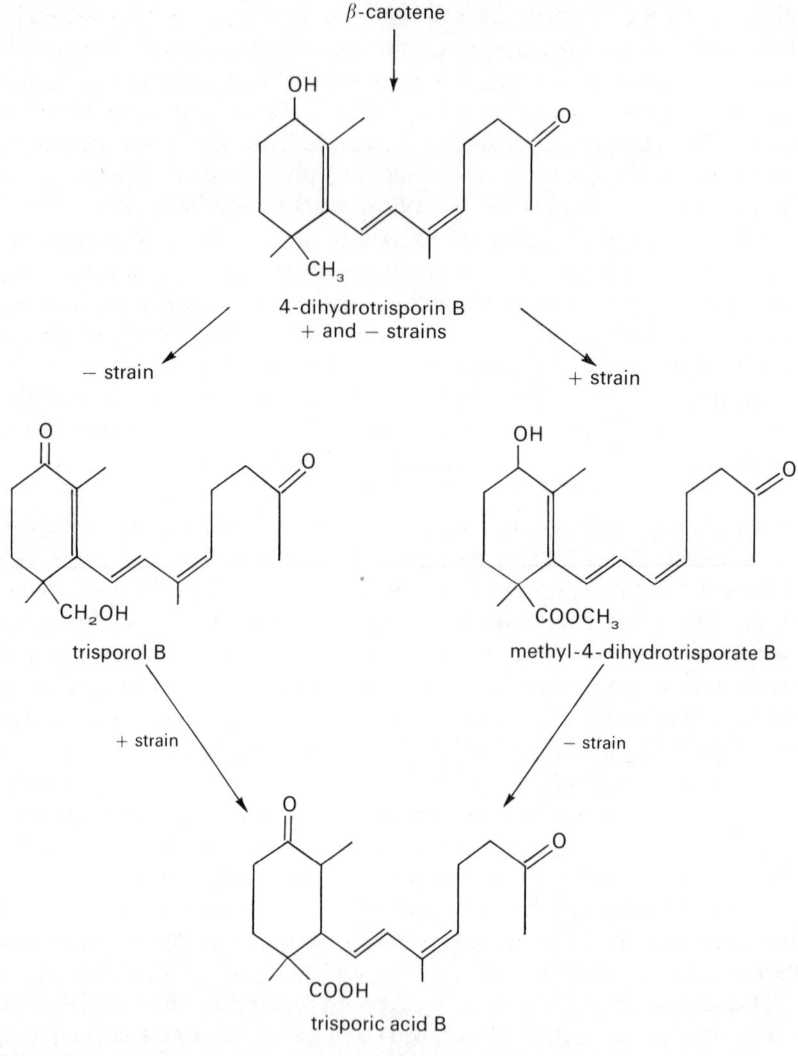

Figure 8.12 Pathways leading to trisporic acid synthesis in *Mucor*.

Ascobolus stercorarius. This is a heterothallic species with *A* and *a* mating types. When the two strains are grown in close proximity differentiation of the male antheridium commences after a few hours with the female ascogonia forming some time later. The trichogynes associated with the latter grow towards the antheridia in a directed manner. In experiments involving the exposure of hyphae of one strain to a culture filtrate from another only the *A* hyphae in the *a* culture filtrate showed any change. Following this the *A* mycelium induces antheridial development in the *a* strain. The compound involved, which is unknown, passes through a membrane and from the observations made it would appear to be produced by the *a* strain as a constitutive metabolite.

The only known hormone in a Basidiomycete fungus has been described in *Tremella mesenterica*. The compound, called tremerogen, has been shown to induce the formation of mating tubes. The homokaryons of this organism grow as a yeast form and when cells of the two mating types are mixed, a tube develops between two compatible cells and from this the dikaryon develops as a mycelial form.

Biochemical events associated with sexual development

Investigations geared to the elucidation of the biochemical basis of sexual development are technically difficult for most fungi. The underlying problems concern the difficulty in establishing synchrony in the developmental process which is necessary for meaningful biochemical analyses and measurements and secondly the fact that most fungi do not exhibit sexual reproduction when grown on liquid media. The significance of the latter problem relates to harvesting the material for analysis and the fact that liquid cultures and their associated physical environment can be more readily manipulated. As a consequence of these several problems information on this aspect of fungal biochemistry remains sparse and fragmentary as will be apparent in the following discussion.

Biochemical changes in Oomycetes
In *Phytopthora* species glucans have an important role in several aspects of development (Bartnicki–Garcia and Hemmes, 1976). The cell walls, of all developmental stages are very rich in glucans which may make up 90 per cent of the wall material. Whilst this total content of glucans remains fairly constant during the life cycle of these fungi, the relative proportions of the two major components, β-1,4-glucan and β-1,3-glucan, with some β-1,6-linkages, do change along with wall ultrastructure. The significance of these changes in the context of sexual development remains to be elucidated.

These fungi also produce another β-1,3-glucan, which has been called mycolaminarin, which is stored in the mycelium as a food reserve. This reserve is mobilised during the development of the sex organs, especially the oogonium which receives a large input of mycelial cytoplasm during its development. The mature oospore that develops following plasmogamy and karyogamy is a thick-walled spore and the wall glucans present have also been shown to be used as a reserve substrate during germination.

A β-1, 3-glucan reserve polymer has also been isolated from *Achlya*. It is utilised during the formation of sex organs and it has been suggested that one role for the sex hormones might be to reverse the glucose induced repression of β-1, 3-glucanase needed to bring about the degradation of the polymer.

Biochemical and metabolic changes in Ascomycetes
Ascus development in *Saccharomyces cerevisiae* is possibly the most extensively studied system in relation to associated biochemical changes. The unicellular nature of this organism is a major virtue for the experimenter to exploit because it makes possible the establishment of synchrony in a cell culture. A fairly high degree of synchrony can be attained in yeast cells induced to undergo ascospore formation.

Sporulation occurs in diploid yeast cells derived from an $a \times \alpha$ mating involving conjugation, or from $a \times a$ and $\alpha \times \alpha$ matings following protoplast fusion. A culture of diploid cells, growing on a rich nutrient medium, can be switched from budding to ascus development by transferring them to semi-starvation conditions which means a medium containing acetate as the carbon source and lacking any form of nitrogen. Diploid cells growing in a less rich medium, i.e. chemically defined, can also be induced to sporulate. The age of the cells at the time of transfer is critical for induction. Cells grown vegetatively on a rich medium have to be grown on to the stationary phase before sporulation can be induced, but log phase cells from the nutritionally poorer medium are used. Not all the cells in the culture develop into asci, the sporulation process is cell-cycle dependent with newly formed buds failing to develop ascospores. This suggests that at least one mitotic division is required in a cell before it can sporulate, why this should be is unknown. Possibly sporulation could be dependent upon certain mRNA that is transcribed late in the cell cycle in the period between nuclear division and septation.

Ascus development in *Saccharomyces cerevisiae* can be divided into several phases on the basis of the recognisable cytological events (figure 8.13) and, as was shown with bacterial sporulation, these provide useful landmarks to which detectable biochemical changes might be related

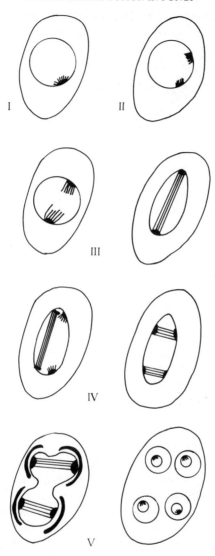

Figure 8.13 Diagrammatic representation of nuclear activity and ascospore formation in *Saccharomyces cerevisiae*. Stage I, single spindle plaque with few microtubules. Stage II, duplicated plaque. Stage III, spindle plaques have come to face one another and are separating during first meiotic division. Stage IV, end of first meiotic division and spindle plaques have duplicated. The plaques then become positioned for the second division. As the second division begins the formation of the spore wall also starts. Stage V, ascospores fully formed. Adapted from Moeus, P. and Rapport, E. (1971) *J. Cell. Biol.*, **50**, 344–361.

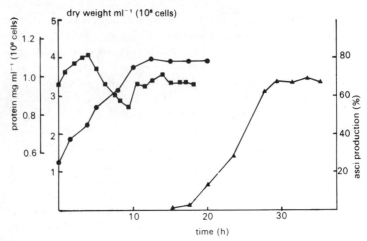

Figure 8.14 Changes in yeast cells during ascospore development; (●) dry weight, (■) protein, (▲) appearance of mature asci. Redrawn from Matur, A. and Berry, D. R. (1978) *J. Gen. Microbiol.*, **109**, 205–213.

(Tingle *et al.*, 1973). Spore formation, which is essentially a reproductive cell division, takes up to 24 h in contrast to vegetative cell division which is completed in 2.3 h. Only a very few biochemical markers have been identified as components of the sporulation process and the most significant of these is DNA synthesis that occurs prior to meiosis at T_4 and T_6 and lasts for 4 h.

RNA synthesis during sporulation has been reported and up to 50 per cent of the RNA in the ascus may be new but its significance is not understood since the RNA species produced are the same as found in the diploid vegetative cell. Most of the RNA that is manufactured is rRNA. Although RNA synthesis continues during sporulation the rate of synthesis declines resulting in a fall in the total RNA in the ascus (see below).

In contrast protein synthesis is a necessary part of ascospore development (figure 8.14). Treatment of asci with cycloheximide up to the stage immediately prior to ascospore delimitation blocks spore formation. Some of the new protein is enzymatic but the roles of many other proteins remains to be unravelled. The synthesis of protein and RNA in developing asci takes place in the absence of exogenous nitrogen. The new molecules are formed therefore at the expense of protein and RNA turnover. As the diploid cells start on spore development the levels of protease and RN-ase increase and are involved in the turnover of up to 50 per cent of the two macromolecules present in the vegetative cells.

Spore formation is highly energy dependent and this is reflected in the involvement of oxidative metabolism. In diploid vegetative cells the tricarboxylic acid cycle is repressed whilst glucose is available but the activity of the enzymes involved in the cycle increases during stage I as a result of de-repression. Isocitrate lyase activity also increases and experiments involving the metabolism of $[1-^{14}C]$- and $[2-^{14}C]$-acetate by spore forming cells, with the highest production of CO_2 from the former molecule, suggests that the glyoxylate cycle is important at this time. Low concentrations of CO_2 are necessary for spore formation but the inclusion of glyoxylate in the sporulation medium releases this requirement.

Both exogenous and endogenous carbon sources are metabolised. At the commencement of sporulation the rate of oxidation of the exogenous substrate is high and then falls away during subsequent stages. Conversely the endogenous rate is low and increases up to stage IV. The early period of rapid utilisation of the exogenous acetate correlates with the timing in the increase of the TCA enzymes and isocitrate lyase. The switch to oxidative metabolism during sporulation is also important in relation to the synthesis of reserves that occurs during this time. Lipids form the major reserve in ascospores in contrast to vegetative cells where the two carbohydrates trehalase and glycogen are more significant. The lipid reserves are synthesised partly from the exogenous acetate and partly from the carbohydrate reserves which are present in the pre-sporulation cell and also produced during the early stages of sporulation.

In other Ascomycetes, e.g. *Neurospora* and *Sordaria*, attempts have been made to relate biochemical changes to the various stages that can be identified in the development of the perithecium, i.e. ascogonial bud, ascogonial hook, ascogonial coil and protoperithecium (Turian, 1978). Selective metabolic inhibitors have been used with these fungi in an attempt to identify the metabolic pathways that are operative at a particular developmental stage and possibly of consequence in the developmental process. Differentiation of the ascogonium in *Neurospora tetrasperma* is blocked by iodoacetate and deoxyglucose, two inhibitors of the glycolytic pathway. In contrast, the later development of the perithecium stage is blocked by the TCA inhibitor, fluoracetate. A similar finding was obtained with *Sordaria fimicola* where cyanide and sodium azide, inhibitors of the terminal cytochrome system, also block perithecium development. Temperature and oxygen tension can affect development, e.g. the complete sequence of perithecium development in *Neurospora tetrasperma* is blocked at 37°C, and growth at low oxygen concentrations block development at the ascogonial coil stage. The conclusion drawn from these observations is that the early stages of differentiation, leading to ascogonium formation, in some way depend on the glycolytic pathway but subsequent development and maturation to the perithecium requires oxidative metabolism.

Macromolecule synthesis is also an important aspect of development in these fungi, the differentiation of new structures being presumably dependent on differential gene transcription and translation. Cytochemical methods have demonstrated active RNA synthesis during ascogonial development in *Neurospora*. 5′fluorouracil, an inhibitor of RNA synthesis, blocks the formation of perithecia in *Sordaria fimicola*, but actinomycin D, another inhibitor of RNA synthesis, and chloramphenicol, which blocks protein synthesis, had no effect.

The appearance of several specific proteins have been reported during sexual development in *Neurospora*; these are tyrosinase, L-amino acid oxidase and a phase-specific perithecial protein (Mishra, 1977). Tyrosinase has a key role in melanin biosynthesis, converting L-tyrosine into the pigment which is present in the ascospores and perithecia but absent from vegetative mycelium. Both this enzyme and L-amino acid oxidase are subject to derepression induced by the starvation conditions that stimulate sexual development. cAMP has been shown to increase tyrosinase activity several-fold.

The phase-specific protein or sex-protein was isolated from perithecia. It occurs only in this organ and not in the ascospores or vegetative mycelium. The concentration of the protein increases dramatically after fertilisation reaching a maximal level at 5–6 days. The role of the protein has still to be resolved as is its origin—it is not clear whether it is formed by *de novo* synthesis or released from some other bound form of protein.

Cell wall synthesis and degradation in Basidiomycetes
The number of Basidiomycete species amenable to biochemical experimentation on sexual development is limited because of technical problems associated with fruit body formation on laboratory media. In those that can be studied changes in hyphal walls and septa are of importance in relation to dikaryon formation and fruit body development in several Basidiomycete species.

In *Schizophyllum commune* the two mating type factors *A* and *B* also have regulatory functions controlling the activities of other structural genes that are involved in the establishment of a dikaryon. Of prime importance is the breakdown of the dolipore septa to allow nuclear migration. The septa are comprised of an alkali resistant glucan, a so-

. called R-glucan, a polymer that also occurs in the hyphal wall. Breakdown of the septa will therefore involve R-glucanase and a comparison was made on the activity levels of this enzyme in monokaryons and dikaryons and various mutant strains with altered A and B factors. The monokaryons were found to have a low R-glucanase activity and this was shown not to be the result of glucose repression. Compatible dikaryons, heterokaryons with common A factors, and mutant strains with an altered B factor all produced high levels of the enzyme and the presence of glucose in the medium had no inhibitory effect. The conclusion from these experiments was that R-glucanase was subject to permanent repression in the monokaryons, but this is reversed by the presence of two compatible B factors in the dikaryotic mycelium. Once the dikaryon is established in the terminal cells the enzyme is no longer required and its activity might then be expected to be subject to further repression.

Sexual reproduction in *Schizophyllum commune* culminates in the formation of fruit bodies on the dikaryotic mycelium with the spore-producing cells, the basidia, located in a hymenial layer that lines the surface of the cup-shaped basidiocarp. Changes in the cell walls of the hyphae, due to polysaccharide breakdown, take place during the later stages of differentiation of the fruit body primordium with the formation of the pileus (Wessels, 1965; Schwalb, 1977). The hyphal wall of this fungus is comprised of two glucans, S-glucan and R-glucan (differentiated on the basis of alkali solubility at room temperature), chitin, protein and other unidentified materials. The R-glucan can be divided into two fractions, R_s (soluble) and R_i (insoluble) after boiling in 2N KOH. The glucans are by far the major component accounting for over 80 per cent of the walls with the chitin content about 3 per cent. Pileus development commences when the exogenous supply of glucose in the culture medium is depleted and simultaneously the amount of R_i glucan in the walls of the hyphae that make up the primordium decreases suggesting a relationship between the two events. Further support can be found in observations made when the dikaryon is grown at 30°C. At this temperature pileus development is blocked and very little of the R_i glucan is degraded. R-glucanase, which is assumed to bring about the R_i glucan breakdown, has been found in both the mycelium and culture filtrates. Whether this is the same enzyme as that involved in septum degradation during the establishment of the dikaryon is unknown. The activity of the R-glucanase, assumed to be of importance during primordium differentiation, is influenced by the presence of glucose in the culture medium whereas the enzyme present in the early stage of dikaryon formation is not.

In the basidiocarps which have two distinguishable parts, the pileus and stipe, elongation of the latter is important in carrying the basidiospores up from the substratum and so assisting in their ultimate dispersal. Studies on *Coprinus cinereus* have shown that wall degradation and synthesis are also important aspects of this part of reproductive development (Gooday, 1975). Elongation of the stipe is an endotrophic process requiring no exogenous nutrient supply. The elongation process involves the synthesis of new chitin microfibrils within the fabric of the hyphal wall. The extensive synthesis that occurs is at the expense of reserves in the hyphae, but the existing wall chitin also has to be partially degraded to allow the insertion of the new microfibrils. The breakdown products from chitin hydrolysis are re-incorporated into the newly formed chitin.

Genetic control of sexual development

Sexual development, like other developmental processes, is primarily subject to genetic control. As stated previously the genetic control involved operates at two levels in many fungi, the genetic significance of mating control has been considered earlier. Mutants showing defective development have been isolated in many fungi and whilst a few of these have been investigated with a view to ascertaining the biochemical lesion, the study of the rest is purely a descriptive one. One complication with sexual sporulation mutants, especially in yeast, is that they are recessive and are therefore only expressed in homozygous diploid cells.

Several types of mutant defective in sexual development have been isolated from *Saccharomyces cerevisiae* (Haber *et al.*, 1975). These are mostly temperature sensitive which sporulate at a permissive temperature of 25°C but not at a higher temperature. One group, the sporulation deficient mutants (*spo* mutants) are cells that fail to complete the budding stage that is taking place when the cells are induced to sporulate. Several cell division cycle mutants (*cdc* mutants) are also deficient for sporulation. These include mutants that are defective in mitotic DNA synthesis, and others that are defective in nuclear segregation. Another class of mutants are those deficient in pre-meiotic DNA synthesis, and do not produce spores as a consequence.

A range of mutants of *Neurospora* have been obtained which exhibit varied characteristics with respect to ascus morphology and ascospore development (Mishra, 1977). One mutation, which has interesting taxonomical consequences, is that affecting spindle orientation in the ascus of *Neurospora tetrasperma*. This species is distinguished from *Neurospora crassa* and other species by having only four ascospores instead of the normal eight. The four-spored ascus is believed to result from the orientation of the spindle parallel to the transverse axis of the ascus during the second and third divisions of the ascus nuclei. The nuclei then end up as pairs in each spore which, as a consequence, are heterokaryotic in terms of mating type, and give rise to self-fertile mycelium. A dominant lethal mutation has been obtained that affects the spindle orientation mechanism with the result that eight spores are formed per ascus, each of which is homokaryotic and producing either *A* or *a* mating type mycelium. Other mutants affect the shape of the ascus, the arrangement of the spores, and the shape of the spores. Biochemical studies on some of these mutants have revealed differences in levels of specific enzymes in comparison to wild-type strains. These studies are still in their infancy and require extension before meaningful conclusions regarding the biochemical significance of the lesions in the context of the overall biochemistry of sexual development can be ascertained.

SUMMARY

1. Sexual reproduction involves three stages, plasmogamy, karyogamy and meiosis. Fungi show wide variations in the mechanisms of plasmogamy and in the duration of the three events.

2. Fungi are haploid organisms so unlike most other eukaryotes that meiotic division follows karyogamy (nuclear fusion) rather than preceding it.

3. Plasmogamy is achieved by gametic conjugation, gametangial contact, gametangial fusion, spermatisation and somatic cell fusion.

4. Karyogamy and meiosis are closely related events with meiotic division occurring very soon after nuclear fusion. The location of these events relates to the mechanism of plasmogamy, thus the location may be the fused gametes or it may be in specialised cells, e.g. the ascus and the basidium, that are produced in specialised fruit bodies.

5. The products of sexual reproduction are spores. Five types of spore are recognised and are representative of the particular taxonomic groups; they are the motile zygotes, the oospores, the zygospore, the ascospore and the basidiospore.

6. In many fungi sexual reproduction is controlled in a manner to promote outbreeding, i.e. heterothallism. The most primitive control involves the formation of male and female

sex organs on separate thalli. In fungi not producing sex organs, e.g. Mucorales, outbreeding is controlled by specific mating factors. In the Ascomycetes mating factor control also operates in species that develop sex organs. In both the Mucorales and Ascomycetes homothalli or self-fertile species are also found. In the Ascomycetes a single mating type gene, with two alleles, controls the compatibility system. In the Basidiomycetes the control is mediated by one or two genes which are multi-allelic.

7. Sex hormones play an important role in the control of sexual reproduction in some fungi. The best documented examples are known in the Phycomycetes. The hormones either function as attractants as in the case of sirenin in *Allomyces* or they are stimulants for sexual differentiation, e.g. antheridiol and oogoniol in Achlya, and the trisporic acids in *Mucor*.

8. Sexual development undoubtedly requires some redirection in metabolism. From a fragmentary knowledge a few general guidelines can be laid down. The switch to oxidative metabolism that occurs at some stage in sexual development in several fungi reflects the need for an increased energy supply. This can be obtained from a non-carbohydrate energy source or probably from the slow hydrolysis of an energy reserve accumulated during vegetative growth. The development of fruit bodies in Basidiomycetes is in part also dependent on materials which are part of the hyphal wall structure or are reserves stored in the hyphae. Sexual development involves the transcription of specific genes as seen in the synthesis of RNA and protein. Much of this synthesis is at the expense of turnover of pre-existing macromolecules.

CHAPTER NINE

SPORE GERMINATION

SPORE GERMINATION IS THE EVENT WHICH COMPLETES THE CYCLE OF VEGETATIVE and reproductive development. The reasons for spore production have been considered in the preceding chapters. It would not be unreasonable to expect that their subsequent germination would be subject to fairly fine environmental control to ensure success. In both ultrastructural and biochemical terms, spore germination involves considerable change (as does spore formation). It is thus a further example of differential gene activity that is associated with developmental processes.

Several definitions have been proposed to describe the process of germination. The most generally accepted states that

"germination occurs when the first irreversible stage is reached, with a form recognisably different from the dormant organism, as judged by physiological and morphological criteria".

Various criteria have been used to estimate germination of bacterial spores, e.g. turbidity changes, manometric methods and microscopic counts. These procedures have frequently been linked with some physical measurement, e.g. changes in refractility of the spores. The most commonly used criterion for germination of fungal spores relates to germ-tube development—a spore is said to have germinated when the germ tube is longer than the diameter of the spore.

Dormancy

Dormancy is an important property of bacterial endospores and many types of fungal spore. Used in a general sense dormancy is a condition in which the spore is characterised by an apparent lack of metabolism.

Where dormant spores are produced the significance of the sporulation process can be interpreted in relation to the survival of the producing organism exposed to unfavourable environmental conditions (Hawker and Madelin, 1976). However, the term dormancy has been freely used even to include dry spores which readily germinate when transferred to water.

Bacterial sporologists have adopted the use of another term, crypto-biosis, to describe the extreme dormant state where metabolic activity is undetectable in the spores (Keynan, 1972). Thus in many studies the respiratory activity of dormant spores has been found to be less than is detectable by conventional Warburg manometry, i.e. $0.3\,\mu l\,O_2\,mg^{-1}$ spores h^{-1}. The mechanism of cryptobiosis is not yet understood. The presence of enzymes involved in outgrowth (see later), in a repressed state in dormant spores, would seem central to the elucidation of this problem. A number of explanations have been presented one of which implicates inhibitor substances which block the *in vivo* activity of these enzymes. Compounds present in fungal spores have been shown to function as self-

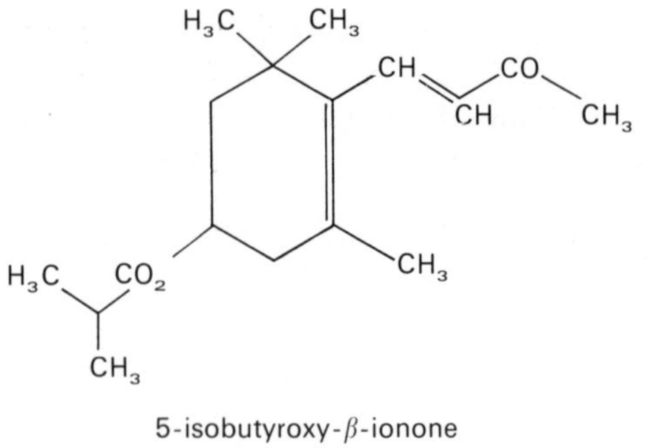

5-isobutyroxy-β-ionone

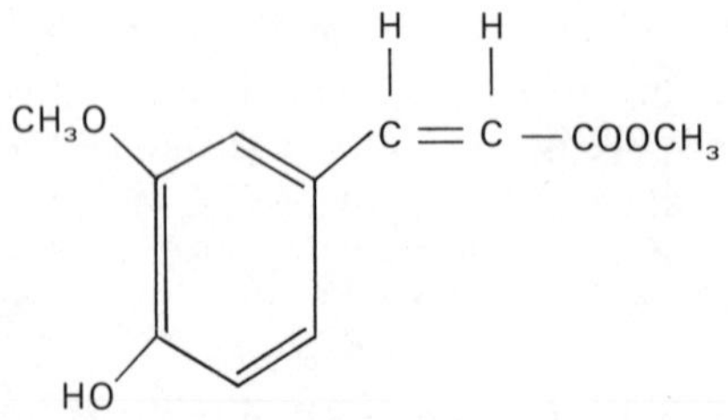

methyl *cis*-ferulate

Figure 9.1   Self-inhibitors of fungal spore germination.

inhibitors. This effect is readily demonstrated when dense spore suspensions are used to inoculate cultures. The active compounds have been identified in two instances, 5-isobutyroxy-beta-ionone in *Peronospora tabacina*, and methyl cis-ferulate in *Puccinia graminis* (figure 9.1). The site of action of these compounds remains to be discovered, they may inhibit some specific germination reaction or some aspect of general metabolism. There are no reports of such specific inhibitor substances in bacterial spores but it has been suggested that the chelation of calcium with DPA could block the activity of Ca^{2+} dependent enzymes. A second view of the mechanism of dormancy and cryptobiosis involves changes in structural features of spores at the termination of the period. Favoured sites are permeability barriers which might prevent entry of nutrients or water into the spore to activate enzymes. Bacterial spores have several coat layers and contain other structures which may be involved in the maintenance of dormancy but there is no convincing evidence to support such a function for any of these spore components. The exception is the cortex for which there is good evidence to suggest that one of its roles is to maintain the spore core in a dehydrated state.

The period of dormancy in spores in their natural state is also a time of maturation. The processes involved in maturation are unknown but the low level of metabolic activity of dormant spores suggests that significant biochemical changes are not involved. The dormant period for spores in their natural environment may last for several months or even years and may be important in relation to survival of the spore. In certain fungi, e.g. teliospores of the rust fungus *Puccinia graminis tritici*, an overwintering period and exposure to low temperature is required to break the dormant state.

Extensive studies in many laboratories have demonstrated that dormant species can be made to germinate following particular treatments. The process has been called activation. The most widely used technique involves the exposure of the dormant spores to sub-lethal heating is very effective for bacterial spores and some fungal spores (figure 9.2). Subsequent research showed that a variety of other techniques are also effective, e.g. low pH, exposure to strong oxidising agents or thiol compounds. Activation is a reversible process and treated spores kept in the absence of their germination requirements ultimately lose their capacity to germinate.

Activated bacterial spores continue to exhibit most of the properties of dormant spores including resistance to heat and irradiation, non-stainability and refractility. Several measurable changes can be

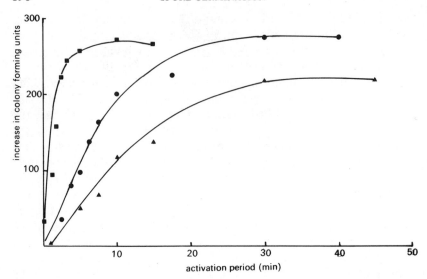

Figure 9.2 Heat activation of endospores of *Clostridium perfringerns*; (▲) 62°C, (●) 65°C, (■) 70°C. Adapted from Levinson, H. S. and Feeherry, F. E. (1978) in *Spores VII* (ed. G. Chambliss and J. C. Vary) American Society for Microbiology, Washington D.C., 34–40.

monitored, e.g. germination frequency and various metabolic processes. A number of theories have been put forward to explain activation, involving:

(i)   Changes in spore permeability.
(ii) Changes in the spore coats.
(iii) The release of factors that stimulate germination.

    Evidence has been suggested for each as a possible mechanism but no single one explains all the facts of activation.

    Dormancy in many fungal spores, mostly asexual spores, is controlled by environmental factors and is known as exogenous dormancy. In these instances fully developed spores can be prevented from germinating by omission of particular nutrients from the medium or by exposure of the spores to unfavourable pH conditions.

Germination of bacterial endospores

Following activation and transfer to a suitable growth medium the bacterial endospore embarks on two phases of development culminating in the formation of a vegetative cell (figure 9.3). The first phase, called

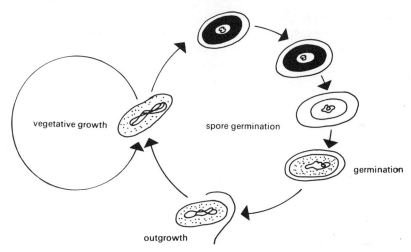

vegetative growth

spore germination

germination

outgrowth

Figure 9.3 Diagrammatic representation of the events associated with endospore germination.

germination, lasts for a few minutes and is followed by the outgrowth phase. The whole process of development following activation takes two hours at the most. The use of the term germination, to describe a part of the whole event of transformation of the endospore to vegetative cell, has caused terminology problems in view of the much broader use of the same term.

The germination phase, although short, involves a variety of metabolic changes as evidenced by the fact that several inhibitors will prevent its occurrence. Exceptions to this rule are inhibitors which specifically block RNA and protein synthesis, these have no effect at all. Further evidence of metabolic events can be found in the loss of the spore cortex and the associated hydrolysis of the peptidoglycan and excretion of DPA and Ca^{2+} ions. The spores also rapidly loose the resistance properties, they show an increase in permeability including the uptake of strains. In *Bacillus cereus* the hydrolysis of the spore coat protein has also been reported. Changes also occur in the spore protoplast; uptake of water and swelling occurs and it loses its refractility. In contrast to the activation process the germination stage is irreversible.

Initiation of germination

What is the stimulus for germination? In different bacterial species specific "trigger reactions" have been described, e.g. the need for a particular amino acid or sugar in the germination medium. The requirement for these substances may be short-lived because removal after an initial period does not block further development. Other evidence also implies that the initiation period is a distinct time at the commencement of the germination phase. Thus different pH and temperature optima have been described for the induction phase and for continued germination.

Two theories have been proposed to explain the nature of the trigger reaction. The first suggests it to be an energy demanding metabolic reaction. Evidence to support this theory is based on experiments using inhibitors for specific metabolic pathways. Other support is claimed from studies on non-sporulating mutants which have also been shown to have lesions in key metabolic pathways.

The second hypothesis suggests that the trigger reaction involves a structural change at an unidentified site in the spore, a possibility being an allosteric change in a protein at the spore surface or in a membrane. Support for this view arises from experiments in which spores supplied with non-metabolisable analogues of glucose or amino acids embark on germination phase.

Differences between the germinated spore and the vegetative cell
Following the germination phase several biochemical events are detectable in the spore protoplast including energy metabolism and macromolecule synthesis. A major difference between energy metabolism in the germinating spore and the vegetative cell is the lack of tricarboxylic acid cycle enzymes and a functional cytochrome system in the spore (Keynan, 1973). In the absence of these components the final transfer of electrons to oxygen is mediated by a flavoprotein dependent NADH oxidase.

Dormant spores lack a functional system for protein synthesis, partly because of the absence of mRNA but also due to defects in the ribosomes affecting their ability to bind aminoacyl to RNA. Many of the spore ribosomal units are smaller than their counterparts in vegetative cells probably due to the detachment of binding proteins. At germination it is assumed that the two components recombine and there is also *de novo* formation of mRNA. Protein synthesis then commences after a lag of a few minutes.

Outgrowth
The process of outgrowth is a continuum of the germination phase provided all the essential nutrients are available, however, germinated

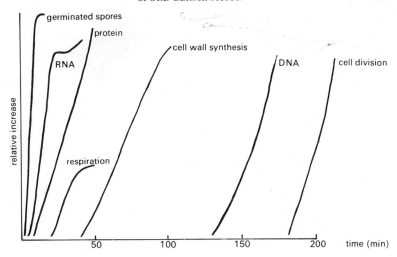

Figure 9.4 Sequence of morphological, physiological and biochemical events during endospore outgrowth.

spores can be held in this state for several days in the absence of the required nutrients. The outgrowth phase is characterised by a clear sequence of events, summarised in figure 9.4, culminating in the development of a vegetative cell. The first morphological change involves a further swelling of the spore protoplast, still enclosed within the spore coats, and the development of the vegetative cell wall partly at the expense of peptidoglycan in the residual cortex. The vegetative cell ultimately appears through the ruptured spore coat or the latter is broken down during the outgrowth phase. Emergence of the vegetative cell can take as little as 50 minutes after the initiation of germination and the subsequent cell division occurs some two hours after germination.

Not unexpectedly macromolecule synthesis is of major importance in the outgrowth phase, many changes are necessary to convert the spore protoplast into a vegetative cell. The absence of stable mRNA requires this to be synthesised prior to any protein synthesis, consequently the latter is under transcription control. An indication of this is seen in the sequential synthesis of different proteins, including specific enzymes. In view of the rapid onset of mRNA synthesis during outgrowth the necessary transcription enzymes, which must be present in the dormant spore, are quickly activated. DNA/RNA hybridisation experiments have shown that the RNA formed during outgrowth is similar to that in

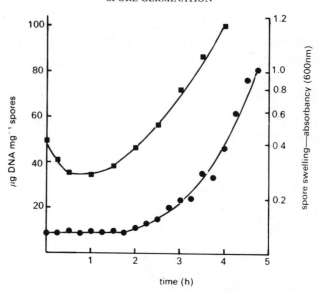

time (h)

Figure 9.5   DNA synthesis during outgrowth of endospores of *Bacillus megaterium*; (●) spore swelling, absorbancy at 660 nm, (■) total DNA. Timing of spore emergence (se), first (d1) and second division (d2) are shown. Redrawn from Lammi, C. J. and Vary, J. C. (1972) in *Spores V* (ed. H. O. Halvorson, R. Hanson and L. L. Campbell) American Society for Microbiology, Washington D.C., 277–282.

vegetative cells but is different from that found in sporulating cells. Similar experiments have substantiated the sequential time-ordered transcription of different RNA forms and indicated that some genes are transcribed at specific times and others continuously. In contrast DNA synthesis does not occur until late into the outgrowth stage, 120–160 minutes after outgrowth depending on the species (figure 9.5).

Synthesis of membrane and cell wall is necessary to contain the growing spore protoplast. Membrane formation, studied by feeding labelled glycerol and phosphate to developing spores, is a discontinuous event with an initial period occurring soon after outgrowth begins and resuming 110 minutes after the onset of germination firstly in a linear manner and then a period of rapid synthesis. The early phase of membrane synthesis does not depend on protein synthesis but the second period, however, is inhibited when chloramphericol is present. Another difference between the two phases of membrane synthesis relates to turnover which is found only in the second period. New cell wall material can also be detected very early in the outgrowth phase. Synthesis of the polymers requires the formation of messenger which has been reported to be formed as early as ten minutes after germination. The enzymes for wall synthesis are produced some 20–40 minutes after the onset of germination.

Germination of Actinomycete spores

The limited studies made with actinomycete endospores indicate that the developmental processes associated with the formation of vegetative

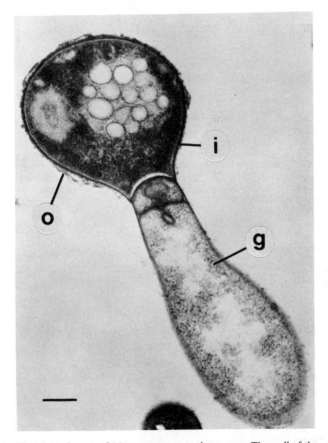

Figure 9.6 Germinated spore of *Micromonospora melanosporea*. The wall of the germ tube (g) develops from an inner wall layer (i) of the spore. When the germ tube is formed the outer wall layer (o) of the spore is ruptured. A septum is present in the germ tube (bar marker 200 nm). From Sharples, G. P. and Williams, S. T. (1976) *J. Gen. Microbiol.*, **96**, 323–332. Reproduced by kind permission of Dr S. T. Williams.

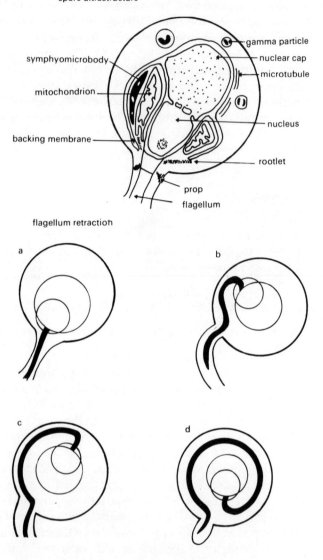

Figure 9.7 Diagrammatic representation of nuclear behaviour during retraction of the flagellum in the encysting zoospore of *Blastocladiella emersonii*. Adapted from E. C. Cantino and G. L. Mills (1976) in *The Fungal Spore* (ed. D. J. Webber and W. M. Hess) Wiley, New York, 501–556.

mycelium are like those described for *Bacillus* and other spore-forming bacteria. Arthrospores are somewhat different in their development because they lack the complex structure of the endospore. Each arthrospore gives rise to 1–4 germ tubes (figure 9.6). The timing of this is environmentally controlled and also differs in different species; it may take anything from 2.5 to 8 hours at 25°C. Information on macromolecular synthesis is still very scanty, but active RNA synthesis occurs and division of the nuclear body probably takes place before germ tube emergence. Evidence for membrane growth has been obtained from electron microscope observations.

Germination of fungal spores

Ultrastructural changes in germinating spores
Three basic mechanisms of spore germination leading to the formation of the vegetative cell or hypha have been recognised in fungi with each being characteristic of certain groups. These are:

(i)   Zoospore encystment involving *de novo* wall synthesis.
(ii) *De novo* formation of a new inner wall layer from which the wall of the germ tube develops.
(iii) The involvement of an existing inner spore wall layer in the early development of the germ tube.

Encystment of zoospores involves a rapid sequence of events commencing with the retraction of the flagellum in some species and its shedding in others. In the spores of *Blastocladiella* species the presence of several unique structures has provided an added interest to the events involved in encystment. In these spores the axenome or core of the flagellum is retracted from its sheath by a coiling process which is associated with a simultaneous rotation of the nucleus and nuclear cap. The membranous sheath of the flagellum appears to become incorporated into the plasma membrane of the spore. The role of the encystosome appears to be in the generation of numerous vesicles. These fuse with the plasma membrane, it is assumed, deposit cell wall material and give rise to the cyst (figure 9.7). Encystment of zoospores of Oomycetes species such as *Pythium* also involves intense vesicle activity (Grove and Bracker, 1978). In this case the discharge of vesicle contents, following their fusion with the plasma membrane, leads to the deposition of an amorphous coat on the spore surface (figure 9.8). This material may function as a physical support for the cellulosic microfibrillar wall that is ultimately produced, or it may

204

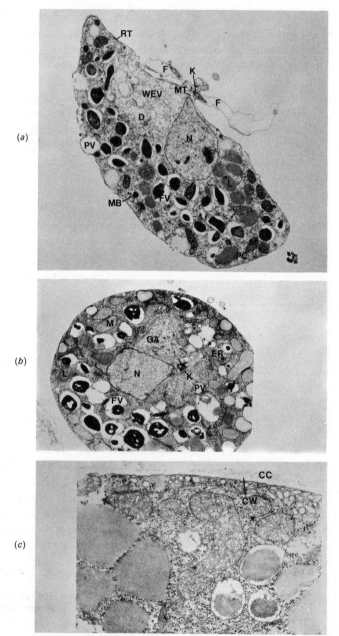

Figure 9.8 Transmission electron micrographs of the zoospore and zoospore development of *Pythium aphanidermatum*; (*a*) near-median longitudinal section of a zoospore (× 15 000),

contain the enzymes necessary for biogenesis of the microfibrils on the cyst surface; this situation still requires resolution.

The ultrastructural changes in spores exhibiting the other mechanisms of germination are considerably simpler. The *de novo* synthesis of a new wall layer has been demonstrated by electron microscopy and autoradiography. As the new layer is formed, the outer layers stretch to accommodate it. The germ tube ultimately appears through a pore or rupture in the outer wall (figures 9.9 and 9.10). This pattern of development has been described in representative species of all fungal groups. The third mechanism of development is more characteristic of Ascomycete, Basidiomycete and Deuteromycete fungi. The inner wall layer, destined to become the germ tube wall, often shows localised thickening at the point of germ tube emergence. The outer wall layers then split at this point allowing the germ tube to emerge (figure 9.9). Analyses on the chemical composition of germ tube walls have not been carried out, but electron microscope studies have revealed differences in the surface texture of the germ tube, and changes in the electron density of wall sections between the wall at the tip and that adjacent to the spore.

Metabolic changes in germinating spores

Nucleic acid and protein synthesis in the germinating spore has demanded the attention of many researchers because it provides a useful system or model for the study of regulation mechanisms in cellular development. The first observable syntheses relate to RNA and protein, but only continued synthesis of protein is essential for germ tube development. The relative timing of the initiation of RNA and protein synthesis varies in different organisms and it is possible to categorise them into three groups on this basis. One group includes the spores where the initiations of RNA and protein synthesis are simultaneous. The second is the group in which protein synthesis begins before RNA synthesis, and the final group is made up of these species in which the reverse situation is found. It follows that certain pre-requisites are necessary in the latter two groups; mRNA

(*b*) section of young cyst showing change in distribution of organelles ($\times 14\,500$), (*c*) periphery of young cyst ($\times 50\,000$).
CC, cyst coat; CW, cyst wall; D, dictyosome; ER, endoplasmic reticulum; F, flagellum; FV, "finger print" vacuole; GA, golgi apparatus; K, kinetosome; L, lipid inclusion; M, mitochondrion; MB, microbody; MT, microtubule; N, nucleus; PC, peripheral flattened cisterna; PV, peripheral vesicles; RT, rootlet; WEV, water expulsion vacuole.
From Grove, S. N. and Bracker, C. E. (1978) *Exp. Mycol.*, **2**, 51–98. Reproduced by kind permission of Dr S. N. Grove.

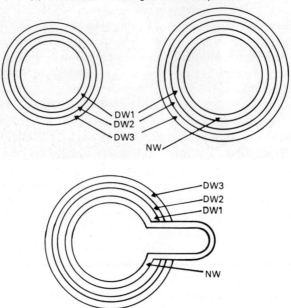

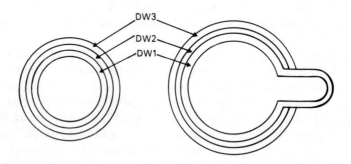

DW—dormant spore wall

NW—new wall

Figure 9.9 Schematic representation of changes in the fungal spore wall during germination.

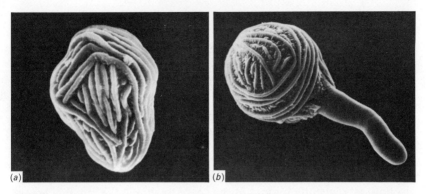

Figure 9.10 Scanning electron micrographs of *Rhizopus stolonifer* spore germination; (a) ungerminated spore ($\times$ 6000), (b) spore with developing germ tube after 5 h ($\times$ 3300). From Van Elten, J. L., Dunkle, L. D. and Freer, S. N. (1977) in *Eucaryotic Microbes as Model Developmental Systems* (ed. D. H. O'Day and P. A. Horgen) M. Dekker Inc., New York, 372–401. Reproduced by kind permission of Dr J. L. Van Elten.

is necessary in spores where protein synthesis starts first and an RNA polymerase is necessary in the third group of spores. Clearly these components must be synthesised during spore development.

Differences in the pattern of synthesis of the various classes of RNA molecules have also been found. In some species a sequential synthesis of the different types of RNA has been reported with a variation in the sequence also. There are probably a similar number of species that show continuous synthesis of all classes of RNA although there may be variation in the rates at different times.

An underlying question pertaining to much of the research on protein synthesis in germinating spores relates to the mechanism of regulation. How is protein synthesis inactivated in dormant spores and quickly activated when germination starts? A possible mechanism would involve the repression of protein synthesis in the dormant spore, caused by the absence of one or more components of the synthetic machinery. This might be achieved either by the spatial separation of the component or its presence in a non-functional state. Investigations into the presence and biological activity of mRNA, tRNA and aminoacyl-tRNA synthetases, and ribosome preparations show there are no defects in the system thus pointing to some method of containment or spatial separation. Evidence for this idea is strong in the very specialised zoospore of *Blastocladiella* species where the ribosomal complex is contained with tRNA and aminoacyl tRNA synthases in the nuclear cap, a membrane bounded organelle—(figure 9.7, Lovett *et al.*, 1977). Similar organelles have not been described in the spores of filamentous fungi, although studies on conidia from *Peronospora tabacina* again suggest that spatial separation could be involved. It was found that some of the ribosomes in dry spores are free of mRNA and are attached to the plasma membrane. When the spore is hydrated the ribosomes are released and combine with mRNA which has some other cytoplasmic location. This union forms an initiation complex which then combines with the large ribosomal sub-unit to initiate protein synthesis.

The synthetic processes discussed above indicate the need for a large energy supply. An energy reserve, e.g. glycogen, lipid, sugars and poly-alcohols, is frequently present in the spore to supply the minimal energy needs during the dormant state and possibly for the first stages of germination as well. In some instances the endogenous reserves are limited and the spore requires an exogenous carbon source for germi-nation. In some instances, e.g. ascospores of *Neurospora crassa*, there is a switch in the substrates utilised as an energy source following activation and subsequent germination. Thus the dormant spores metabolise a lipid reserve, whereas after activation trehalose is used. Carbohydrate meta-bolism in spores involves the three well known pathways, and in many reports it has been shown that a functional TCA cycle and terminal electron transport system are also operative to maximise energy production.

Modifications to the normal pattern of spore development

The normal pattern of development of both bacterial and fungal spores can be blocked and abnormal development encouraged by the modifi-cation of certain environmental factors. In both groups of organisms this involves another immediate cycle of spore development, hence the term microcycle sporulation has been used to describe the events.

Spores of several *Bacillus* species cultured in a diluted complex medium or in a medium lacking glucose are induced to undergo the microcycle. A variety of other nutritional factors, e.g. phosphate limitation, will induce the same effect. The spores formed by microcyclic development appear to be normal except for the DNA content which can be up to three times that of the normal spore.

The outgrowing cells have to be at a certain state of development before the microcycle can be induced. Using specific inhibitors it was shown that the capability for acetate oxidation must have developed in the cells.

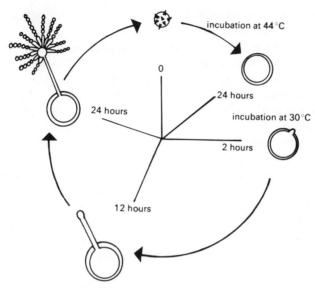

incubation at 44 °C

0

24 hours

24 hours

incubation at 30 °C

2 hours

12 hours

Figure 9.11 Microcyclic conidiation in *Aspergillus niger*. Adapted from Smith, J. E. and Anderson, J. G. (1973) *Symp. Soc. Gen. Microbiol.*, **23**, 295–337.

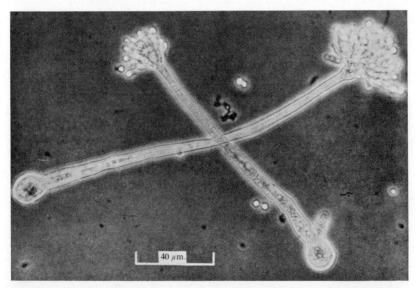

40 μm.

Figure 9.12 Growth of conidiophores from the enlarged conidium during microcyclic development in *Aspergillus niger*. From Anderson, J. G. and Smith, J. E. (1971) *J. Gen. Microbiol.*, **69**, 187–197. Reproduced by kind permission of Prof. J. E. Smith.

Other research has suggested that the optimal time for induction is the same as the time for DNA replication.

Microcyclic development has been described for asexual spore formation in several fungi (figures 9.11 and 9.12). The cycle is frequently induced by a specific temperature regime. Initially the spores are kept at elevated temperatures and during this period they exhibit spherical growth which is frequently very extensive. After a holding period at this high temperature the spores are switched to a lower temperature and this initiates the production of a germ tube which rapidly differentiates into a spore bearing structure.

These altered patterns of development provide interesting models for the study of the interaction between environmental factors and the control mechanisms associated with the development process (Duncan *et al.*, 1978). In one case, *Aspergillus niger*, it has proved possible to initiate the cycle in large scale culture in a fermenter. The provision of large amounts of material by this method presents an opportunity for investigations into the basis of the control mechanisms.

SUMMARY

1. Spore germination completes the cycle of vegetative and reproductive development.

2. Dormancy is a property of many types of spore. It is characterised by a state of very low metabolic activity which, in the case of bacterial endospores, is beyond the lower limits of detection. Spores in the dormant state are capable of surviving extremes in environmental conditions that are unfavourable to vegetative cells.

3. Dormancy can be broken artificially by various treatments, which are known as activation. The activation process is reversible, and spores not supplied with their particular germination requirements lose their capacity for germination.

4. Following activation, bacterial endospores pass through two stages prior to the formation of the vegetative cell. These are the germination phase and the outgrowth phase. The germination phase is short, and involves changes in spore structure and spore components but no macromolecule synthesis. Different bacterial species have different germination stimuli, e.g. specific amino acids. During the germination phase, some of the differences between the spore and the vegetative cell begin to be altered. Under suitable conditions, the germinating spore proceeds directly into the outgrowth phase. When conditions are unfavourable, outgrowth does not occur, but the germi-

nation phase changes are not reversible. During outgrowth the spore exhibits ultra structural and biochemical changes. In particular, active mRNA synthesis is a necessary pre-requisite for all the new proteins required for embarkation into active growth.

5. Spore germination in fungi involves a change in cell form in the unicellular types, or germ tube outgrowth leading to hyphal development in the filamentous forms. In the latter instance a period of cell wall synthesis may be a necessary pre-requisite, as in the case of the naked zoospore and some other types which have walled spores. The wall of the germ tube is derived from the newly formed wall material or from a pre-existing inner wall layer.

6. Most fungal spores contain some stable mRNA, produced during spore development. However, there are differences between fungal species in the relative timing of RNA and protein synthesis, depending on whether any stable message is present. This is clearly the case in fungal spores that synthesise RNA and protein simultaneously, or protein before RNA, but not when RNA synthesis occurs before protein synthesis. In any case, certain enzymes must be present in the spore, and it is thought that these are spatially separated from other components of the synthetic system prior to germination.

7. The normal development of spores can be blocked in some organisms by altered environmental conditions. The spores develop abnormally by embarking on another cycle of spore development. This is known as microcyclic sporulation. In bacteria this is under nutritional control, and in fungi the temperature at which the spores are germinated is the determinant.

FURTHER READING

Chapter 1

Cooper, S. and Helmstetter, C. E. (1968) "Chromosome replication and the division cycle of *Escherichia coli* B/r", *J. Mol. Biol.*, **31**, 519–540.

Costerton, J. W., Ingram, J. M. and Cheng, K-J (1974) "Structure and function of the cell envelope of Gram-negative bacteria", *Bact. Rev.*, **38**, 87–110.

Donachie, W. D. (1968) "Relationship between cell size and time of initiation of DNA replication", *Nature*, **219**, 1077–1079.

Donachie, W. D., Jones, N. C. and Tether, R. (1973) "The bacterial cell cycle", *Symp. Soc. Gen. Microbiol.*, **23**, 9–44.

Doyle, R. J., Streips, U. N. and Helman, J. R. (1977) "Zones of cell wall enlargement in *Bacillus subtilis*", in *Microbiology* (1977) ed. D. Schlessinger, American Society for Microbiology, Washington, 44–49.

Ensign, J. C. and Wolfe, R. S. (1964) "Nutritional control of morphogenesis in *Arthrobacter crystallopoietes*", *J. Bact.*, **87**, 924–932.

Henning, U. (1975) "Determination of cell shape in bacteria", *Ann. Rev. Microbiol.*, **29**, 45–60.

Higgins, M. L. and Shockman, G. D. (1971) "Prokaryotic cell division with respect to wall and membranes", *Crit. Rev. Microbiol.*, **29**, 29–73.

James, R. (1978) "Control of DNA synthesis and cell division in bacteria", in *Companion to Microbiology* (ed. A. T. Bull and P. M. Meadow), Longman, London, 59–76.

Kleppe, K., Ovrebö, S. and Lossius, I. (1979) "The bacterial nucleoid", *J. Gen. Microbiol.*, **112**, 1–13.

Mendelson, N. H. (1977) "Cell growth and division: a genetic viewpoint", in *Microbiology* (1977) ed. D. Schlessinger, American Society for Microbiology, Washington, 5–24.

Ohya, S., Yamakazi, M., Sugawara, S. and Matsuhashi, M. (1979) "Penicillin-binding proteins in *Proteus* species", *J. Bact.*, **137**, 474–479.

Pettijohn, D. E. (1976) "Procaryotic DNA in nucleoid structure", *C.R.C. Crit. Rev. Biochem.*, **4**, 175–202.

Sargent, M. G. (1978) "Surface extension and the cell cycle in Prokaryotes", *Adv. Microb. Physiol.*, **18**, 106–176.

Shapiro, L. (1976) "Differentiation in the *Caulobacter* cell cycle", *Ann. Rev. Microbiol.*, **29**, 45–60.

Slater, M. and Schaechter, M. (1974) "Control of cell division in bacteria", *Bact. Rev.*, **38**, 199–221.

Sonntag, U., Schwarz, H., Hirota, Y. and Henning, U. (1978) "Cell envelope and shape of *Escherichia coli* multiple mutants missing the outer membrane lipoprotein and other major outer membrane proteins", *J. Bact.*, **136**, 280–285.

212

Spratt, B. G. (1975) "Distinct penicillin binding proteins involved in the division, elongation and shape of *Escherichia coli* K12", *Proc. Nat. Acad. Sci.*, USA, **72**, 2999–3003.
Torti, S. V. and Park, J. T. (1976) "Lipoprotein of Gram-negative bacteria is essential for growth and division", *Nature*, **263**, 323–326.
Whittenbury, R. and Dow, C. S. (1978) "Morphogenesis in bacteria", in *Companion to Microbiology* (ed. A. T. Bull and P. M. Meadow), Longman, London, 221–264.
Zaritsky, A. and Woldringh, C. L. (1978) "Chromosome replication rate and cell shape in *Escherichia coli*: lack of coupling", *J. Bact.*, **135**, 581–587.

Chapter 2
Biely, P. (1978) "Changes in the rate of synthesis of wall polysaccharides during the cell cycle of yeasts", *Arch. Microbiol.*, **119**, 213–214.
Byers, B. and Goestch, L. (1975) "Behaviour of spindles and spindle plaques in the cell cycle and conjugation of *Saccharomyces cerevisiae*", *J. Bact.*, **124**, 511–523.
Cabib, E. (1975) "Molecular aspects of yeast morphogenesis", *Ann. Rev. Microbiol.*, **29**, 45–60.
Carter, B. L. A. (1978) "The yeast nucleus", *Adv. Microb. Physiol.*, **17**, 244–302.
Duran, A. and Cabib, E. (1979) "Chitin synthetase distribution on the yeast plasma membrane", *Science*, **203**, 363–365.
Farkas, V. (1979) "Biosynthesis of cell walls of fungi", *Microbiol. Rev.*, **43**, 117–144.
Hartwell, L. E. (1974) "*Saccharomyces cerevisiae* cell cycle", *Bact. Rev.*, **38**, 164–198.
Hartwell, L. H., Mortimer, R. K., Culotti, J. and Culotti, M. (1973) "Genetic control of the cell division cycle in yeast. V. Genetic analysis of *cdc* mutants", *Genetics*, **74**, 267–286.
Johnson, B. F., Calleja, G. B. and Yoo, B. Y. (1977) "A model for controlled autolysis during differential morphogenesis of fission yeast" in *Eucaryotic Microbes as Model Developmental Systems* (ed. D. H. O'Day and P. A. Hergen), Marcel Dekker Inc., New York, 212–229.
Lopez-Romero, E. and Ruiz Herrera, J. (1978) "Properties of β-glucan synthetase from *Saccharomyces cerevisiae*", *Ant. Van Leeuw.*, **44**, 329–339.
Minet, M., P., Thuriaux, P. and Mitchison, J. M. (1979) "Uncontrolled septation in a cell division cycle mutant of the fission yeast *Schizosaccharomyces pombe*", *J. Bact.*, **137**, 440–446.
Mitchison, J. M. (1973) "The cell cycle of a eukaryote", *Symp. Soc. Gen. Microbiol.*, **23**, 189–208.
Phaff, H. J., Miller, H. W. and Mrak, E. M. (1978) *The Life of Yeasts*, Harvard University Press, Cambridge, Massachusetts. Chapters 2 and 3.

Chapter 3
Bartnicki-Garcia, S. (1968) "Cell wall chemistry, morphogenesis and taxonomy of fungi", *Ann. Rev. Microbiol.*, **22**, 87–108.
Bartnicki-Garcia, S. (1973) "Fundamental aspects of hyphal morphogenesis", *Symp. Soc. Gen. Microbiol.*, **23**, 245–267.
Dominguez, J. B., Goni, F. M. and Uruburu, F. (1978) "The transition from yeast-like to chlamydospore cells in *Pullularia pullulans*", *J. Gen. Microbiol.*, **108**, 111–117.
Dow, J. M. and Rubery, P. H. (1977) "Chemical fractionation of the cell walls of mycelial and yeast-like forms of *Mucor rouxii*: A comparative study of the polysaccharide and glycoprotein components", *J. Gen. Microbiol.*, **99**, 29–41.
Farkas, V. (1979) "Biosynthesis of cell walls of fungi", *Microbiol. Rev.*, **43**, 117–144.
Gooday, G. W. (1971) "An autoradiographic study of hyphal growth of some fungi", *J. Gen. Microbiol.*, **67**, 125–133.
Gooday, G. W. (1977) "Biosynthesis of the fungal wall—mechanisms and implications", *J. Gen. Microbiol.*, **99**, 1–11.

Gooday, G. W. (1978) "The enzymology of hyphal growth", in *The Filamentous Fungi*, Vol. III (ed. J. E. Smith and D. R. Berry), Arnold, London, 51–77.

Grove, S. N. (1978) "The cytology of hyphal tip growth", in *The Filamentous Fungi*, Vol. III (ed. J. E. Smith and D. R. Berry), Arnold, London, 28–50.

Gull, K. (1978) "Form and function of septa in filamentous fungi", in *The Filamentous Fungi*, Vol. III (ed. J. E. Smith and D. R. Berry), Arnold, London, 78–93.

Hunsley, D. and Burnett, J. H. (1970) "The ultrastructural architecture of the walls of some hyphal fungi", *J. Gen. Microbiol.*, **62**, 203–218.

Peberdy, J. F. (1978) "Protoplasts and their development", in *The Filamentous Fungi*, Vol. III (ed. J. E. Smith and D. R. Berry), Arnold, London, 119–131.

Prosser, J. I. and Trinci, A. P. J. (1979) "A model for hyphal growth and branching", *J. Gen. Microbiol.*, **111**, 153–164.

Polacheck, I. and Rosenberger, R. F. (1978) "Distribution of autolysins in hyphae of *Aspergillus nidulans*—evidence for a lipid-mediated attachment to hyphal walls", *J. Bact.*, **135**, 741–747.

Rosenberger, R. F. (1976) "The cell wall", in *The Filamentous Fungi*, Vol. III (ed. J. E. Smith and D. R. Berry), Arnold, London, 328–344.

Ruiz-Herrera, J., Lopez-Romero, E. and Bartnicki-Garcia, S. (1977) "Properties of chitin synthetase in isolated chitosomes from yeast cells of *Mucor rouxii*", *J. Biol. Chem.*, **252**, 3338–3343.

Stewart, P. R. and Rogers, P. J. (1978) "Fungal dimorphism, a particular expression of cell wall morphogenesis", in *The Filamentous Fungi*, Vol. III (ed. J. E. Smith and D. R. Berry), Arnold, London, 164–196.

Sypherd, P. S., Borgia, P. T. and Paznokas, J. L. (1978) "Biochemistry of dimorphism in the fungus *Mucor*", *Adv. Microb. Physiol.*, **18**, 68–105.

Trinci, A. P. J. (1978) "Wall and hyphal growth", *Sci. Prog. Oxford*, **65**, 75–99.

Trinci, A. P. J. (1978) "The duplication cycle and vegetative development in moulds", in *The Filamentous Fungi*, Vol. III (ed. J. E. Smith and D. R. Berry), Arnold, London, 132–163.

Chapter 4

Bachrach, H. L. (1978) "Comparative strategies of animal virus replication", *Adv. Virus Res.*, **22**, 163–186.

Bishop, D. H. L. and Flamand, A. (1975) "Transcription processes of animal RNA viruses", *Symp. Soc. Gen. Microbiol.*, **25**, 95–152.

Dales, S. (1973) "Early events in cell–animal virus interactions", *Bact. Rev.*, **37**, 103–135.

Eisen, H. (1975) "Regulation mechanisms involved in bacteriophage development", *Symp. Soc. Gen. Microbiol.*, **25**, 79–93.

Hruby, D. E., Guarino, L. A. and Kates, J. R. (1979) "Vaccinia virus replication. I. Requirement for the host cell nucleus", *J. Virol.*, **29**, 705–715.

Murialdo, H. and Becker, A. (1978) "Head morphogenesis of complex double-stranded deoxyribonucleic acid bacteriophages", *Microbiol. Rev.*, **42**, 529–576.

Newton, A. A. (1970) "The requirements of a virus", *Symp. Soc. Gen. Microbiol.*, **20**, 323–358.

Newton, A. A. (1974) "Viruses", in *Companion to Biochemistry* (ed. A. T. Bull, J. R. Lagnado, J. O. Thomas and K. F. Tipton), Longman, London, 277–306.

Sambrook, J. F. (1975) "Transcription of the smaller DNA tumour viruses", *Symp. Soc. Gen. Microbiol.*, **25**, 153–181.

Shepherd, R. J. (1976) "DNA viruses of higher plants", *Adv. Virus Res.*, **20**, 305–339.

Showe, M. K. and Kellenberger, E. (1975) "Control mechanisms in virus assembly", *Symp. Soc. Gen. Microbiol.*, **25**, 407–438.

Chapter 5

Cross, T. and Attwell, R. W. (1975) "Actinomycete spores", in *Spores VI* (ed. P. Gerdhardt, R. N. Costilow and H. L. Sadoff), American Society for Microbiology, Washington, 3–14.

Doi, R. H. (1977a) "Genetic control of sporulation", *Ann. Rev. Genet.*, **11**, 29–48.

Doi, R. H. (1977b) "Role of ribonucleic acid polymerases in gene selection in prokaryotes", *Bact. Rev.*, **41**, 568–594.

Doi, R. H. and Leighton, T. J. (1972) "Regulation during initiation and subsequent stages of bacterial sporulation", in *Spores V* (ed. H. O. Halvorson, R. Hanson and L. L. Campbell), American Society for Microbiology, Washington, 225–232.

Dunn, G., Jeffs, P., Mann, N. H., Torgensen, D. M. and Young, M. (1978) "The relationship between DNA replication and the induction of sporulation in *Bacillus subtilus*", *J. Gen. Microbiol.*, **108**, 189–195.

Ensign, J. C. (1978) "Formation, properties and germination of Actinomycete spores", *Ann. Rev. Microbiol.*, **32**, 185–220.

Freese, E. (1977) "Metabolic control of sporulation", in *Spore Research* (1976) Vol. 1 (ed. A. N. Barker, J. Wolf, D. J. Ellar, G. J. Dring and G. W. Gould), Academic Press, London, 1–32.

Freese, E. and Fujita, Y. (1976) "Control of enzyme synthesis during growth and sporulation", in *Microbiology* (1976) ed. D. Schlessinger, American Society for Microbiology, Washington, D.C., 164–184.

Ginsberg, D. and Keynan, A. (1978) "Independence of *Bacillus subtilis* spore outgrowth from DNA synthesis", *J. Bact.*, **136**, 111–116.

Gould, G. W. and Dring, G. J. (1975) "Role of expanded cortex in resistance of bacterial endospores", in *Spores VI* (ed. P. Gerdhardt, R. N. Costilow and H. L. Sadoff), American Society for Microbiology, Washington, 541–546.

Hardisson, C. and Suarez, J. E. (1979) "Fine structure of spore formation and germination in *Micromonospora chalcea*", *J. Gen. Microbiol.*, **110**, 233–237.

Hanson, R. S. (1975) "Gene expression during bacterial sporogenesis", in *Microbiology* (1975) ed. D. Schlessinger, American Society for Microbiology, Washington, 475–483.

Keynan, A. (1978) "Spore structure and its relations to resistance, dormancy and germination", in *Spores VII* (ed. G. Chambliss and J. C. Vary), American Society for Microbiology, Washington, 43–53.

Piggot, P. J. and Coote, J. G. (1976) "Genetic aspects of bacterial endospore formation", *Bact. Rev.*, **40**, 908–962.

Prestidge, L., Gage, V. and Spizizen, J. (1971) "Protease activities during the course of sporulation in *Bacillus subtilis*", *J. Bact.*, **107**, 815–823.

Ryter, A. (1965) "Etude morphologique de la sporulation de *Bacillus subtilis*", *Ann. Inst. Pasteur*, **117**, 40–60.

Sadoff, H. L. (1972) "Sporulation antibiotics of *Bacillus* species", in *Spores V* (ed. H. O. Halvorson, R. Hanson and L. L. Campbell), American Society for Microbiology, Washington, 157–166.

Sadoff, H. L. (1973) "Comparative aspects of morphogenesis in three prokaryotic genera", *Ann. Rev. Microbiol.*, **27**, 133–153.

Sadoff, H. L., Page, W. J. and Reusch, R. N. (1975) "The cyst of *Azotobacter vinelandii*: comparative view of morphogenesis", in *Spores VI* (ed. P. Gerdhardt, R. N. Costilow and H. L. Sadoff), American Society for Microbiology, Washington, 52–60.

Sonenshein, A. L. and Campbell, K. M. (1978) "Control of gene expression during sporulation", in *Spores VII* (ed. G. Chambliss and J. C. Vary), American Society for Microbiology, Washington, 179–192.

Szulmajster, J. (1973) "Initiation of bacterial sporogenesis", *Symp. Soc. Gen. Microbiol.*, **23**, 45–84.

Tipper, D. J. and Gauthier, J. J. (1972) "Structure of the bacterial endospore", in *Spores V* (ed. H. O. Halvorsen, R. Hanson and L. L. Campbell), American Society for Microbiology, Washington, 3–12.

Warth, A. D. (1978) "Molecular structure of the bacterial endospore", *Adv. Microb. Physiol.*, **17**, 1–45.

White, D. (1975) "Myxospores of *Myxococcus xanthus*", in *Spores VI* (ed. P. Gerdhardt, R. N. Costilow and H. L. Sadoff), American Society for Microbiology, Washington, 44–51.

Chapter 6

Darmon, M., Barra, J. and Bracket, P. (1978) "The role of phosphodiesterase in aggregation of *Dictyostelium discoideum*", *J. Cell. Sci.*, **31**, 233–243.

Durston, A. J. (1977) "The control of morphogenesis in *Dictyostelium discoideum*", in *Eucaryotic microbes as Model Developmental Systems* (ed. D. H. O'Day and P. A. Horgen), Marcel Dekker Inc., New York, 294–321.

Durston, A. J. and Vork, F. (1979) "A cinematographical study of the development of vitally stained *Dictyostelium discoideum*", *J. Cell. Sci.*, **36**, 261–279.

Gerisch, G. and Wick, U. (1975) "Intracellular oscillations and the release of cAMP from *Dictyostelium* cells", *Biochem. Biophys. Res. Comm.*, **65**, 364–376.

Hutterman, A. (1973) "Biochemical events during spherule formation of *Physarum polycephalum*", *Ber. Deut. Botanisch. Gesell.*, **86**, 55–76.

Konjin, T. M., Barkley, D. S., Chang, Y. Y. and Bonner, J. T. (1968) "Cyclic AMP: a naturally occurring acrasin in cellular slime moulds", *Amer. Nat.*, **102**, 225–233.

Lechevalier, H. A. (1978) "The Gymnomyxa (Myxothallophytes, Myxofungi, Mycetozoans", in *C.R.C. Handbook of Microbiology* 2nd ed. **Vol. II** (ed. A. I. Laskin and H. A. Lechevalier), C.R.C. Press, Florida, USA, 71–79.

Loomis, W. F., Dimond, R. L., Free, S. J. and White, S. S. (1977) "Independent and dependent sequences in development of *Dictyostelium*", in *Eucaryotic Microbes and Model Developmental Systems* (ed. D. H. O'Day and P. A. Horgen), Marcel Dekker Inc., New York, 177–194.

McCullough, C. H. R. and Dee, J. (1976) "Defined and semi-defined media for the growth of amoebae of *Physarum polycephalum*", *J. Gen. Microbiol.*, **95**, 151–158.

Newell, P. C. (1978) "Cellular communication during aggregation of *Dictyostelium*", *J. Gen. Microbiol.*, **104**, 1–13.

Newell, P. C., Franke, J. and Sussman, M. (1972) "Regulation of four functionally related enzymes during shifts in the developmental programme of *Dictyostelium discoideum*", *J. Mol. Biol.*, **63**, 373–382.

Oohata, A. and Takeuchi, I. (1977) "Separation and biochemical characterisation of the two cell types present in the pseudoplasmodium of *Dictyostelium discoideum*", *J. Cell Sci.*, **24**, 1–9.

Sauer, H. W. (1973) "Differentiation in *Physarum polycephalum*", *Symp. Soc. Gen. Microbiol.*, **23**, 375–405.

Sauer, H. W. (1978) "Regulation of gene expression in the cell cycle of *Physarum*", in *Cell Cycle Regulation* (ed. J. R. Jeter, I. L. Cameron, G. M. Padilla and A. M. Zimmerman), Academic Press, New York, 149–166.

Schaeffer, B. M. (1975) "Secretion of cAMP induced by cAMP in the cellular slime mould *Dictyostelium discoideum*", *Nature*, **255**, 549–552.

Schindler, J. and Sussman, M. (1977) "Ammonia determines the choice of morphogenetic pathways in *Dictyostelium discoideum*", *J. Mol. Biol.*, **116**, 161–169.

Sussman, M. and Schindler, J. (1978) "A possible mechanism of morphogenetic regulation in *Dictyostelium discoideum*", *Differentiation*, **10**, 1–5.

Wendelberger-Schieweg, G. and Hutterman, A. (1978) "Amino acid pool and protein turnover during differentiation (spherulation) of *Physarum polycephalum*", *Arch. Microbiol.*, **117**, 27–34.

Wright, B. E. and Thomas, D. A. (1977) "Enzyme turnover in *Dictyostelium*", in *Eucaryotic Microbes as Model Developmental Systems* (ed. D. H. O'Day and P. A. Horgen), Marcel Dekker Inc., New York, 194–212.

Wurster, B., Shubiger, K., Wick, U. and Gerisch, G. (1977) "Cyclic GMP in *Dictyostelium*: oscillations and pulses in response to folic acid and cyclic AMP signals", *FEBS Lett.*, **76**, 141–144.

Zaar, L. and Kleinig, H. (1975) "Spherulation of *Physarum polycephalum* ultrastructure", *Cytobiol.*, **10**, 306–328.

Chapter 7

Bartnicki-Garcia, S. and Hemmes, D. E. (1976) "Some aspects of the form and function of oomycete spores", in *The Fungal Spore* (ed. D. J. Webber and W. M. Hess), Wiley, New York, 593–639.

Bracker, C. E. (1966) "Ultrastructural aspects of sporangium formation in *Gilbertella persicaria*", in *The Fungus Spore* (ed. M. F. Madelin), Butterworths, London, 39–60.

Cantino, E. F. and Lovett, J. S. (1964) "Non-filamentous aquatic fungi: model systems for biochemical studies of morphological differentiation", *Adv. Morphog.*, **3**, 33–93.

Clutterbuck, A. J. (1978) "Genetics of vegetative growth and asexual reproduction", in *The Filamentous Fungi*, Vol. III (ed. J. E. Smith and D. R. Berry), Arnold, London, 214–239.

Gay, J. L. and Greenwood, A. D. (1966) "Structural aspects of zoospore production in *Saprolegnia ferax* with particular reference to the cell and vacuolar membranes", in *The Fungus Spore* (ed. M. F. Madelin), Butterworths, London, 95–108.

Kozakiewicz, Z. (1978) "Phialide and conidium development in the Aspergilli", *Trans. Brit. Mycol. Soc.*, **70**, 175–186.

Lovett, J. S. (1975) "Growth and differentiation of the water mold *Blastocladiella emersonii*: cytodifferentiation and the role of ribonucleic acid and protein synthesis", *Bact. Rev.*, **39**, 345–404.

Mishra, N. C. (1977) "Genetics and biochemistry of morphogenesis in *Neurospora*", *Adv. Genet.*, **19**, 341–405.

Smith, J. E. (1978) "Asexual sporulation in filamentous fungi", in *The Filamentous Fungi*, Vol. III (ed. J. E. Smith and D. R. Berry), Arnold, London, 214–239.

Tan, K. K. (1978) "Light-induced fungal development", in *The Filamentous Fungi*, Vol. III (ed. J. E. Smith and D. R. Berry), Arnold, London, 334–357.

Turian, G. E. (1975) "Differentiation in *Allomyces* and *Neurospora*", *Trans. Brit. Mycol. Soc.*, **64**, 367–380.

Turian, G. (1976) "Spores in Ascomycetes, their controlled differentiation", in *The Fungal Spore* (ed. D. J. Webber and W. M. Hess), Wiley, New York, 716–786.

Turian, G. E. and Bianchi, D. E. (1972) "Conidation in *Neurospora*", *Bot. Rev.*, **38**, 119–154.

Webber, D. J. and Hess, W. M. (1975) "Diverse spores in fungi", in *Spores VI* (ed. P. Gerdhardt, R. N. Costilow and H. L. Sadoff), American Society for Microbiology, Washington, 97–111.

Chapter 8

Barksdale, A. W. and Lasure, L. L. (1973) "Induction of gametangial phenotypes in *Achlya* and other fungi", *Science*, **166**, 831–837.

Bartnicki-Garcia, S. and Hemmes, D. E. (1976) "Some aspects of the form and function of oomycete spores", in *The Fungal Spore* (ed. D. J. Webber and W. M. Hess), Wiley, New York, 594–639.

Bu'Lock, J. D. (1976) "Hormones in fungi", in *The Filamentous Fungi*, Vol. II (ed. J. E. Smith and D. R. Berry), Arnold, London, 345–368.

Casselton, L. A. (1978) "Dikaryon formation in higher Basidiomycetes", in *The Filamentous Fungi*, Vol. III (ed. J. E. Smith and D. R. Berry), Arnold, London, 275–297.

Crandall, M. (1976) "Mechanisms of fusion in yeast cells", in *Microbial and Plant Protoplasts* (eds. J. F. Peberdy, A. H. Rose, H. J. Rogers and E. C. Cocking), Academic Press, London, 161–175.

Crandall, M., Egel, R. and Mackay, V. L. (1977) "Physiology of mating in three yeasts", *Adv. Microb. Physiol.*, **15**, 307–398.

Fletcher, J. (1978) "Timing of events during oospore genesis in *Saprolegnia diclina*", *Trans. Brit. Mycol. Soc.*, **70**, 417–422.

Fowell, R. R. (1975) "Ascospores of yeast", in *Spores VI* (ed. P. Gerdhardt, R. N. Costilow and H. L. Sadoff), American Society for Microbiology, Washington, 124–131.

Gooday, G. W. (1975) "The control of differentiation in fruit bodies of *Coprinus cinereus*", *Reports of Tottori Mycol. Inst. (Japan)*, **12**, 151–160.

Grove, S. N. (1976) "Form and function in zygomycete spores", in *The Fungal Spore* (ed. D. J. Webber and W. M. Hess), Wiley, New York, 560–589.

Haber, J. E., Esposito, M. S., Magee, P. T. and Esposito, R. E. (1975) "Current trends in genetic and biochemical study of yeast sporulation", in *Spores VI* (ed. P. Gerdhardt, R. N. Costilow and H. L. Sadoff), American Society for Microbiology, Washington, 132–137.

Hopper, A. K. and Hall, B. D. (1975) "Control of yeast sporulation by the mating type locus", in *Spores VI* (ed. P. Gerdhardt, R. N. Costilow and H. L. Sadoff), American Society for Microbiology, Washington, 138–146.

Matur, A. and Berry, D. R. (1978) "The use of step enzymes as markers during meiosis and ascospore formation in *Saccharomyces cerevisiae*", *J. Gen. Microbiol.*, **109**, 205–213.

Mishra, N. C. (1977) "Genetics and biochemistry of morphogenesis in *Neurospora*", *Adv. Genet.*, **19**, 341–405.

Nasrallah, J. B. and Srb, A. M. (1978) "Immunofluorescent localisation of a phase-specific protein in *Neurospora tetrasperma*", *Exp. Mycol.*, **2**, 211–215.

Phaff, H. J., Miller, M. W. and Mrak, E. M. (1978) *The Life of Yeasts*, Harvard University Press, Cambridge, Massachusetts, chapter 4.

Schekman, R. and Brawley, V. (1979) "Localised deposition of chitin on the yeast cell surface in response to mating phenomone", *J. Biol. Chem.*, **76**, 645–649.

Schwalb, M. (1977) "Cell wall metabolism during fruiting of the Basidiomycete *Schizophyllum commune*", *Arch. Microbiol.*, **114**, 9–12.

Sutter, P. R. (1977) "Regulation of the first stage of sexual development in *Phycomyces blakesleeanus* and other mucoraceous fungi", in *Eucaryotic Microbes as Model Developmental Systems* (ed. D. H. O'Day and P. A. Horgen), Marcel Dekker Inc., New York, 251–272.

Tingle, M., Singhklar, A. J., Henry, S. A. and Halvorson, H. O. (1973) "Ascospore formation in yeast", *Symp. Soc. Gen. Microbiol.*, **23**, 209–244.

Turian, G. (1976) "Spores in Ascomycetes, their controlled differentiation", in *The Fungal Spore* (ed. D. J. Webber and W. M. Hess), Wiley, New York, 716–786.

Turian, G. (1978) "Sexual morphogenesis in the Ascomycetes", in *The Filamentous Fungi*, Vol. III (ed. J. E. Smith and D. R. Berry), Arnold, London, 315–333.

Van den Ende, H. (1978) "Sexual morphogenesis in the Phycomycetes", in *The Filamentous Fungi*, Vol. III (ed. J. E. Smith and D. R. Berry), Arnold, London, 257–274.

Wessels, J. G. H. (1965) "Biochemical processes in *Schizophyllum commune*", *Wentia*, **13**, 1–113.

Chapter 9

Duncan, D. B., Smith, J. E. and Berry, D. R. (1978) "DNA, RNA and protein biosynthesis during microcycle conidiation in *Aspergillus niger*", *Trans. Brit. Mycol. Soc.*, **71**, 457–464.

Gould, G. W. and Dring, G. J. (1972) "Biochemical mechanisms of spore germination", in *Spores V* (ed. H. O. Haworson, R. Hanson and L. L. Campbell), American Society for Microbiology, Washington, 401–408.

Grove, S. N. and Bracker, C. E. (1978) "Protoplasmic changes during zoospore encystment and cyst germination in *Pythium aphanidermatum*", *Exp. Mycol.*, **2**, 51–98.

Hardisson, C., Manzanal, M-B., Salas, J-A. and Suarez, J-E. (1978) "Fine structure, physiology and biochemistry of arthrospore germination in *Streptomyces antibioticus*", *J. Gen. Microbiol.*, **105**, 203–214.

Hawker, L. E. and Madelin, M. F. (1976) "The dormant spore", in *The Fungal Spore* (ed. D. J. Webber and W. M. Hess), Wiley, New York, 1–72.

Kalakoutskii, L. V. and Agre, N. S. (1973) "Endospores of Actinomycetes: dormancy and germination", in *Actinomycetales: Characteristics and Practical Importance* (ed. G. Sykes and F. A. Skinner), Academic Press, London, 179–195.

Keynan, A. (1972) "Cryptobiosis: a review of the mechanisms of the ametabolic state in bacterial spores", in *Spores V* (ed. H. O. Halvorson, R. Hanson and L. L. Campbell), American Society for Microbiology, Washington, 355–362.

Keynan, A. (1973) "The transformation of bacterial endospores into vegetative cells", *Symp. Soc. Gen. Microbiol.*, **23**, 85–123.

Lovett, J. S. (1976) "Regulation of protein metabolism during spore germination", in *The Fungal Spore* (ed. D. J. Webber and W. M. Hess), Wiley, New York, 189–240.

Lovett, J. S., Gong, C-S. and Johnson, S. A. (1977) "Zoospore germination and early development of *Blastocladiella emersonii*", in *Eucaryotic Microbes as Model Developmental Systems* (ed. D. H. O'Day and P. A. Horgen), Marcel Dekker Inc., New York, 402–424.

Van Etten, J. L., Dunkle, L. D. and Knight, R. H. (1976) "Nucleic acid and fungal spore germination", in *The Fungal Spore* (ed. D. J. Webber and W. M. Hess), Wiley, New York, 243–299.

Van Etten, J. L., Dunkle, L. D. and Freer, S. N. (1977) "Germination in *Rhizopus stolonifer* sporangiospores", in *Eucaryotic Microbes as Model Developmental Systems* (ed. D. H. O'Day and P. A. Horgen), Marcel Dekker Inc., New York, 372–401.

INDEX

(Where a page number is italicised the entry referred to occurs in a table or figure.)